FACTS, VALUES AND THE POLICY WORLD

Phil Ryan

First published in Great Britain in 2022 by

Policy Press, an imprint of
Bristol University Press
University of Bristol
1–9 Old Park Hill
Bristol
BS2 8BB
UK
t: +44 (0)117 954 5940
e: bup-info@bristol.ac.uk

Details of international sales and distribution partners are available at
policy.bristoluniversitypress.co.uk

British Library Cataloguing in Publication Data
A catalogue record for this book is available from the British Library

ISBN 978-1-4473-6454-2 hardcover
ISBN 978-1-4473-6456-6 ePub
ISBN 978-1-4473-6457-3 ePdf

Cover design: Liam Roberts
Front cover image: Robert Keane, unsplash
Bristol University Press and Policy Press use environmentally responsible
print partners.
Printed by CPI Group (UK) Ltd, Croydon, CR0 4YY

Contents

Acknowledgments and dedication

My colleague Les Pal suggested that this work might find a home at Policy Press. Once I followed his advice, Laura Vickers-Rendall welcomed the manuscript with encouragement and exemplary professionalism. Laura called on four anonymous readers who got back to me with insightful comments in record time. The other members of the production team at Policy Press were also a delight to work with.

Before all of that could happen, of course, the book had to be written. A work such as this emerges from a long process of chewing over things. Many of my students helped me tremendously in this journey. Others were willing to put up with my classroom digressions, my thinking aloud, my uncertainties. And so, to all my students, I dedicate this book.

Introduction

The training of social scientists, including future policy analysts, is always a training in technique and *culture*. Training into a culture involves the transmission – intentional or unintentional, explicit or tacit – of ways of seeing the world and ways of behaving. For social scientists trained in a certain way, a key element of this cultural acquisition is to recognize a no-go zone: 'theories are positive – about how the world really is – and not normative – about how we want the world to be' (Remler and Van Ryzin, 2015); 'Research questions should not ask about what ought to be, but rather seek to understand what is' (Barakso et al, 2014). One methods textbook advises: 'In scientific writing, avoid words or phrases such as "should," "must," "ought to," "good," and "bad," which imply moral imperatives and value judgments.' If one fails to heed this advice, one will fall into 'a messianic approach that is more appropriate for an evangelist than a scholar' (Gebremedhin and Tweeten, 1994, 19).

But cultures, of course, are never fully consistent. Consider the advice just cited: we are being told that we *should* or *must* avoid words such as 'should' or 'must'. So there is an explicit message, but also an unspoken one: we must learn to *disguise* our 'moral imperatives and value judgments', as the authors themselves have done.

But just what's wrong with using 'should'? The counsel points to a broad and deeply rooted outlook, which I will call the binary view. This view holds that:

a) There is a gulf between two entirely different types of phenomena. On the one hand, we have: facts, positive or empirical statements, and so on. In an entirely different realm are values or norms, value judgments or normative statements, and so on. These different types of phenomena are 'absolutely heterogeneous in character', as Max Weber put it (1949, 12).

b) The validity of fact claims can, in principle, be objectively tested. This is not always easy, but is generally possible. Value claims, on the other hand, can be neither verified nor falsified. Being untestable, they are inherently subjective, enjoying 'no objective validity whatsoever' (Ayer, 1946, 108). We may thus liken them to mere tastes or preferences.

c) It is vital to recognize the distinction between these types of phenomena, as it constitutes a logical gulf that all rigorous thought must respect: one cannot deduce an 'ought' from an 'is', values from facts, nor vice versa.

1

d) All disciplined thought must strive for objectivity, to be as free of values as possible. (A variant of the binary view replaces (d) with the requirement that our value-commitments be transparent and explicitly declared.)

The binary view affects the way many social scientists go about their work. It also structures social roles in important ways. 'The Expert', according to the binary view, should provide clarity about facts, about the way the world is, but leave matters of value to citizens or elected officials. Such an outlook will certainly structure many policy analysts' understanding of their mission.

Though presented in many textbooks, the binary view is not a mere concoction of academics. We have all, I imagine, had the experience of getting into an argument about some public issue that we considered important. It may have concerned recent questions, such as the building of a border wall or pandemic mask mandates, or perennial controversies such as abortion, gay rights or gun control. In such discussions, we may experience little movement and much anger, more heat than light, as the saying goes. This can lead us to conclusions that are very popular in our age: that we are inevitably divided by our deepest values, and that arguments that touch on those values are likely to be fruitless. We may well feel, on the other hand, that we can generally resolve disagreements about factual matters: we can often, for example, simply look things up somewhere or other. Given this, the view that a profound gulf exists between facts and values seems justified by our own personal experience.[1]

Yet someone might reasonably object that, while the binary view reflects part of our experience, it certainly doesn't reflect *all* of it. This is true. Indeed, I suspect that no one can fully *live* the binary view. The victim of racial discrimination, for example, is unlikely to believe that the ideal of fair treatment is a merely personal preference. And you would be taken aback by someone who said they eat only vanilla ice cream because it would be morally wrong to enjoy any other flavor. You'd be just as perplexed by someone who said they oppose euthanasia because they find the word hard to pronounce. Our reactions to such puzzling statements show that we do draw distinctions between questions of right and wrong and mere tastes or preferences.

Nevertheless, even beliefs that we don't fully believe can have a great impact. They may be activated in particular contexts, and influence important choices and decisions. The dichotomy of fact and value, in particular, 'has assumed the status of a cultural institution', as philosopher Hilary Putnam puts it (1981, 127). Cultural patterns shape much of what we do *without thinking*: that is, a cultural norm can guide us, unless we take conscious pains to act otherwise, whether or not we fully believe it. Of particular importance are propositions that become lodged in methodologies and complex models: they may exercise great influence even if no one can endorse them when they are made explicit. We may thus classify adherence to the binary view as a half-belief.

But what's wrong with the binary view? ...

Since this book proceeds on the basis that the binary view is mistaken, I should offer a brief justification of that position. A first difficulty with the view is that it is not entirely clear on just which side of the positive–normative divide certain types of claims should be located. Consider some basic distinctions offered by various proponents of the binary view. An introductory economics book tells us that 'The positive concerns what *is*, *was*, or *will be*, and normative statements concern what *ought to be*' (Lipsey et al, 1973, 15, emphasis in original). In like fashion, philosopher Rebecca Goldstein confidently declares that 'Philosophers use the word "normative" to refer to any propositions that contain the word "ought"' (2014, 7). The quotes from various methods textbooks with which we began understand the divide in the same way.

But these simple distinctions are not reliable. 'Ought' and 'should' may be used in ways clearly free of normative content (eg in probabilistic statements). And what are we to do with evaluative claims of the form 'Harry *is* a jerk'? Most people would view this as a subjective value judgment, but the simple rules just presented would classify it as a positive claim. One might supplement the ought–is rule by classifying all such statements as normative, yet this strategy also presents difficulties, as it is unclear just what 'all such statements' might mean. If 'Mr X is a crook' is a normative statement, does it change its status to factual once Mr X has been convicted? (The jury would certainly not see things this way: they are trying to determine whether Mr X is *in fact* a crook, prior to their judgment: it is not their view that their decision *makes* him a crook.)[2]

But the binary view faces a more fundamental problem than the classification challenge just examined. Because it focuses our attention on individual statements, considered in isolation, the binary view misunderstands the nature of both positive and normative claims. We must shift our attention to a different level, and consider claims taken in conjunction with their supports. If I declare that capital punishment is wrong and you ask me why, I can support my position by presenting *other* claims I hold to be true. This illustrates how every particular belief we hold is part of a network of beliefs. Some beliefs in that network are normative, others positive.

Normative beliefs depend upon other beliefs, some of which are positive. If we ask someone why they think we should limit immigration, for example, their reasons will include some fact claims. It may be less obvious that positive beliefs in turn depend upon normative ones. There is an objective 'world out there' that does not depend upon our values.[3] But *our* facts, the set of beliefs about the world to which we consciously or unconsciously assent, do depend upon values. Let us briefly examine three forms of this dependence.

First, our conscious attention is narrowly focused. As Berger and Luckmann put it: 'My knowledge of everyday life has the quality of an instrument that cuts a path through a forest and, as it does so, projects a narrow cone of light on what lies just ahead and immediately around; on all sides of the path there continues to be darkness' (1967, 45). That we find something worth paying attention to, or making a statement about, depends upon our value-based interests, broadly understood. 'Only a small portion of existing concrete reality', insisted Max Weber, 'is colored by our value-conditioned interest and it alone is significant to us' (1949, 76). This is striking, as Weber is one of the most influential exponents of value-neutrality in social science. But Weber always recognized, unlike many later advocates of value-free social science, that our choice of topics for analysis, many of the concepts we forge to grapple with them, and indeed our general grasp of reality itself, are all shaped by our value commitments.

Second, most of what we know, or think we know, is taken on trust. In trusting someone's assertion, we assume that the fact in question has been generated in conformity with a norm of basic honesty. For the sorts of facts we trust in formal intellectual work, we also assume respect for other norms, such as the norm that there be careful consideration of the relevant evidence. The centrality of trust for our grasp of reality is highlighted by the giant experiment being carried out in the age of Trump: personal decisions concerning who is worthy of trust have become so polarized that even a shared sense of reality seems to be dissolving.

Finally, values are involved even in those facts that we grasp with our 'own eyes'. We perceive the world through a set of labels, and our labeling of the world is not random: it develops throughout our lives, in function of our interests. Thus, for example, 'a cat-lover has many more words with which to classify domestic felines than I do; the Queen of England no doubt has a rich vocabulary to describe the subtle distinctions between types of forks' (Ryan, 1995, 101).

Because our beliefs form a network, each belief being supported by others, we can say that no fact is *merely* factual, no norm is *merely* normative. By fixating our attention on the status of individual statements, considered in isolation from one another, the binary view misses this complex quality of our facts and values. This fixation encourages intellectual carelessness. Slotting a statement into the 'Fact' pigeonhole easily leads to neglect of its normative underpinnings: 'Who exactly do I have to *trust* in order to accept this fact, and do I have *good reasons* for trusting them?'; or 'What are the *values* that have led me to consider this fact worthy of interest?' When a claim is classified as normative, on the other hand, it can be too easy to dismiss as *merely* normative, perhaps even 'ideological'. The binary view thus facilitates the dismissal of uncongenial values, which are dogmatically assumed to lack rational supports.[4]

… And what's the alternative to it?

No matter how dubious the central claims of the binary view, it will not be buried merely by pointing out its defects. It is a commonplace among philosophers of science that a theory can only be defeated by an alternative theory.[5] An influential alternative in policy theory today – which travels under different labels (eg post-positivism, constructionism) – is based on the assumption that the root of the problem is our excessive trust in our access to facts, in our knowledge of objective reality. Given this, a natural response is to challenge the gulf between facts and values by, as it were, dragging down our factual beliefs, by arguing that we know much less than we think, that objectivity is an illusion, that 'truth' should always be put in quotation marks, that scientific discourse is just one form of rhetoric among others, and so on.

Like the binary view that it opposes, this approach receives some support from our lived experience. We all know how some firm truths of one age can be viewed as quaint superstitions in the next. And it is certainly true that phrases such as 'You have to face the facts' or 'Try to be objective about this' are often used in an attempt to impose a particular point of view – one that need not be particularly objective. But to conclude from such phenomena that one should adopt a sneering attitude towards the very idea of truth is to indulge in runaway inductivism, to jump from some observations to an unsupported generalization. This skeptical alternative, moreover, has consequences of which its original advocates were almost certainly unaware. It leaves thought powerless, for example, in the face of climate change denial, creationism or when confronted with the whole rhetoric of 'alternative facts'. (A fuller critique of 'post-positivist' policy analysis is presented in Ryan, 2015.)[6]

The critique of the binary view offered in the previous section points to a very different alternative. If every belief is part of a network of beliefs, then a reasonable response in the face of claims that strike us as problematic is to explore the networks of which they are a part: to inquire into their bases, their supports. And this response is every bit as appropriate for apparently normative claims as it is for positive ones. I say apparently normative because one of the things we will find when we start to explore underlying networks of beliefs is that a 'should' claim is usually an incompletely formulated 'if–then' claim, one that says something about the way the world is. To return to an earlier example: someone claims that we should not have capital punishment. We ask them to explain their view, and we find that their position can be stated: '*If* we don't want to execute innocent people, *then* we should not have capital punishment.' And that is certainly a claim about the way the world *is*: in our world, criminal trials are not infallible, and wrongful convictions will never be entirely prevented. So by having the person 'fill in' their initial claim, by bringing its underlying assumption to light, the claim itself seems to have changed its nature.

Suppose someone replies: 'Ah, but all we've found out is that your normative claim about capital punishment rests upon a second normative claim: we should not execute innocent people. So your original claim is still normative.' In fact, though, we've found that the original claim *also* rests on a claim concerning the imperfections of criminal trials. Further, even the apparently normative claim about executing innocent people itself can be supported with further claims.

And this points to a vital quality of our networks of belief: they do not 'bottom out'. There is no foundation that, once reached, allows of no further questions. Even the evidence of the senses does not constitute a foundation for fact claims. One can always ask of a particular piece of sensory evidence whether it was obtained under conditions that would make it reliable, whether the labels with which it is understood and communicated are adequate, and so on. Further, it would be a serious misunderstanding to view sense-data as foundational within the modern sciences. As Thomas Kuhn put it: 'Are theories simply man-made interpretations of given data? ... The operations and measurements that a scientist undertakes in the laboratory are not "the given" of experience but rather "the collected with difficulty"' (1970b, 126). In a similar vein, Marx had earlier commented that 'all science would be superfluous if the outward appearance and the essence of things directly coincided' (rpt. 1959, 817).

As with fact claims, there is no final foundation for normative claims. Many insist that religious beliefs provide a firm foundation for such claims. But religious beliefs are also caught up in networks of belief (see Chapter 1). Nor is the statement 'I want to be happy' a final resting place for normative claims, as some thinkers believe. We need not bother asking 'Why do you want to be happy?'[7] But one can always ask other things: 'What do you *mean* by happiness?'; '*How* have you come to understand the word that way?'; 'Are you aware of *other* understandings of the concept, ones that have been held by other people?'; and so on.[8]

To say there is no ultimate foundation for either factual or normative claims does not mean that they float unsupported in the air. Claims rest on multiple supports. But there is no ultimate unsupported support.[9] An important consequence of this is that *there is always something to talk about, if we're willing to talk*. Because our networks of belief do not bottom out, dialogue need not reach a final impasse: further questions can always be asked, further reasons can (eventually) be supplied. *If*, that is, we are willing to continue a discussion. (We will return to this in Chapter 1.)

I say that further reasons can *eventually* be supplied, because we are often not certain of our reasons for holding a particular view. This points to a vital quality of our personal network of beliefs: it is not entirely transparent to us. We did not consciously endorse each proposition that we believe. Many were picked up casually from our various milieux, many arise from our past experiences, generalizations of which we may be unaware, until they are somehow drawn to our attention. Thus, we do not fully know just what beliefs we hold, and it may take some reflection to uncover the grounds on which we endorse a particular position. (This has important implications for the practice of policy analysis, which will be explored in Chapter 6.)

To sum up: the approach recommended here is more relaxed with respect to certain concerns linked to the binary view, yet more rigorous in other respects. We can simply abandon, for example, an obsession with taxonomy, with pigeonholing statements in one camp or another: it actually matters little whether a particular claim is ultimately normative or positive. Why not? Because we can follow a similar procedure in the face of any claim that strikes as problematic, whatever its nature: inquire into its bases, its supports, learn something about the network of beliefs of which it is a part.

Imagine an objection: 'I'm sorry, but you can't evade the ontological question: do facts and values have fundamentally different natures, or do they not?' The simplest answer is: 'Why do you want to know? For what practical purposes would the answer to that question be important?' Someone who insists on the fact–value dichotomy might answer that we need a clear understanding of the distinction in order to avoid jumping from 'is' to 'ought'. They might also argue that the dichotomy is essential to prevent one's objective analysis being 'contaminated' by values, allowing, for example, one's view of what the world should be to hide the world as it really is.

I will argue in Chapter 5 that both these concerns misunderstand the requirements for rigorous thought. For now, consider the second one. First, we need to be in the grip of certain values even to *want* to understand reality. It is unlikely today, for example, that one will be willing to confront the full implications of the climate crisis unless one is gripped by deep value commitments: to future generations, to nature or something else. Further, there are so many ways that attempts to understand reality can be led astray that to fixate on one of those will almost certainly make it harder for us to detect the others.[10]

On the other hand, the alternative pursued here is more rigorous in important ways. The binary view's belief that values are ultimately subjective gives license simply to stipulate that this or that value will be taken as axiomatic. In the alternative approach, the concept of a network of beliefs that does not bottom out entails that no value claim is truly axiomatic: any norm may be pulled into what Jürgen Habermas terms the 'vortex of argumentation' (1996, 339). Furthermore, as we will see in Chapter 5, some concerns traditionally linked with the binary view are not so much abandoned as *extended*.

In sketching out a viable alternative to the binary view, I have moved quickly over various points: they will be further developed as we proceed, and as we apply various insights sketched out in this Introduction to a variety of issues.

A note on terminology

Values and norms

This work uses a deliberately loose language, referring interchangeably to values and norms. My usage is tailored to address the binary view, which does not attribute subjectivity to values *as opposed to* some other normative dimension, but throws all these phenomena into the same bin. This does not mean that no distinctions can be drawn within the realm of values/norms. But these should not be laid down by terminological fiat. Rather, just as sculptors and carpenters have accumulated much knowledge concerning the properties of materials by working with them, so do we uncover the nature of various types of values/norms by 'working' with them: probing their supports, identifying their implications and so on.

Belief

I do not use 'belief' to denote something *opposed* to knowledge or reason. In this work, a belief is simply something that a person takes to be true or valid.[11] The most rigorous scientist, for example, has many beliefs about the nature of reality, some of which are well supported by the edifice of science.[12]

Policy world

I will make frequent reference in this work to the 'policy world'. Like the arts world, or the world of sports, this is not a physical place, but a set of activities. Almost everyone steps into the policy world at least occasionally, when we discuss or write about things that governments are doing, or might do, to address public problems, to prevent problems from arising, to preserve the good things in our society and world, and so on.

How the policy world works – how it is shaped and constrained, for example, by ideologies, conceptual baggage, status hierarchies and so on – is thus important for anyone interested in public affairs in general or in specific issues of public concern. Indeed, as I will immodestly suggest at the end of Part I, the limitation imposed on the policy world by the influence of the binary view has implications for civilization itself.

Within that broad policy world, there is a set of people engaged on an ongoing basis in some type of formal policy analysis. One can find them in government, academia, civil society organizations and so on. For readers unfamiliar with this field, you can think of policy analysis as social science focused on the question 'What is to be done?' (by governments in particular).

Plan of this work

Anyone familiar with the policy world will tell you that it could not possibly function on the basis of a strict binary view. So why waste time exploring the relation of that view to the policy world? Is this not as pointless as developing a biting critique of alchemy?

Part I will answer that objection, showing how an outlook that seems impossible to embrace in any strict fashion can still wield great influence. As a down payment on that argument, let me point out that the binary view, which proclaims the subjectivity of all norms, is nevertheless a normative outlook. It prescribes how social scientists *should* work, how policy analysts *should* analyze. It is also the basis for a view of how the policy analyst *should* relate to elected officials.

Now, in any sphere of action, actual practice will find its way between normative notions of an ideal practice and various real-world pressures. So Part I will argue that many of the ideas about how policy analysis should be undertaken have been influenced by the binary view, and this has a demonstrable effect upon actual policy practice. We will also see that even reactions against traditional visions of ideal policy analysis have been affected by the binary view: that view is so rooted in our broader culture that its 'gravitational pull' can capture even those who seek to distance themselves from it. Part II will show that when we decisively break free of the set of prejudices that constitutes the binary view, our understanding of the nature and scope of policy analysis is transformed. The policy analyst must pay attention to new questions, and challenge a widespread understanding – rooted in the binary view – of the relation between analyst and elected official. Finally, Part III forthrightly discusses some of the dangers that might emerge from a consistently non-binary policy practice.

PART I

The binary view: effects and durability

In considering the impact of the binary view upon the policy world, we must acknowledge that the most interesting and important effects turn up in writers who do not begin their work with a declaration of allegiance to the view itself. Its key claims are often considered obvious, and most writers try to avoid stating the obvious. So while Part I will consider the impact of some explicit statements of the binary view, it will also proceed inferentially, examining certain types of practices and statements that can reasonably be held to flow from that view.

Note that I will be citing passages from particular authors. No claim is being made that the authors themselves are poor thinkers or that their work is without value. We are all, to a greater or lesser extent, children of our time and context. And we can all make use of the default assumptions of our time and yet do valuable work.

Chapter 1 will examine some specific effects of the binary view. Chapter 2 will consider a broader effect, one that shapes the practice of policy analysis in various ways: the dilemma created by viewing values as merely arbitrary preferences, while needing to find *some* source of values if policy analysis is to have any direction at all. Chapter 3 will argue that elements of the binary view prove quite durable, surviving even in intellectual milieux that appear hostile to the view. Finally, we will examine the ways in which the binary view is a very *convenient* one for many actors in the policy world.

Note that I make no claim concerning the precise prevalence of the binary view in the policy world. That world is too vast and heterogeneous to permit a systematic and persuasive content or discourse analysis, or anything similarly rigorous. But I urge the reader to reflect on this question, taking as your data the slice of the policy world with which you are personally familiar. Part One will present various 'symptoms' of the binary view at work. As you proceed through these chapters, ask yourself how often you run across these symptoms.[1] How often, on the other hand, do you come across reasoned argumentation concerning the norms relevant to a policy? How often are normative positions *explicitly* argued for, as opposed to being taken for granted? (Explicit normative argument is never entirely absent from the policy world, but how common is it? How influential?)

1

Some effects of the binary view

The great divide

The binary view is, obviously, binary. It introduces supposedly clear divides, not just between statements, but between overall approaches to reality. It dictates which sorts of beliefs may find a home within rigorous thought and which may not. One methods text thus declares that 'Ideologies contain many normative assumptions, statements, and ideas.' The social sciences, on the other hand, 'offer descriptive statements ('this is how the world operates') and explanations' (Neuman, 2011, 59). In like spirit, another methods book states that 'today social theory has to do with what is, not with what should be' (Babbie, 2013, 6). For some authors, this does not mean that normative issues are unimportant: they are simply someone else's concern. Levitt and Dubner's popular *Freakonomics* tells us that morality 'represents the way that people would like the world to work – whereas economics represents how it actually *does* work' (2005, 13, emphasis in original).[1]

At times one gets the impression that the binary view exercises a gravitational pull, dragging down thinkers on the brink of escaping its orbit. Consider the following argument from polymath Herbert Simon:[2]

> In the realm of economics, the proposition 'Alternative A is good' may be translated into two propositions, one of them ethical, the other factual:
> 'Alternative A will lead to maximum profit.'
> 'To maximize profit is good.'
> The first of these two sentences has no ethical content, and is a sentence of the practical science of business. The second sentence is an ethical imperative, and has no place in any science. Science cannot tell whether we *ought* to maximize profit. (Simon, 1965, 249, emphasis in original)

As recommended in the Introduction to this work, Simon 'fills in' the statement 'Alternative A is good.' He recognizes that one can *give reasons* for a value claim. This, obviously, sits uneasily with his claim that value judgments can only be validated by 'human fiat' (1965, 56). How does he resolve the contradiction? By assuming that reason-giving can descend *one level and only one level*. One can answer the question 'Why is alternative

A good?' but not the obvious follow-up question, 'Why is it good to maximize profit?' But of course the claim that profit maximization is good could be broken down as well. One might say, for example, (a) to maximize profit maximizes the company's chances of survival, employees' chances of continued employment and so on; and (b) these things are, in turn, good. And that last sentence could itself be further broken down. But Simon fails to acknowledge this. That as brilliant a thinker as Simon should have been satisfied with such an untenable position testifies to the power of the binary view.

The binary view's great divide misunderstands all that it excludes: it ignores the rational content of values and it misses the distinction between moral norms and mere subjective whims. Just as importantly, the great divide encourages an uncritical attitude toward all that it *includes*: toward facts, 'positive' disciplines and so on. Thus, it weakens our understanding of *facts*, by silencing important critical questions, such as 'What are the *values* that lead me to consider *this* fact worthy of attention?' It likewise silences the question, so important for certain types of phenomena: 'Just which values enter into the very constitution of this fact?'

The latter question is particularly important for what I will call straddling terms, concepts that inevitably straddle the line between facts and values. Such concepts, *once defined*, can be treated as matters of fact. But controversial values necessarily enter into their very definition.[3] One cannot define concepts such as freedom, free press, sexism, racism and so on without inclusion of some value component. Such concepts are hardly trivial in the world of policy. Consider, as a further example, Steven Haines's claim that 'while order is a matter of fact, justice will invariably be a matter of opinion. In essence, one can be objective about order but only subjective about what is just' (2010, 71). But order itself is a value-laden concept. Historian John Lukacs's *Five Days in London: May 1940* tells of a meeting of the French War Committee on 25 May 1940 to discuss how to respond to the disastrous military situation. President Lebrun argued that France was honor-bound not to sign a separate peace with Hitler. But General Weygand, says Lukacs, 'had the last word. The total destruction of the French armed forces, fighting to the end only to save their honor? "We must preserve the instruments of order. What troubles would result if the last organized force, that is the Army, is destroyed?"' (1999, 89). For the general, having France under Nazi occupation was compatible with order. Needless to say, many would consider this to be a condition of unsurpassable disorder. Our values necessarily enter into our assessment of the presence or absence of order.[4] One can apply the same analysis to related terms, such as 'national interest' or 'the common good'.

As many critics have pointed out, the binary view's claim that a scholarly discipline deals in facts alone likewise encourages insensitivity to the value-foundations of that discipline. Here is Paul Samuelson's influential introduction to economics:

> 'Beauty is in the eye of the beholder' is an aphorism reminding us that judgments of better or worse involve *subjective* valuations. But this does not deny that one person's nose may be *objectively* shorter than another's. Similarly, there are elements of valid reality in a given economic situation, however hard it may be to recognize and isolate them. There is not one theory of economics for Republicans and one for Democrats, one for workers and one for employers, one for the Russians and still another for the Chinese. (Samuelson, 1976, 7, emphasis in original)

That is, economics simply studies economies, factual realities as objective as the length of one's nose. Economists may disagree about policy matters, of course, because 'Basic questions concerning right and wrong goals to be pursued cannot be settled by mere science as such. They belong in the realm of ethics and "value judgments"' (Samuelson, 1976, 7). But the science of economics itself depends upon the simple ability to 'observe things as they are' (7).

We see here that the heirs of Weber's arguments for value-neutrality often lack his nuanced understanding. Weber insisted that 'The problems of the social sciences are selected by the value-relevance of the phenomena treated' (1949, 21). Modern economics proceeds on the basis of values such as growth and efficiency. One can certainly imagine an alternative economics, equally deductive and mathematical in its methods, founded on values such as social cohesion or egalitarianism.[5] One's starting point in this matter, as Weber recognized, is not dictated by 'science', nor by what Samuelson calls 'things as they are'.

A related effect of the claim that one's discipline is simply positive is the neglect of all normatively 'tainted' disciplines. William Riker and Peter Ordeshook titled their textbook on rational choice theory *An Introduction to Positive Political Theory* (1973). Such an introduction required no familiarity at all with the history of political thought, which was, it seems, merely normative. Elsewhere, Riker explicitly argued for ignorance of all previous political thought. Political scientists must resist the 'intellectually trivial' focus on the 'so-called giants of the past', since only 'contemporary theory' was 'important in guiding political research' (1964, 341). The development of political theory in our century was 'unmatched in any previous era' (1992, 5). In fact, 'until recently', nothing had existed that could be called theory 'with etymological justification' (1983, 47). While such claims might strike those familiar with the history of political thought as laughable, they are more plausible for those who come to 'positive' political theory from other disciplines.[6]

Thus, the great divide can encourage an uncritical attitude towards the status of facts, and towards the normative underpinnings of one's scholarly discipline. A further unfortunate effect is the encouragement of a spirit of *subterfuge*, as we saw in the introduction when considering the advice offered by Gebremedhin and Tweeten to social science students. Methodological advice rooted in the binary view's great divide can thus encourage what philosopher Jürgen Habermas terms 'cryptonormative' scholarship (1987a, 282). Faced with this phenomenon, it may help to recall Robert Dahl's wry observation that 'Much could be gained if the clandestine smuggling of moral values into the social sciences could be converted into open and honest commerce' (1947, 1–2).

The end of the line

In this section, I wish to consider a certain type of statement, one that is common in the policy world. We need to consider not merely the literal meaning of each statement examined here, but its *force*, 'the practical implications of its use' (Toulmin, 2003, 28). Here are two examples:

> In experiments used to identify which concept of inequality is held by people, it was found that 40 per cent of participants thought about inequality in absolute terms. It is not that one concept is 'right' and one 'wrong'. They simply reflect different value judgements about what constitutes higher 'inequality'. These value judgements carry considerable weight for the position one takes in the globalization debate. (Ravallion, 2003, 742)

> Critics of industrial agriculture are on stronger ground when they argue that the food it produces is deceptively cheap: it costs less at the supermarket, but only because governments provide industrial agriculture with all sorts of subsidies ... But there is nothing inherently wrong with government subsidies of the food system; virtually every country in the world engages in some form of them. Subsidies merely reflect the policy decisions and underlying value judgments a society chooses to embrace. (Hertsgaard, 2011, 196–197)

At the level of literal meaning, both statements assert that value judgments are weighty: they influence policy choices. It is hard to disagree with this. But there is a further quality to both statements, one that grants them their particular force. In both cases, once weighty value judgments have been identified, there is *nothing to be said* about them: they just *are*. When we reach a value judgment, we've reached the end of the line. Note that neither of the authors goes on to *assess* the value judgment in question, to consider whether it is reasonable or not, well supported or not.

Now we might be quite dismayed to come across a similar sort of thinking with respect to *facts*: 'We just disagree on whether weapons of mass destruction were found in Iraq, and that's all there is to it.'[7] The fact that the just-cited arguments from Ravallion and Hertsgaard can strike us as reasonable while the hypothetical sentence just offered seems absurd suggests a general guideline for teasing out at least some effects of the binary view. Take a statement about values or norms. Transpose it into the realm of facts and examine it carefully: does the transposed statement seem highly problematic, perhaps even absurd? If so, then the original statement is probably influenced by the binary view. Further, when the transposed statement is problematic, we should subject the original statement to critical scrutiny, however commonsensical it may appear at first blush.

End-of-the-line thinking is also invoked when an author states that this or that is a matter of opinion:

> Whether a person who uses drugs is worth less than a person who does not is a matter of opinion. Whether it is fair to give less of societal resources to people who are involved with particular drugs defined as illegal and more to people who instead use other drugs that are defined as legal is not a testable question. As a result it is almost necessary to ground a drug policy based on values in ideology. Theory is part of the scientific process of building evidence and advancing knowledge, so the policymaker making drug policy based on values has more limited use for theory. In summary, it is difficult to justify with reason and knowledge a drug policy based on values. There is less empirical evidence and more assumption. (Brownstein, 2013)

Here we see a number of the binary view's simple oppositions at work. On one side of the great divide stand science, knowledge, evidence, reason. On the other, distant, side, we find opinion, values, ideology, assumption. It is simply assumed that the gulf between these spheres is unbridgeable.

One last marker of end-of-the-line thinking can be noted: the invocation of 'reasonable people' and their inevitable disagreement over value issues. Thus:

> Although it is sometimes implied or even asserted that if enough analysis were done, if enough facts and data were gathered, all 'right-thinking' people would agree on the appropriate course of action to handle a problem, this is not the way the world works. Quite reasonable people can disagree on policy issues because they have differing interests, values, and affiliations. (Anderson, 2011, 5)

Estimated medical expenditures for sequelae of alcohol abuse and alcoholism have been consistently placed in the neighborhood of $10 billion annually ... Even if this kind of information were available for all the effects of drinking, however, the question of which effects are most important would remain ambiguous. The reason is simply that 'social importance' is *ultimately* a value question about which reasonable people can disagree. (Panel on Alternative Policies, 1981, 24, emphasis added)

Again, there is little to disagree with at the level of literal meaning: reasonable people can disagree about all sorts of things. But the *force* of the statement is almost always to suggest that the matter ends there: as the second quote suggests, there is something ultimate about value differences. And so, as economists Lipsey, Sparks and Steiner put it: normative arguments 'will turn on value judgments about how one ought to behave. These are questions on which reasonable people sometimes just have to agree to disagree' (Lipsey et al, 1973, 16).[8] Again, this is not how we generally view factual disagreements.

Finally, we should recognize that end-of-the-line thinking grips even theorists who have rejected some elements of the binary view. Lindblom and Cohen argue that normative analysis is 'overwhelmingly empirical in form', which clearly recognizes that normative claims can be rationally discussed, supported or critiqued (1979, 46). Yet even they accept that 'one is eventually driven back to end-of-the-line propositions that have to be treated as axioms, or as articles of faith, or as expressions of preference or emotion' (46).

Fatal divisions

One of the key claims to emerge from the Introduction is that 'There is always something to talk about, if we're willing to talk.' Clearly, end-of-the-line thinking rejects this. It holds, to the contrary, that pushing normative debates too far is unwise: we are bound, eventually, to reach a foundation of 'fundamental differences in basic values, differences about which men can ultimately only fight', as Milton Friedman put it (1953, 5).[9]

I would wager that this view, which I will call foundational pessimism, is more widely held than the claim that dialogue need never come to an impasse. Certainly, foundational pessimism has been proclaimed by many influential thinkers. Karl Popper, for example, held that our beliefs concerning the 'ideal form of social life' can be known 'only from our dreams and from the dreams of our poets and prophets. They cannot be discussed, only proclaimed from the housetops. They do not call for the rational attitude of the impartial judge, but for the emotional attitude of the impassioned preacher' (rpt. 2002a, 486). For Joseph Schumpeter, the world is full of 'rifts on questions of principle which cannot be reconciled by rational argument because ultimate values – our conceptions of what life and what society should be – are beyond the range of mere logic' (rpt. 1976, 251).[10]

While foundational pessimism may seem plausible, even self-evident, note how much it assumes: (a) that our beliefs and actions have a logical structure, such that they are rooted in some foundational views; (b) that we *know* what those foundational views are; (c) that they are meaningful, in the sense that when asked to clarify them we can do so; and (d) that they provide guidance for specific choices and beliefs.[11] The approach sketched out in the Introduction challenges much of this, developing the suggestion that our beliefs form a bottomless network, rather than a vertical structure.

Which image, network or tower, is more accurate? One way to answer this is to search out some of those 'fundamental differences' about which we supposedly 'can ultimately only fight'. When we look at examples that the prophets of foundational pessimism themselves offer of supposed bedrock differences, we often find ourselves faced with competing abstractions, pale shadows of uncertain meaning and import. Friedman himself offers eloquent examples of this.

Why, for example, do many critics consider the 'free market' policies espoused by Friedman somewhat extreme? Friedman knows: 'Underlying most arguments against the free market is a lack of belief in freedom itself' (1962, 15). *This* would seem to be a fundamental difference: some believe in freedom, some do not. His critics could answer, however, that they were *at least* as committed to freedom as Friedman, and that the important issue concerns not the choice between freedom and totalitarian coercion,[12] but just *which* freedoms a modern society must respect and how competing freedoms are to be balanced.

As evidence that Friedman himself accepted that not all freedoms could be tolerated, we can note his comment that 'it is important to preserve freedom only for people who are willing to practice self-denial, for otherwise freedom degenerates into license and irresponsibility' (1962, 18). Perhaps it was this fear of license and irresponsibility' that led Friedman to what many have seen as an excessively indulgent stance towards the extensive human rights violations of Chile's Pinochet regime, a regime with which his name was often associated.[13]

Friedman was, of course, opposed to what he saw as violations of *economic* freedom. In his influential *Free to Choose*, he lamented the fact that 'we are not free to buy cyclamates or laetrile' (1979, 57). We are not free to *buy* them, of course, because no one is free to *sell* those products. So Friedman was upset that the state would interfere with the marketing of carcinogenic sweeteners and ineffective cancer treatments.

Can such questions not be debated? Can we not discuss whether government should interfere in the marketing of carcinogens or whether massive human rights violations are an acceptable price to pay for 'pro-market' economic reforms? Of course we can. And in such debates, what is at stake is not whether one believes in freedom or not, but just which freedoms are most vital. This is not a question about which we can 'only fight'.

An analogous point can be made concerning the fundamental value of equality. Friedman proclaimed his support for equality of opportunity: 'No arbitrary obstacles should prevent people from achieving those positions for which their talents fit them and which their values lead them to seek' (1979, 123). Unfortunately, 'In some intellectual circles the desirability of equality of outcome has become *an article of religious faith*: everyone should finish the race at the same time' (125, emphasis added). Friedman did not actually cite anyone advocating 'equality of outcome', but his reference to 'religious faith' connotes a belief that is beyond debate.[14]

As with freedom, the real issue here is not between those who believe in one fundamental value and those who don't: the question is just what that value entails. A rather different liberal thinker, John Rawls, also advocated equality of opportunity, but drew radically different policy positions from that value. For Rawls, such equality required ongoing measures to equalize life chances: 'the accumulated results of many separate and seemingly fair agreements entered into by individuals and associations are likely over an extended period to undermine the background conditions required for free and fair agreements' (2001, 53). That is, Rawls held that an entirely free market of the sort advocated by Friedman will, over time, undermine both freedom and equality of opportunity, because those born into relatively poor circumstances find their life opportunities seriously narrowed, through no fault of their own. Hence, both freedom and ongoing equality of opportunity require that government guarantee equal access to education, for example, as well as various distributional measures, involving 'a number of inheritance and gift taxes' (1971, 101, 277).

So are Friedman and Rawls divided by a fundamental difference in basic values? Can there be no dialogue between their respective positions? Not at all. Were we to explore each position, we would find a welter of differences on *factual* matters. These differences need not generally involve contradictory fact claims as such. The Friedmanite and the Rawlsian, for example, need not differ in their quantitative estimates of current income inequality. Rather, they would most probably differ over the *sorts of facts* that are most relevant to the issue. Friedman, for example, can argue that government efforts at redistribution will inevitably be accompanied by 'fraud, abuse, and waste' (1979, 118), and that 'Wherever the free market has been permitted to operate, wherever anything approaching equality of opportunity has existed, the ordinary man has been able to attain levels of living never dreamed of before' (137).[15] A Rawlsian, on the other hand, might point to the difference between the probability of a child born of poor parents going to university and that of a rich child, in order to argue that the market, left to its own devices, does not provide equality of opportunity. The Rawlsian might also point to evidence concerning the impact of inequality on mental and physical health. The relevance of that *factual* point, in turn, depends upon the *normative* claim that such health effects are unacceptable. The Friedmanite might respond with a blithe 'Life is not fair' (Friedman, 1979, 127).[16]

On both the issues of freedom and equality, then, we have found that the supposedly irreducible values are vague abstractions, whose content for the person espousing them needs to be filled in, by seeing how they are applied in particular contexts, how those particular applications are defended and so on.[17] The meaning of the supposedly fundamental value can only be ascertained through the exploration of particular issues. Finding the concrete meaning of an abstract value in this way is something that dialogue can do very well.[18]

This is not a new insight. In truth, foundational pessimism ignores some long-standing wisdom. Think, for example, of a typical Socratic dialogue, in which an interlocutor gives a confident answer to a question such as 'What is justice?' or 'What is virtue?' – only to have the answer deconstructed through a consideration of concrete examples. The practical importance of this insight was also discussed by one of the American Founders, James Madison: 'All new laws, though penned with the greatest technical skill, and passed on the fullest and most mature deliberation, are considered as more or less obscure and equivocal, until their meaning be liquidated and ascertained by a series of particular discussions and adjudications' (Hamilton, Jay, and Madison, rpt. 1937, 229).[19]

In the policy world, the insight has been most clearly stated by the incrementalists. Thus, against the view that a work of policy analysis can begin with a clear statement of relevant values, Lindblom and Cohen argue that 'it appears to be impossible to articulate values with any precision prior to empirical analysis of issues to which the values are relevant' (1979, 47).[20] Other policy theorists have articulated similar insights. Discussing a British royal commission on capital punishment, Geoffrey Vickers notes that 'The commissioners used the norms which they brought with them to the conference table; but these norms were changed and developed by the very process of applying them' (1965, 64).[21]

Let us summarize the argument against foundational pessimism with a hypothetical example. Imagine two policy theorists. One says 'I believe that public policy should aim above all to promote social equality.' The other answers: 'No, the first task of policy is to preserve freedom.' Is this an irreducible difference in fundamental values, about which they can 'only fight'? It is not. Upon hearing their respective declarations, we must begin by asking: just what do they *mean*? And this can only be ascertained by examining the choices each theorist would make on specific issues. The *texture* of freedom and equality for each person will only be discovered in concrete cases. At this point, we will have discovered that each theorist's fundamental value is bound up with all sorts of other normative and factual beliefs, and that, as a result, there is much to talk about. *If*, and this condition must always be kept in mind, they are willing to talk.

But let us consider the other side of the coin: imagine two policy theorists who *both* say 'I believe that public policy should aim above all to promote social equality.' Can we assume that they are fundamentally in agreement with one another? The logic of the preceding argument forces a negative answer. Understanding the intricacy of our networks of belief helps guard against the illusion that a simple verbal agreement on a phrase means much. For us to agree that equality is important is roughly the same as two scientists agreeing that physics is good.

Deborah Stone's textbook *Policy Paradox: The Art of Political Decision-making* contains a wonderful discussion of the shades of meaning of a value such as equality, illustrated by a debate over how to divide a chocolate cake among a group of students. Everyone agrees that the cake should be divided equally. But what does this mean? An equal slice for everyone? Or perhaps those who had a more substantial lunch before class should get less? Or perhaps men as a group should get as much as women as a group? Or perhaps equality of opportunity should reign: 'Give everyone a fork and let us go at it,' suggest some students. And so on. Some of the interpretations of equality presented by Stone seem fanciful, yet each of them has a real-life analogue in the world of policy debates (1997, 39–42). To those who believe that societies are bound together by their shared convictions (eg Walzer, 1990), Stone offers the sobering reminder that we constantly struggle over the meaning of the very ideals to which we pledge our allegiance.

The fact that general values may be interpreted in a variety of ways, however, does not render them meaningless, empty containers into which anything at all might be poured. The practical meaning of a specific value for a particular person must be fleshed out in specific applications. But it must be fleshed out in ways that are plausible, given one's initial understanding of the value, however vague that may be. Whatever one's feelings about the military overthrow of Egypt's democratically elected Islamist government in 2013, it is hard to agree with John Kerry's defense of the military: 'In effect, they were restoring democracy' (qtd in Fisher, 2013). A reasonable observer is unlikely to feel that Kerry was rendering his personal understanding of democracy more precise. We are more likely to conclude instead that he was engaging in Orwellian newspeak. Thus, general values may be vague, but they are not all-embracing; they are not entirely devoid of meaning.

These general values are meaningful in another sense as well, a practical sense. To say, as Friedman does, that one endorses equality of opportunity, as opposed to unnamed liberals who allegedly advocate equality of outcome, is to provide a useful *slogan* for a political group. It provides a group with a somewhat illusory sense of its own unity and its difference from others. If this sense of difference is pushed far enough, the group may have little inclination to debate with others. Once again, we must recognize that this is not because debate is impossible, because we have reached the end of the line, but simply because it is deemed *undesirable*.

This last observation is relevant to a particularly fertile source of foundational pessimism, the cultural divide between belief and secularism. 'New Atheist' Richard Dawkins sees little point debating with 'dyed-in-the-wool faith-heads', as they are 'immune to argument, their resistance built up over years of childhood indoctrination' (2006, 5–6). Conservative Catholic Edward Feser responds in kind: 'where ordinary commonsense judgments about what is real and what is right are concerned, there is almost no common ground left between religious believers and secularists' (2008, 227). These statements are best understood as efforts to circle the wagons by sharpening the sense of difference between one camp and the other (Ryan, 2014a).

One may doubt this. Don't the normative positions of the believer bottom out with their particular sacred scripture? Isn't it impossible to enter a dialogue with someone who says that 'I know homosexuality is wrong, because the Bible tells me so'? It may be painful, it may be frustrating, but it is not impossible if the will to dialogue exists. Scriptural commands are filtered through a process of interpretation. There are thus many questions one may put to the person who cites the Bible to defend a position, concerning the legitimacy of their interpretation, the justification for their emphasis upon some commands and their neglect of others, and so on. As I argued in *After the New Atheist Debate*:

> For someone to say 'I believe we must do X because God calls on us to do it' would not be the end of the discussion, but simply another claim up for debate. One might ask: Just what are your grounds for believing that God calls us to this? If the answer referred to this or that biblical verse, a number of follow-up questions would suggest themselves: But is this particular biblical call, as you understand it, consistent with the central thrust of the biblical message? What do you understand that central thrust to be, and what are your grounds for thinking that? (Ryan, 2014a, 136)

'Whose values will prevail'?

Sophocles's *Antigone* centers on a conflict of imperatives. Polynices has died in an attack on Thebes. Creon, king of Thebes,

> Says he is not to be buried, not to be mourned;
> To be left unburied, unwept, a feast of flesh
> For keen-eyed carrion birds. (rpt. 1947, 127)

Polynices's sister, Antigone, disobeys the order. For Creon, this disobedience is a clear attempt by Antigone to put her norms in place of his own, the norms of the duly appointed authority. And he vows that 'We'll have no woman's law here, while I live' (140). Antigone has a different view of matters. She tells Creon that

> I did not think your edicts strong enough
> To overrule the unwritten unalterable laws
> Of God and heaven, you being only a man. (138)

For Antigone, there is no question of following her own *preferences*, as we might say today, but of obeying 'the holiest laws of heaven' (128).

One might answer that Antigone is acting only upon her *interpretation* of the 'holiest laws of heaven'. This is true. Indeed, she does not always seem certain of her interpretation.[22] Nevertheless, for Antigone, it is question of interpreting *something objective*, the actually existing 'unwritten unalterable laws' (128). For Creon, on the other hand, the issue is *whose norms* will carry the day.[23]

The modern reader is likely to bridle at Creon's claim that

> He whom the State appoints must be obeyed
> To the smallest matter, be it right – or wrong. (144)

Nevertheless, someone who holds the binary view must necessarily side with Creon's position in one crucial respect: since values are subjective, every normative claim is *someone's*. In a normative conflict, the question, for those who hold the binary view, really is *whose* values will prevail.

Thus, policy theorist Michael Carley argues that, when dealing with 'large-scale policy decisions and broad resource allocations, for example, between competing project areas like housing and health', the analyst's role is limited to 'outlining broad alternatives and elucidating the value choices and the values sets of participants relevant to the problem'. 'Rational analysis', says Carley, has little else to contribute, because the important issue is simply 'whose values are going to prevail?' (1980, 28, 30). In a similar vein,

Milton Friedman argues that '"Fairness," like "needs," is in the eye of the beholder. If all are to have "fair shares," someone or some group of people must decide what shares are fair' (1979, 126).[24] In a 1964 talk at Harvard's Young Conservative Club, Friedman condemned the Civil Rights Bill as '"wrong in principle," because it attempts to make people "conform to the values of the majority"' (qtd in Harvard Crimson, 1964). This underlines the impact of the personalization of values: the Civil Rights Act is not a matter of fundamental justice, but of some people's values.

Now there is an element of truth in such formulations. For example, in a decision-making body in which a unified majority has no desire to enter into serious normative dialogue with the minority, it is reasonable to say that the values that prevail are the values of the majority alone. But that does not mean that normative decisions must always represent the triumph of someone or other's values. We can again come at the issue through an analogy from the realm of facts. Imagine a committee of politicians or officials who review what will be taught in science textbooks. Some of the members have little concern for scientific accuracy.[25] They believe that all science is political.[26] Thus, they view the committee's debates precisely as a question of whose science will prevail. Other members of the committee, and many outside observers, view the matter rather differently. For them, what is at stake is whether *science itself* will prevail. They believe there is a qualitative difference between science and the pseudo-science promoted by this or that lobby group.

Analogously, members of a decision-making body who are uninterested in dialogue, who seek only the triumph of their pre-set position, will view the outcome as deciding whose values will prevail. Others will be asking whether serious deliberation will prevail. Will the outcome be the fruit of dialogue, and of a serious critique of initial views, or will it simply reflect the will of whoever had the votes to impose their pre-set views? Again, there is a qualitative difference between those types of outcomes.

The belief that all values are *someone's* values has an important implication for views of the proper role of the policy analyst, an implication foreshadowed in *Antigone*. As we saw, Creon viewed Antigone's actions as an expression of simple defiance, an attempt to impose 'woman's law'. Similarly, belief in the subjectivity of norms leads to the view that 'the morally self-conscious analyst [is] an arrogant sort who wants to substitute his or her own personal values for society's values' (McPherson, 1983, 77).[27] This view is nicely expressed in a Vietnam-era *New Yorker* cartoon. A young soldier stands in front of a panel of officers, one of whom tells him: 'Aren't you being a little arrogant, son? Here's Lieutenant Colonel Farrington, Major Stark, Captain Truelove, Lieutenant Castle, and myself, all older and more experienced than you, and we think the war is *very* moral' (rpt. Mankoff, 2004 [1968], 467, emphasis in original).[28]

This personalization of values creates a great barrier to critical dialogue. The policy analyst challenging a particular normative assumption can be viewed as challenging those who hold the assumption: a boss, perhaps, or a client. If, as often happens, such a perceived challenge provokes a hostile response, the whole experience gives added plausibility to the binary view itself, by demonstrating that normative debates are a mug's game, to be avoided as best we can. The binary view thus has a self-reinforcing quality.

We have considered four broad effects of the binary view: (a) Its 'great divide' generates misunderstanding of *both* sides of the divide. It encourages a lack of critical scrutiny, for example, of the value elements in one's scholarly discipline. (b) End-of-the-line thinking assumes that, when something is a matter of opinion, our ability to reason and critique has somehow reached a dead end. This suggests that: (c) we are ultimately divided from one another by differences about which we can 'only fight'. Finally, the binary view encourages (d) a subjective view of values, so that normative differences are perceived as a matter of *who* will win.

We now turn to a more diffuse effect, one that manifests itself in various core strategies of policy analysis.

2

The quest for exogenous values

The binary view presents policy analysis with a sharp dilemma. We may approach this through a piece of research textbook advice that is typical of the binary view: 'Ultimately, deciding the best or most desirable application of knowledge is a subjective, individual activity' (Manheim and Rich, 2006, 2). While many social scientists may nod their heads at this piece of folk wisdom, policy analysis faces a difficulty, because it is *intrinsically* concerned with 'the best or most desirable application of knowledge'. Policy analysis is practical reflection, reflection on the question 'What is to be done?' Hence it is involved in its *essence* with matters of value, since 'What is to be done?' always involves the question, 'What is *worth* doing?' – along with other value-laden questions.[1]

This value-centric quality of policy analysis is highlighted by Wildavsky's classic definition: policy analysis is about 'finding a problem about which something can and ought to be done' (1979, 3). As Anderson points out,

> Problems are not just 'out there' waiting to be resolved. The first act of evaluation is to make a distinction between 'problems' and 'the way things are.' Poverty is not a problem for a society that believes that 'the poor are always with us' – or that they get precisely what they deserve. (1979, 712)

So how does analysis governed by the binary view manage, if it seeks to be 'scientific' and 'objective', and understands this to involve keeping values at bay? Escape from the dilemma is provided by having guiding values come from *somewhere else*. Thus, a key effect of the binary view is to spark a quest for sources of value, exogenous sources that allow the analyst to bypass the task of making explicit normative arguments.

This process need not be as conscious as the foregoing might suggest. The exogenous values do not have to come labeled as such: they can arrive embedded in specific policy choices. Thus, 'If the Department of Defense desires a given amount of transport capability, alternative systems may be investigated to determine which of them is the lowest cost method of providing that capability' (Stokey and Zeckhauser, 1978, 153). Armed with the prior choice of some amount of transport capability, a would-be value-free analyst can get down to work. All sorts of disciplinary and other values will still shape the analysis, but there need be no *explicit* reflection on normative matters.

A qualifier should be kept in mind throughout this chapter: since, as the Introduction noted, adherence to the binary view is a half-belief, we should say that *in so far* as policy analysis is shaped by the binary view, it must seek for exogenous values. An analyst might seek to build explicit normative arguments into their work, and make a case for them. More problematically, another analyst might *feign* adherence to the binary view, pursuing a value-driven analysis that merely *appears* to be value-neutral. In this case, there will be no sincere search for exogenous values.

The decision maker as a source of values

Herbert Simon writes that 'A subordinate is said to accept authority whenever he permits his behavior to be guided by the decision of a superior, without independently examining the merits of that decision' (1965, 11). Simon's careful formulation does not assume that the subordinate *internally* accepts the values embodied in the superior's decision, they simply proceed *as if* they did. Accordingly, policy analysis can take the values, or the particular policy choices, of the elected official as axioms for a given piece of policy analysis or decision. As Simon puts it: 'Democratic institutions find their principal justification as a procedure for the validation of value judgments. There is no "scientific" or "expert" way of making such judgments, hence expertise of whatever kind is no qualification for the performance of this function' (56).

I do not wish to claim that this view is an accurate general description of the relation between elected officials and bureaucrats.[2] I am not considering a typical situation here, but one in which an analyst really seeks to provide analysis while respecting the constraints of the binary view, and finesses that constraint by turning to the elected official for axioms.

At times, as many observers have pointed out, this is harder than one might expect. Caidan and Wildavsky quote an Argentinian official who explained that 'The President travels around the country making speeches in small localities expressing what he would hope to do in terms of services for the area. Through this type of content analysis, we would hope to arrive at a list of priorities for each ministry' (1980, 114). We are not told how the president felt about this way of setting priorities. Were he to find out about it, he might well exclaim: 'Who told you to take my speeches seriously?'

This illustrates the problem that the analyst who truly looks to the elected official for guidance naturally expects clarity, while the politician will often have good reasons for cultivating ambiguity. Discussing the challenge of incorporating distribution into cost-benefit analysis (CBA), Stokey and Zeckhauser comment that 'Our problem would be easier if the decision maker could state his preferences in such a form as "In my opinion, \$3 in redistribution benefits are worth \$1 in net efficiency benefits'" (1978, 157). This wistful desire for a decision maker who presents opinions and preferences in a form that can easily be used as axioms for analysis is doomed to be frustrated, particularly on a matter as sensitive as income distribution.

At times, the view that valid normative guidance can come from elected officials takes on an almost mystical quality: 'Managers who serve a jurisdiction for an extended period come to understand this community's values, traditions, and goals. Yet, the manager must remember that the council represents the community, and they must defer to the elected officials as representing the policy wishes of the citizenry' (Hansell, 2007, 114). It is not clear just how the elected official can communicate the 'wishes' of the public on issues about which the public has not in fact thought. Certainly, anyone with even limited knowledge of the workings of modern political systems will have doubts about just what, or whom, electoral winners might represent.

Moreover, as was suggested earlier, the elected official may not even *want* to give clear guidance on many issues. Indeed, one contemporary school of thought says that rational politicians are not terribly interested in specific policy outcomes. They merely seek to get elected, and stay elected, and the policies they espouse are the means to that end. In this view, 'the department store cannot be defined in terms of its brands and a party cannot be defined in terms of its principles', as Joseph Schumpeter put it (1976, 283). Just as products are but a means to the store's goal of profit, policies and principles are only a means to the goal of power. One may find that view too cynical, or inapplicable to many politicians, yet recognize that in many instances the policy analyst will not receive clear guidance from the decision maker or guidance that they can even pretend to consider legitimate.[3]

Summation strategies

Naturally, then, policy analysis shaped by the binary view requires other sources of exogenous values. One such source arises from a summation strategy. Values will not be the fruit of critical reflection, but the result of summing up individual, uncoordinated, often unreflective choices. One relies, as Mishan and Page put it, on 'the orderings, or the subjective valuations, of the individual members of society, *and nothing more*' (1992, 62, emphasis added).

The classic summation procedure is CBA. Nothing in what follows should be read to suggest such analysis is useless. It can be extremely valuable, particularly when applied to relatively narrow matters, where it can, for example, help to 'weed out the abysmally unjustifiable projects' (Stokey and Zeckhauser, 1978, 176). Even on broader, more complex issues, CBA can help guide the search for 'relevant information' and discipline reflection (Sunstein, 2001, 5). Thus, the target here is not CBA as such, but the belief that it can allow policy analysis to bypass the task of critical reflection on values.

What Dan Durning calls 'one of the first and most widely used policy methods textbooks' (Durning, 1999, 392), Stokey and Zeckhauser's *A Primer for Policy Analysis*, insisted that economists 'are neither the creators nor the dictators of values. They merely provide a procedure for inferring and pursuing existing values; their role is descriptive or "positive" rather than prescriptive or "normative"' (1978, 259). In the case of CBA, this inferring of values can be quite creative.

At its most ambitious, CBA will attempt to put a price on *anything*. What is the value of a human life? Cass Sunstein notes that the Environmental Protection Agency 'used a value of a statistical life of $6.1 million. That figure was derived by calculating the average of over two dozen studies, mostly in the 1970s, generally designed to show how much an employer had to pay employees to compensate for a statistical risk of death' (2001, 22).[4] Similarly, a study mentioned by Stokey and Zeckhauser estimated the cost of air pollution by examining 'housing prices and wage differentials in areas with differing pollution levels to estimate people's willingness to pay for reduced tailpipe emissions' (1978, 151). Stokey and Zeckhauser go on to comment that this is superior to 'most political decision making procedures' because 'the interests of individuals who are poorly organized or less closely involved are counted' (151).

Clearly, what Stokey and Zeckhauser present as a modest exercise in 'inferring and pursuing existing values' is in truth shaped by various values. In estimating the value of a human life on the basis of the choices of individuals who accept employment in hazardous workplaces, for example, CBA holds that such individuals *should* be allowed to represent the choices of everyone else. But are they in fact representative? As Steven Kelman argues, 'To use the wage premiums accorded hazardous work as a measure of the value of life means to accept as proxies for the rest of us the choices of people who do not have many choices or who are exceptional risk-seekers' (1992, 159). Further, to estimate people's 'willingness to pay' for clean air on the basis of housing or wage patterns, as Stokey and Zeckhauser advocate, assumes that people have adequate information concerning pollution differentials and concerning the health effects of those differentials. Both assumptions are improbable.

Consider now the values that can be smuggled into a CBA that seeks to put a dollar value on the harms inflicted upon *some* people by the actions of *others*. In their analysis of the potential costs of climate change, Nordhaus and Boyer argue that 'Among regions, the climate-related years of life lost [YLL] are quite small (0.63 percent of YLLs) in established market economies, but they rise to a significant fraction (11.76 percent of YLLs) in Sub-Saharan Africa.'[5] And they go on: 'To value YLLs, we assume that a YLL is worth two years of per capita income' (2000, 80–82). So, the 'cost' of a death of a child in Niger from climate change represents roughly 1.2 percent of the cost of a Swiss child's death.[6] Well then: an objective, dispassionate, policy analyst must conclude that climate change is simply not as serious an issue as it would be if most of its victims lived in the global North, because *some human beings are simply worth less than others*. A number of nasty adjectives could be applied to this modus operandi. Nordhaus and Boyer might defend themselves by citing Stokey and Zeckhauser's claim that they are merely 'inferring and pursuing existing values'.[7] To which one could reasonably reply: if your method leads you to give the lives of 85 children in Niger the same value as that of a single Swiss child, *find another method*.[8] (Assuming, that is, that one even *needs* to put some price on life in order to formulate a sane policy response to climate change.)[9]

More generally, CBA is shaped by its fundamental value choice, to maximize net benefit. Invoking the Kaldor-Hicks criterion, Stokey and Zeckhauser argue that maximizing net benefit 'guarantees that the benefits of any project undertaken will be large enough so that those who gained by the project *could* compensate those who lose, with everyone thus made better off' (1978, 137). The argument, in effect, is that following the criterion will increase the size of the pie, which we are then free to divide up according to our income distribution preferences. But where is the evidence that 'we' are somehow free to reshape the distribution of social wealth in any way we choose? How many market societies have sharply redistributed wealth?[10] If this is rarely in fact done, then we should assume that it is unlikely for it to be done, and not use this unlikely possibility as a justification for maximizing net benefit. In fact, when policy choices affect the concentration of wealth and income, they are also affecting the concentration of political power: decisions that concentrate wealth, in general, can make the redistribution of that wealth even less likely.

So the standard justification for the net benefit approach is a truly curious normative argument. Elsewhere in economics, rationality involves weighting possible outcomes by their likelihood. In the present case, however, the net benefit focus is justified by something that merely *could* happen, with no evidence provided concerning the likelihood of its actually occurring. Reflection on that probability, of course, would draw policy analysis into consideration of the existing political climate and on the relations between economic and political structures, which could undermine the very attempt to avoid critical value reflection.

Conventional CBA procedures also have normative implications for a very different distributional issue: between the interests of the living and people who have yet to be born. As is well known, CBA discounts future costs and benefits. Why? There is a deceptively simple answer: 'everyone, under almost any circumstances, would prefer $1 now to $1 a year from now' (Stokey and Zeckhauser, 1978, 160). An evaluation has entered in, but it is not tainted with an aura of subjectivity because it is one upon which 'everyone' agrees. Given this universal evaluation, it is apparently sensible to discount *future* benefits from a project, relative to *current* costs: 'The funds expended for a government project are not funds that would otherwise stand idle … If left in the private sector, they will be put to use there, and in that use will earn a rate of return that measures the value that society places on that use of the funds' (1978, 170).

Once again, the analyst has not 'created' values, she has simply *discovered* them, in the choices that 'society' makes. This convenient discovery of ready-to-use valuations is facilitated by two questionable moves. First, the aggregate results of choices made by those with funds to invest and those with reasons to borrow are allowed to represent the decision of society.[11] Second, it is claimed that financial rates of return should be used to discount *all* future costs and benefits.

Let us focus on that second claim. As we have seen, 'everyone' is said to prefer $1 today to $1 in a year. As Cass Sunstein points out, 'money can be invested and will grow, and because of that simple fact a dollar today is worth more than a dollar in a year' (2001, 34). This is true, under *some* circumstances.[12] But that 'simple fact' hardly applies to other types of goods. If faced with the choice between a piece of chocolate today or one tomorrow, for example, I cannot 'invest' today's chocolate to make it grow. Yet, even here, people generally discount future goods and ills, relative to the present.

This reflects, in part, 'pure time preference', a 'preference for the present unit simply because it is present' (Fetter, 1927, 249). As Carl Menger put it, 'All experience teaches that a present enjoyment or one in the near future usually appears more important to men than one of equal intensity at a more remote time in the future' (rpt. 2007, 153–154).[13] The question is whether this greater value that individuals give to the present over the future should guide *social* decisions. Granted that the cost-benefit analyst 'discovers' this value in society, should she *respect* it? That is, of course, an unavoidable normative question.

It is worth noting, first, Adam Smith's argument that it was society's job to *counteract* our preference for the present:

> The pleasure which we are to enjoy ten years hence interests us so little in comparison with that which we may enjoy to-day, the passion which the first excites, is naturally so weak in comparison with that violent emotion which the second is apt to give occasion to, that the one could never be any balance to the other, unless it was supported by the sense of propriety, by the consciousness that we merited the esteem and approbation of every body. (Smith, rpt. 2009, 221)

That is, the 'sense of propriety', sustained through social interactions, attenuates the individual's time preference. Smith certainly did not believe that one should uncritically infer the values that guide social decisions from the behavior of myopic individuals.

Pure time preference is an even more questionable value-basis for analysis when we consider social decisions whose effects stretch well into the future. George Monbiot suggests that 'Given a choice between a new set of matching tableware and the survival of humanity, I suspect that most people would choose the tableware' (2004, 8). Two distinct factors are at work here. We have, again, pure time preference at the individual level: I have difficulty imagining, and taking seriously, the impact that climate change may have on *my* future life. But there is also an unwillingness to take seriously a threat that, rightly or wrongly, many believe will largely affect other people.

Adam Smith had something to say about this factor as well: 'Let us suppose', Smith suggested, 'that the great empire of China, with all its myriads of inhabitants, was suddenly swallowed up by an earthquake, and let us consider how a man of humanity in Europe, who had no sort of connexion with that part of the world, would be affected upon receiving intelligence of this dreadful calamity'. Smith's prediction is sobering:

> he would pursue his business or his pleasure, take his repose or his diversion, with the same ease and tranquillity, as if no such accident had happened. The most frivolous disaster which could befal himself would occasion a more real disturbance. If he was to lose his little finger to-morrow, he would not sleep to-night; but, provided he never saw them, he will snore with the most profound security over the ruin of a hundred millions of his brethren. (rpt. 2009, 158)

Smith was writing about current calamities that occur somewhere else, but his observation can be extended to future ones.

So both myopia and egotism lead us to downplay the importance of future ills. This led philosopher John Rawls to argue that 'In the case of the individual, pure time preference is irrational ... In the case of society, [it] is unjust' (1971, 295).[14] The fact that 'everyone' may give greater weight to the present, then, does not provide the cost-benefit analyst with an uncontroversial value upon which to base calculations.[15] This is particularly relevant to today's most urgent challenge: because the harms from climate change are of such long duration, any time discounting at all values the suffering of many future victims at next to nothing.[16]

The claim here is not that this or that method for dealing with time in CBA should be used. The point is simply that the typical arguments for time discounting insert some questionable normative judgments into the analysis, which will go unexamined so long as they are believed to be the judgments of society, simply inferred by analysts. The judgments that society pronounces, whether through democratic procedures or through uncoordinated market choices, may be irrational, unjust or both.[17] They cannot provide an unquestioned value basis for analysis. Just what the analyst should *do*, when faced with a social decision that is irrational and/or unjust, is another matter, to which we return in Part II.

One final point concerning CBA: the foregoing discussion bypasses the question of how CBA is actually used. The question is vital, when considering just how problematic are the normative assumptions made by cost-benefit analysts in any particular case. There is a longstanding complaint among CBA's proponents that critics have caricaturized it, painting it as naive and simplistic, and ignoring its real-life sophistication. Rosemarie Tong offers an interesting reply: the complaint assumes that 'policymakers eagerly turn to the margins and footnotes of their experts' analyses, expecting to find there the really important policy recommendations'. It is possible, Tong suggests, that the qualitative caveats that analysts include in their conclusions 'are regarded by policymakers and experts alike as some sort of cloying frosting that detracts from the taste of an elegant numerical cake' (1986, 17–18). Is this fair? I don't really know. We need an ethnography of CBA, which would study just how it is used in practice. This cannot be gleaned from analysts' reports alone: we need to understand just how the various components in those reports get used downstream of the analyst.

Perhaps nothing demonstrates the cultural influence of the binary view as much as the fact that a thinker as far removed from technocratic CBA as Michel Foucault also flees from normative judgment by appealing to the supposed values of society. Tunisian interviewer J. Hafsia, responding to Foucault's critique of the penal system as a mechanism by which society divided the 'good' from the 'bad', commented that Foucault himself must base his critique on some 'moral discourse', some notions of good and bad. Not at all, insisted Foucault. 'One thing is certain', he went on, that the penal system is 'no longer tolerated by people' ('n'est plus supporté par les gens') (1994, 2:208). But the same could be said of taxation. Does that mean the decades-long anti-tax revolt is justified? On its own, widespread dissatisfaction – which in this case may or may not have existed – is not a sufficient normative foundation for judgment.

Values are subjective ... with one exception

CBA is governed by one value: we should maximize net benefits. Money is the ultimate yardstick, as all non-marketed goods and bads must be translated into monetary quantities. There is a paradox here: a philosophy that assumes values to be subjective tacitly grants maximum net benefit the status of an objective value: it is objective, because *everyone* can supposedly agree on it. The belief that *one* value can be exempted from the claim that all values are subjective exists in a variety of forms. In some variants, it provides policy analysis with another solution to the challenge of finding direction in a world of (supposed) subjectivity.

One interpretive clue for detecting this belief in *one* objective value is to scrutinize use of the term 'rational', and related words, as well as terms opposed to it ('irrational', 'foolish', 'ideological'). In different fields, scholars regularly refer to the 'rational firm', which seeks only to maximize profits, the 'rational politician', who seeks only to win and retain office, not any 'material or ideological value' (Riker, 1962, 207–208), or the 'rational voter', who seeks optimal 'streams of utility derived from government activity' (Downs, 1957, 36).[18] In all these phrases, the implication is that, within a given context, one value is of such overriding and self-evident importance that anything other than its single-minded pursuit is foolishness. In the same spirit, some policy theorists will speak of 'rational' and 'irrational' public policy. For William Easterly, for example, 'irrational policies' are those that 'create poor incentives for growth' (2001, 237). In all these cases, the operative value is 'not explicitly presented as a value, since it is seen as equivalent to rationality as such' (Habermas, 1989a, 37).

The claim that, in specific contexts, one and only one value is objective, is often supported by invoking a world of cut-throat competition. In his influential essay, 'The Methodology of Positive Economics',[19] Milton Friedman reasoned that:

> unless the behavior of businessmen in some way or other approximated behavior consistent with the maximization of returns, it seems unlikely that they would remain in business for long. Let the apparent immediate determinant of business behavior be anything at all – habitual reaction, random chance, or whatnot. Whenever this determinant happens to lead to behavior consistent with rational and informed maximization of returns, the business will prosper and acquire resources with which to expand; whenever it does not, the business will tend to lose resources and can be kept in existence only by the addition of resources from outside. (Friedman, 1953, 22)

Just as the economic market supposedly forces actors to maximize or perish, 'politicians who do not behave according to the specified goals are eliminated from the system' (Riker, 1977, 32).

The competition assumption can obviously be applied at the level of the nation. Public policy would thus be rational if it promotes national survival.

Ironically, this was the outlook of the founder of supposedly value-free social science. As Wolfgang Streeck notes:

> Weber's own social science was anything but *wertfrei*. His passionate rejection of the social policy advocacy of the economists of his time was that of a liberal nationalist for whom – what he thought were – the coming struggles for national survival and international supremacy, in particular with Britain, were of paramount importance. Social policy, just as democracy, was not for making people happy, but to help the newly formed German Reich to brace itself for an anarchic, conflict ridden international world. That Weber could consider his position to be *wertfrei* was due to his conviction that *Realpolitik* was an objective fact and not something one was free to choose. (2016, 243)

In the modern age, the focus on national strength as the one objective value has come to entail an emphasis not just on military readiness but on economic growth, now seen as an essential component of national strength.[20]

To insist, however, that one and only one value is rational, on the basis of the competition argument, requires problematic unstated assumptions. In the economic case, it assumes 'perfect' competition, the theoretical ideal of mainstream economists that, if ever fully realized, would choke off economic growth altogether, as Schumpeter demonstrated.[21] The models of the 'rational' politician and voter, for their part, generalize some observed facts, but resolutely ignore others. For example: if voters were *only* concerned about their narrow interests, why would politicians so often resort to a rhetoric of principled argument?

In the specific sphere of public policy, it is hard to deny that economic growth is widely taken to be *the* ultimate goal. This focus is built into our structure of political carrots and sticks. If the gross national product (GNP) shrinks over two consecutive quarters, the economy is considered to be in a recession, a threatening state of affairs for political incumbents. The economic obsession is hardly new. Aristotle wrote that 'some men turn every quality or art into a means of getting wealth; this they conceive to be the end, and to the promotion of the end they think all things must contribute' (*Politics*, 1258a). The observation sounds like a description of many modern-day discussions of the role of higher education. Even that most humane of economists, John Maynard Keynes, endorsed this narrow focus. He looked to a day when 'We shall once more value ends above means' and honor 'the delightful people who are capable of taking direct enjoyment in things'. Yet he warned:

> But beware! The time for all this is not yet. For at least another hundred years we must pretend to ourselves and to every one that fair is foul

and foul is fair; for foul is useful and fair is not. Avarice and usury and precaution must be our gods for a little longer still. For only they can lead us out of the tunnel of economic necessity into daylight. (rpt. 1963, 371)

Long after Keynes wrote, economic growth is still treated by many as *the* objective value, *the* exception to the doctrine that all values are subjective.

Only happiness matters

An interesting variant of the one-objective-value approach is offered by economist Richard Layard, who advocates that public policy be based on the classic utilitarian principle 'the right action is the one which produces the greatest happiness' (2003, 3.16). Layard explicitly states that we need to escape from ethical conflict by embracing a single ethical good: 'The problem with [having] many goals is that they often conflict, and then we have to balance one against the other. So we naturally look for one ultimate goal that enables us to judge other goals by how they contribute to it' (2005, 112–113).

Layard's desire to avoid ethical trade-offs is linked to a distaste for 'politics'. He writes that, in Amartya Sen's view, conflicts between social objectives such as political freedom and social opportunities 'should be resolved through the political process. *I am more hopeful that evidence can be brought to bear*, evidence that tells us about how achieving these objectives affect[s] people's feelings' (2005, 260, emphasis added). 'Evidence', for Layard, does not inform or enrich the 'political process', it is an *alternative* to it. Layard's quest is for an overarching public ethics that stands beyond political debate. Indeed, his public ethics will even be shielded from critical reflection: 'in recent decades it has become increasingly difficult for teachers to teach moral values as established truths, rather than as interesting topics for discussion. We have to pull back from this situation and teach the wisdom of the ages as well-established principles' (2005, 200).

Layard finds the single good he seeks in happiness, 'feeling good – enjoying life and wanting the feeling to be maintained' (2005, 12):

Happiness is that ultimate goal because, unlike all other goals, it is self-evidently good. If we are asked why happiness matters, we can give no further, external reason. It just obviously does matter. As the American Declaration of Independence says, it is a 'self-evident' objective.

By contrast, if I ask you why you want people to be healthier, you can probably think of reasons why – people should not be in pain, they should be able to enjoy life and so on. Similarly, if I ask you about autonomy you will point out that people feel better if they can control their own lives. Likewise, freedom is good because slavery, prison and the secret police lead to nothing but misery.

So goods like health, autonomy and freedom are 'instrumental' goods – we can give further, more ultimate reasons for valuing them. And that is why we are sometimes willing to sacrifice one of these goods for the sake of another. (Layard, 2005, 113)

The passage is revealing on a couple of counts. Most striking is Layard's misquotation of the Declaration of Independence. What is 'self-evident', according to the Declaration, is not the unique status of happiness, but that we all enjoy 'unalienable Rights', including 'Life, Liberty and the pursuit of Happiness'. In this formulation, liberty and the *pursuit* of happiness, not happiness itself, enjoy equal status. Not so for Layard: freedom is a merely instrumental value, while happiness is an 'ultimate' one. But this view of freedom arises from a logical error on his part: the fact that we can identify goods that flow from autonomy or freedom does not, as Layard believes, prove they are merely instrumental goods.

This error of inference is the second revealing aspect of Layard's argument: like so many thinkers who seek a neat and tidy ethical 'system', Layard implicitly denies the possibility of things that are both goods in themselves and means to other goods.[22] Ignoring such mixed goods is not a trivial mistake: it allows one to dismiss any particular good as a mere means, merely instrumental, as soon as one has identified *any* other good that is serves. Because human goods are interrelated, any good could be dismissed in this way, including happiness itself.[23]

Having arrived at his one true good through a dubious reasoning process, Layard proceeds to dismiss concerns traditionally raised by critics of utilitarianism. A key issue is the problem of protecting rights: as philosopher John Rawls argued, utilitarianism leaves rights at the mercy of 'uncertain and speculative actuarial calculations' (1971, 160). Layard offers no argument to counter this, and simply asserts that utilitarian calculations will always protect rights (2003, 2005, 123).

We have reviewed various attempts to treat *one* overarching value as objective. Layard's attempt is revealing in an important respect. He wishes to break away from orthodox economics' traditional obsession with material growth. But he does so as an economist who has internalized many core assumptions of that system of thought, including the deep fear of the subjectivity of values. This illustrates how breakaway thinking can reproduce much of the system it ostensibly seeks to escape. This is a central theme of Chapter 3.

Conclusion

This chapter has examined the basic dilemma of a policy analysis shaped by the binary view: that view holds that analysis must not be 'contaminated' by values, yet policy making and policy analysis are intrinsically shaped by values. Various stratagems to address the dilemma have been examined and their problematic nature has been argued. We must keep in mind that the dilemma is grounded in the binary view itself: abandon the view, recognize that values can be subjected to critical scrutiny and rational assessment, that they do not contaminate rigorous thought but are in truth essential to it, and the dilemma vanishes. We will return to this in Part II, when we examine non-binary analysis.

3

The durable flotsam of the binary view

It is not so easy to escape the effects of the binary view. Even approaches that depart sharply from elements of the view can, paradoxically, rely on some of its most problematic underlying assumptions and implications. Some believe that the binary view has been sunk by decades of criticism. This is, in general, untrue. But even in intellectual circles where the binary view seems to have vanished, the flotsam that has survived its wreckage proves durable. We will examine a few of these survivals here.

Before examining examples of flotsam within policy theory itself, I wish to take up an example of a broader cultural influence that has a powerful impact on education policy in particular. The example will help tease out an important distinction between a consistent rejection of the binary view and a widespread outlook that superficially resembles such rejection.

Many histories

There are various directions in which one may head after accepting that thought is inevitably value-laden. One might opt for 'confessional statements of value preferences', as Mary Hawkesworth termed them (1992, 325).[1] As Hodgson and Irving argue, the ideal of value-neutrality 'seems ever more untenable given the now widespread acceptance that all inquiry is value-laden. Here the job for researchers is to be able to recognise the values we bring to bear, and use these to work for explicit ends' (2007, 201). But even if one succeeds in identifying one's operative values, the crucial question is what comes next. Philosopher Eric Voegelin observed in the 1950s that

> If science was defined as exploration of facts in relation to a value, there would be as many political histories and political sciences as there were scholars with different ideas about what was valuable … As a matter of fact, the idea was advanced, and could find wide consent, that every generation would have to write history anew because the 'values' which determined the selection of problems and materials had changed. (1952, 13)

This notion would seem quite close to the approach advocated in this book. But let us note where it can lead. Much controversy was sparked in Japan when the government approved a revisionist history text. Among other omissions, its coverage of World War II ignored the 'comfort women' forced into prostitution by the army. One of the authors declared that 'Every nation is entitled to interpret history in its own way, and to hand it down to its children as it sees fit' (qtd in Pedroletti, 2001).

The Japanese example is cited here only because an author gave such a frank defense of historical bias. Examples could be given from around the globe, including North America, of how history textbooks are pressed into the service of political values. The Florida Education Act of 2006, for example, stipulates that history courses will instruct students about 'The nature and importance of free enterprise to the United States economy' (Section 21). In Texas, history students must learn about 'efforts by global organizations to undermine U.S. sovereignty through the use of treaties' (Texas Education Agency, 2010).

What is the remnant of the binary view in this? The values that found all these different approaches remain *unquestioned*. They just *are* the values that a particular group of decision makers happens to have embraced, and are not subject to scrutiny. And so one can set up parallel histories, with no dialogue between them. One no longer tries to exclude values from thought, as the 'pure' binary view recommends, but they remain *outside* the process of critical reflection and reflexivity.[2]

There are scholars today for whom the belief that all history is inevitably political, and the associated denial of objectivity, are viewed as progressive and cutting edge. This is ironic. In 1927, French philosopher Julien Benda published an explosive little book, *La Trahison des Clercs*. Benda argued that intellectuals – who in his view had traditionally sought to restrain hatreds between nations, classes and races – had betrayed this mission from the late nineteenth century onwards, and 'given themselves over to the game of political passions' (rpt. 1975, 167). Among other targets, Benda took aim at widespread cynicism concerning the ideal of objectivity. He noted how *useful* this cynicism had been for propagandists on both sides of World War I. Power, and unjust power in particular, always stands in need of illusions. And the belief that there is no such thing as objective truth is a helpful aid to such illusions.[3]

So should we aim for an apolitical teaching of history? That is not the argument here. We need to make distinctions. One can recognize the political implications of any form of thought without seeking to put thought *at the service of* a political agenda. One can further distinguish between putting history at the service of political goals, *which are treated as beyond question*, and allowing historical insight itself to challenge our understanding of political goals.

Binary social constructionism?

Sociologist Alfred Schutz's analysis of our 'typification', or labeling, of phenomena around us, by which we construct our lived reality, shows how even the simplest element of factual knowledge is part of a network of beliefs.[4] His approach thus has a strong affinity with the one developed in this work. Moreover, his analysis also had a great influence on Berger and Luckman's *Social Construction of Reality*, perhaps the best-known work of social construction theory. So one might think that social constructionism would be naturally hostile to the binary view. Some of its insights, however, can be appropriated in a way that manages to reproduce that view.

Policy theorists Anne Schneider and Helen Ingram critique the 'social construction of target populations'. Target populations are 'persons or groups whose behavior and well-being are affected by public policy' (1993, 334). These target populations have 'empirically verifiable' boundaries (335). The 'social construction' of these populations refers *only* to 'the cultural characterizations or popular images of the persons or groups whose behavior and well-being are affected by public policy. These characterizations are normative and evaluative' (1993, 334). Our *factual* knowledge, then, is not socially constructed, only our *normative* attitudes.

To define something is to make it stand out against that which it is *not*. When rigorous, a definition of X says something about X *and* about not-X.[5] Thus, Schneider and Ingram's narrow definition of social construction carries the implication that everything outside the 'normative and evaluative' dimension is something *other* than socially constructed. As the concept becomes a narrow beam, everything outside its light is *naturalized*.

To this framework, clearly grounded in the dichotomy of fact and value, Schneider and Ingram add a special twist: negative attitudes towards target populations are *inherently unjustifiable*. Thus, 'True empowerment and equality would occur only if all target populations had social constructions that were positive' (1993, 345). The assumption seems to be that, precisely since they are *mere* value judgments, these 'social constructions' are inherently arbitrary and subjective. So why should any social group be put at a disadvantage by judgments of that sort?

In a book published a few years after their initial article, Schneider and Ingram appeared to have arrived at a broader understanding of social construction, which had come to denote 'world making or the varying ways in which realities of the world are shaped' (1997, 73). Yet their reference to 'the social constructions of target populations, and other value-laden messages' (11) made it clear that with respect to target populations they continued to limit the concept of social construction to the 'normative and evaluative' elements stressed in their earlier work.

Most importantly, they end up at roughly the same conclusion: 'In truly democratic and discursive systems, virtually all social groups would carry generally positive constructions' (1997, 145). As their examples of social groups include 'fascists', 'criminals', 'drug kingpins', 'gangs' and 'right-wing militia', the injunction is rather startling (1997, 107ff). Rarely does one find such a forthright appeal for society and policy analysis to enter the proverbial night where all cows are black.

Recall that a target population is merely the correlate of a particular policy: it is the set of 'people, groups, and/or organizations whose behavior or capacity the policy is intended to change or effect' (1997, 82). Thus, drunk drivers constitute a target population only relative to any policy meant to affect their actions. Any particular member of the target population also belongs to various other populations. It should be clear that negativity towards a target population often reflects a judgment regarding the actions that define that population. If one disapproves of drunk driving, then 'drunk drivers' *must* carry a negative connotation, which can only be shed at the expense of abandoning the underlying judgment. Thus, uniformly positive constructions of target populations require the refusal to engage in any normative judgments at all.

The binary view's suspicion of value judgments thus permeates Schneider and Ingram's analysis. They might have broken decisively with that view by reflecting on the qualities that make normative judgments justifiable. They needed to reflect, for example, on the basis for a distinction between *unjust* negative stereotypes, such as those related to 'young black men' (1997, 111), and legitimate ones, such as those related to 'drug kingpins', who are 'constructed as violent, dangerous, threatening' (109).

I argued earlier that the binary view's 'great divide' often gives rise to 'cryptonormative' scholarship (Habermas, 1987a, 282). Schneider and Ingram's work is typical in this respect. Their own underlying norms are touched on in passing, as if their meaning will be clear to all readers. Thus: people's 'selection for benefits or burdens should reflect the *legitimate* political power and preferences of groups within the society' (1997, 84, emphasis added). Policy should be 'sensible' rather than 'illogical' (122). It is impossible either to disagree with such claims or to understand just what they mean.

Incommensurability

The insight that we can only observe facts with the aid of theoretical frameworks, most commonly associated with Thomas Kuhn, undermines the commonsensical claim that we have easy access to 'brute' facts, which is a vital support for the binary view. Yet insights from the philosophy of science can also be appropriated in a way that reproduces not the binary view as such, but one of its central implications. In practice, Thomas Kuhn's notion of 'incommensurable' paradigms can extend foundational pessimism, the view that we are inevitably divided from each other by our foundational beliefs, from the realm of values into that of facts.

Incommensurability is a useful concept when understood literally. It denotes the impossibility of measuring two phenomena against each other. One example is the difficulty in claiming unambiguous progress for a civilization as a whole.[6] I have elsewhere argued that cultures are also incommensurable with one another. This does *not* mean that all cultures are 'equal': if A and B cannot be measured against one another, we cannot affirm that one is better than another, *nor* that they are equal (Ryan, 2010b).

Kuhn often used the term 'incommensurable' in that literal fashion. In a 1973 lecture, he noted that a 'good scientific theory' manifests various qualities, such as accuracy, consistency, broad scope, simplicity and fruitfulness. Kuhn went on to comment that 'Individually the criteria are imprecise: individuals may legitimately differ about their application to concrete cases. In addition, when deployed together, they repeatedly prove to conflict with one another; accuracy may, for example, dictate the choice of one theory, scope the choice of its competitor' (rpt. 1998, 103). Lacking some agreed-upon way to weight the conflicting qualities of a good theory, we cannot conclusively 'measure' them against one another.

At times, however, Kuhn pushed the concept of incommensurability farther than this, apparently suggesting that the difference between outlooks is so profound that there is no basis for discussion between them: scientists holding different paradigms 'inevitably talk through each other' (1970b, 109). The 'inevitably' is highly problematic. One cannot prove the claim on the basis of historical data: looking back at a scientific controversy, one cannot know whether dialogue was impossible or merely difficult, or whether people simply did not wish to engage in it.

Kuhn's claims led Imre Lakatos to declare that 'in Kuhn's view scientific revolution is irrational, a matter for mob psychology' (1970, 178). Kuhn accepted that 'my own past rhetoric is doubtless partially responsible' for some confusion (1970a, 259). He thus restated the incommensurability argument: 'In a debate over choice of theory, neither party has access to an argument which resembles a proof in logic or formal mathematics' (260); and then he clarified it: 'Nothing about this relatively familiar thesis should suggest that scientists do not use logic (and mathematics) in their arguments, including those which aim to persuade a colleague to renounce a favoured theory and embrace another' (261). He later advanced a judicial analogy to scientific debates (rpt. 1998, 111). We know that court judgments are often not unanimous: this does *not* mean that debate among the judges is irrelevant. Even in this more modest form, Kuhn's claim should be viewed as an invitation to further study of the history of science, rather than a proven truth. Pearce Williams observes that both Kuhn and Popper used the history of science to build their arguments. Yet the history of science, suggests Williams, 'cannot bear such a load at this time. We simply do not know enough to permit a philosophical structure to be erected on a historical foundation' (1970, 50).

Given the controversial nature of the incommensurability claim, it is surprising how influential it has been within the social sciences. Oddly, many social scientists take the claim that science cannot arrive at conclusive proof as itself conclusively proven.[7] Further, the incommensurability claim has often been interpreted in its more extreme form: paradigms are a prison from which escape is unlikely. Authors who wield the paradigm concept in this way regularly tie themselves in knots.

Burrell and Morgan's influential work on organization theory paradigms, for example, claims that each such paradigm leads those who hold it to 'view the world in a particular way'. As a result, one cannot hold two paradigms simultaneously, and even 'inter-paradigmatic journeys' are rare (1979, 24–25). Now if paradigms really are so all-embracing, this makes perfect sense. But Burrell and Morgan then proceed to give detailed analyses of each paradigm. The question is: if each paradigm belongs 'to a quite different reality' (400), where did *they* acquire the ability to hop from one 'reality' to another, an ability that they deny to the theorists they are studying? Donald Davidson points to the same paradox in Kuhn's own work: 'Kuhn is brilliant in saying what things were like before the [scientific] revolution using – what else? – our postrevolutionary idiom' (1985, 130).

Turning to policy theorists in particular, we find similar depictions of paradigms as prisons.[8] But those who wield the imagery of the paradigm prison appear not entirely to believe what they are saying. Kelly and Maynard-Moody, for example, firmly declare that 'We cannot escape our historically and culturally determined theoretical positions' (1993, 136). Yet faced with concrete issues one can 'bring together various stakeholders' and seek 'intersubjective agreement through the outsider's facilitation' (137– 138). This is done by 'getting participants to look beyond their own valid yet parochial views and interests' (140). So while we may not be able to 'escape' our frameworks, with the help of the analyst-as-facilitator we can 'look beyond' them. But when the prison is a mental one, does not peering over the wall itself constitute an escape?

Marie Danziger's 'postmodernized' policy analysis presents the same difficulty. After declaring that 'a scientist's working paradigms determine the shape of the facts he can never observe neutrally' (1995, 436), she claims that once students 'can define the conflicting paradigms available to them, they are more likely to recognize the crucial weaknesses of any particular perspective, model, or system' (446). Here it seems that the well-trained student has a choice of prisons.

In all this, it often seems forgotten that Kuhn offered not an account of paradigm prisons, but of scientific *change*. That change, for Kuhn, flowed from the very nature of scientific paradigms. Precisely by restricting the scientist's field of vision, a paradigm gives the scientist very precise expectations regarding the results of ongoing observation and experiment. These expectations in turn allow anomalies to emerge. Hence, far from constituting a static and hermetically sealed framework in which theory is immunized from disproof, what Kuhn calls normal science 'prepares the way for its own change' (1970b, 65). So while paradigms appear self-protecting in the short run, they are eventually self-undermining.

Peter Hall, the policy theorist whose work on policy paradigms has perhaps been the most influential, does address the dynamism of science in Kuhn's philosophy, but misunderstands it. For Hall, incommensurability means that

> the process whereby one paradigm comes to replace another is *more sociological than scientific*. It may be set in motion by an accumulation of anomalies, but the ensuing competition between paradigms is likely to be resolved only through a process that involves *exogenous* shifts in the power of key actors and a broader struggle among competing interests in the community. (1990, 61, emphases added)

Hall certainly did not find this in Kuhn. For Kuhn, a revolution is *scientific* only if its outcome can be decided by the community of scientists itself:

> If authority alone, and particularly if nonprofessional authority, were the arbiter of paradigm debates, the outcome of those debates might still be revolution, but it would not be *scientific* revolution. The very existence of science depends upon vesting the power to choose between paradigms in the members of a special kind of community. (1970b, 167, emphasis in original)

Kuhn never argued that revolutions in science were something *other than* scientific: he sought, rather, to change our understanding of what it means for science to be science.

By misrendering Kuhn's concept of scientific revolution, Hall can liken that process to the sort of transition that took place in the UK's macroeconomic policy in the 1970s and 1980s. Politicians became involved in the 'confrontation between Keynesian and monetarist ideas' in 1970s Britain, and 'official decisions' concerning which paradigm to use for policy guidance were 'heavily influenced by political considerations' (1990, 66). Politics being politics, it is hard to imagine this *not* being the case. But for Hall, 'this outcome was *dictated* by the nature of social science itself. The economic doctrines of monetarism and Keynesianism were premised, as competing theories in social science often are, on fundamentally different conceptions of the world' (66, emphasis added).

Hall lists a few differences between monetarism and Keynesianism, neglects their similarities (eg both take the goal of capitalist growth as a given), and then declares that 'It should be apparent that these were two quite different policy paradigms' (1990, 67). But to catalogue differences says nothing about the possibility of discussing those differences and arriving at some shared understanding. Indeed, an endnote calls into question Hall's whole presentation of Keynesianism and monetarism as irreconcilable paradigms:

> by the mid-1980s, both paradigms had been revised to some extent in the light of the claims of the other and intervening economic developments. As they began to converge on some points, it became easier to assess the validity of their tenets, and something of a synthesis between the two doctrines began to emerge. (1990, 75)

One does not normally expect a 'synthesis' of 'fundamentally different conceptions of the world'.

For Pierre-Marc Daigneault, Hall is at the origin of the 'ideas matter' approach in policy theory, and has 'inspired a whole generation of scholars' (2014, 453), yet it is not clear from Hall's work whether the concept of 'paradigm' actually helps us understand the event he is studying. The account of the rise of monetarism in the UK could be told as a simple case in which an inconsistently-applied Keynesianism ran into serious difficulties, which created an opening for a new political tendency.[9] To transfer language from Kuhn's philosophy of science and refer to such policy difficulties as 'anomalies', as Hall does, does not add much if any insight. The more traditional political account, in which economic difficulties created a political opening, provides a satisfactory explanation of the transition from Keynesianism to monetarism, a transition that bears little if any resemblance to Kuhn's concept of 'scientific revolution'. Recall, in particular, Kuhn's insistence that a revolution could only be scientific if the community of researchers enjoys some autonomy. Hall, on the other hand, recognizes that the Keynesian–monetarist struggle did not take place in an autonomous context: 'Over time, an aggressive policy of promoting civil servants who were pliable or sympathetic to monetarist views helped to establish the new paradigm in Whitehall, and many civil servants soon saw the advantages of conversion to the new approach' (1990, 72). The case thus tells us nothing about the possible fruitfulness of dialogue in situations in which people have both the autonomy and the willingness to discuss their differences.

This chapter has identified various residual elements of the binary view, even in approaches that depart from it. Examination of these residues has also helped to clarify the nature of a true alternative to the binary approach. To take one example: as we saw, to say that historical accounts should deliberately be shaped by each nation's values *seems* to depart from the binary view, yet reproduces that view's postulate of the arbitrary nature of values. A true alternative will not do this, and will thus be as critical of many pseudo-alternatives to the binary view as it is of that view itself.

4

Convenient belief

Within the policy world, some people face strong incentives to embrace the binary view, whether or not their belief in it runs particularly deep. Douglas Amy's 'Why policy analysis and ethics are incompatible' (1984) presents an important inventory of the motives for keeping policy analysis free of serious normative reflection. Though the article is three decades old, Amy's argument remains relevant today.

Amy notes that critical ethical reflection can threaten the 'analyst–client relationship': 'Most analysts work for clients who have a strong commitment to a set of goals or programs and who would not be pleased by a report that raised questions about the basic desirability or worth of those programs' (1984, 580). Closely related to this is the threat that ethical reflection might present to the profession of policy analysis itself. The legitimacy of that profession currently resides upon an image of analysts as 'purely technical advisors whose work is value free and apolitical' (1984, 581).[1] Two factors are at work here. One concerns democratic norms: the policy role of these unelected experts 'was politically acceptable because they were never involved in setting policy goals' (1984, 581). The other factor concerns the personal interests of people trained in a particular way. Consider the plight of a young analyst. He has been trained in techniques. He has *not* been trained in thinking about messy things, such as competing values, social norms and so on. In fact, he probably believes that all these other matters concern 'value judgements', questions about which, he assumes, no training is possible. That is, his lived world is shaped by the binary view, even though he's never heard the term before. Naturally, he wants to demonstrate that he is worth his salary. But on the rare occasions when he opens his mouth on value questions, he reveals that he has nothing of real interest to say. Nothing of interest, in particular, to his boss, who from time to time wonders just why she hired him. And so, perhaps unconsciously, he focuses on what he knows best: number crunching. And if number crunching is better for some dimensions of a problem than for others, he focuses on those dimensions that are easier to handle. This almost unconscious bias is often termed 'technique-driven thinking': our techniques shape the very things we take into account when tackling a problem, and the things we ignore.

Amy points to various other reasons why it is convenient for actors in the policy world to avoid normative reflection. When a policy decision is controversial, he notes, officials generally prefer to defend it as a purely technical matter: 'When confronted with a group of inquisitive reporters, irate citizens, or hostile congressmen, it would make little political sense for bureaucrats to follow the advice of some scholars and begin discussing the various ethical deliberations involved in their decision' (1984, 582). Politicians, too, will prefer 'technocratic styles of policy analysis and justification' (583), at least on some issues. On other issues, as Amy notes, politicians loudly proclaim their commitment to 'values' (584). But the binary view points to an underlying similarity between technocratic justification and the proclamation of values such as 'the defense of the family': in both approaches, values remain beyond reflection. We see once again the close ties between the binary view and something ostensibly opposed to it.

Two reminders are in order here. First, none of these convenience benefits of the binary view requires that actors in the policy world truly believe its claims. They may half-believe them, or they can simply respect the 'culture' of their organization and behave *as if* they adhered to the binary view. Second, even feigned adhesion to the binary view need not operate universally. Should an individual analyst be inclined, however, to raise serious normative questions about the direction of policy, bureaucratic filters may well kick in. As Amy notes, 'analysts who try to raise serious questions about basic agency policy are very quickly perceived as threats to their superiors' (1984, 580). Naturally, perceptions that the analyst is 'unsound' will be heightened should their critique 'question the basic tenets of American ideology' (585). The young analyst, in particular, may thus be tempted to at last feign passionless objectivity.[2] Indeed, the benefits to a technocratic and supposedly value-neutral stance being so great, one may be tempted to conclude that it is nothing more than a half-believed performance. One may further come to view *all* forms of objectivity in the same light.[3] This reduction of all objectivity to its most problematic form is a dangerous error.

But if Amy is right, and I think there is much truth to his argument, if the binary view is held because it is an extremely *convenient* view, is the rational critique of that view pointless? To be more blunt: is this work not engaged in a fool's quest? Only time will tell. But we should keep in mind that there is a reason why unacknowledged motives are unacknowledged. One will never hear a politician say: 'I'm going to pretend that my experts are offering me purely factual, scientific, value-free advice, because that way voters are less likely to pay attention to what I'm up to.' The defense of *any* belief or action is more effective when it can point to certain widely valued goods that are thought to be supported by it, or when it can claim to be held on intellectually defensible grounds. Thus, even if unacknowledged motives are the truly determining ones, critique of publicly acknowledged reasons is vital, since they serve as rationalizations for action.[4]

Consider, for example, the invasion of Iraq. Let us suppose that there were decision makers who knew very clearly that claims concerning Saddam

Hussein's link to al-Qaeda, or his support for the 9/11 attacks, were simply not true. For them, these false beliefs were a rhetorical pretext for action, rather than a true reason for it. Now imagine that the general public had come to know, prior to the invasion, that the claims were false. Clearly, this would have left decision makers who were firmly set on an invasion in a difficult position: congressional support would have weakened, the political price of an invasion would have risen. Thus, as Jürgen Habermas puts it, careful critique can limit the 'pool' of rationalizations that are available to decision makers (1996, 484). Analogously, in the case of the binary view, critique can:

- attack, once again, the intellectual credibility of the binary view;
- show that important normative goods are not threatened by its abandonment; and
- show that there is an alternative to the binary view that does not rely on the abandonment of concern for truth and objectivity.

All these points weaken the defenses of the binary view, and can lead at least some policy actors to reconsider that view and think about what life would be like without it.

That said, there is no question that the analyst who wishes to challenge the binary view consistently will need patience, a strong sense of tactics, a clear understanding of the context in which she finds herself and a solid analysis of that context's structure of interests. We will return to this challenge in Part II.

Conclusion to Part I:
A world on autopilot

Prior to examining the durability of the binary view (Chapter 3) and its attractive qualities for many policy actors (Chapter 4), Part I surveyed some of its effects within the policy world. We considered both specific effects, such as end-of-the-line thinking and foundational pessimism (Chapter 1), and a broader impact, the quest for exogenous values (Chapter 2).

But the policy world, of course, is simply an aspect of the world. I wish to end Part I by musing on the various relations that the world of policy might have with our civilization as a whole. I say 'musing' because what follows is clearly speculative. I wish to reflect on the sort of civilization that 'fits' with the binary view, while recognizing that, as has been argued throughout this work, the binary view is half-believed and coexists in this world with other beliefs, which also have their effects.

One can reasonably argue that the policy world is, even now, a space in which at least some of a society's collective aspirations are 'translated', expressed as a series of practical actions. It *could* also be a place where reflection on the implications of those concrete actions, and on their likely side effects, could in turn lead us to second thoughts about our collective aspirations. In doing this, it would contribute to our world's capacity for disciplined normative reflection. This potential role was nicely expressed in Wildavsky's suggestion that 'Analysis teaches us not only how to get what we want ... but what we ought to want' (1979, 18). Thus, policy analysis could serve as part of humanity's 'compass', one of the means by which we reflect upon *where* we are headed and where we *should* be headed (not just how we can get there quicker).

This is not to say that, in an ideal world, every analyst would be as proficient in philosophical reflection as in quantitative modeling techniques, or that we would all be thinking simultaneously about how to get this done and why is this worth doing. To use an analogy: there will always be emergency-room nurses and physicians whose job is to fix immediate problems. But no reasonably functional society would limit its healthcare to this. In the same way, there will always be policy analysts who take the preferences of clients as given, as axioms for action. There is nothing wrong with this, so long as policy analysis as a whole is not limited to that narrow task, and so long as those who perform that narrow task do not enjoy more prestige than analysts engaged in more foundational work.

But what happens when society has little appetite for a form of reflection that goes deeper, that raises normative questions, that refuses to take the 'preferences of society' (whatever that might mean) as axioms for analysis? What happens when policy analysts are trained in such a way that they are unfit for such reflection? When policy reflection *as a whole* is truncated in this way, a civilization's reflection is affected as well.[1] We witness the apotheosis of 'instrumental' or 'means–end' rationality.[2] As philosopher Max Horkheimer put it, *reason* becomes identified with 'subjective reason' alone, a form 'essentially concerned with means and ends, with the adequacy of procedures for purposes more or less taken for granted and supposedly self-explanatory. It attaches little importance to the question whether the purposes as such are reasonable' (rpt. 2004, 3). Elsewhere, I have depicted the difference in forms of reason:

> A stupid dog chases a car. At each instant, it aims at the current location of the vehicle. Since the car is moving, the dog's path traces out a curve, and it runs farther than necessary. Thus the stupid dog. A clever dog chases a car. It makes a rough estimate of its speed and that of the car, and runs in a straight line to where the car will be when the paths of the dog and car intersect. Thus the clever dog. And the wise dog? It calmly watches the car pass by, saying to itself 'Just what would I do with a car were I to catch it?' (Ryan, 2010a)

In so far as our civilization fails to ask just why it is chasing all that it is chasing, we are stuck at the level of the clever dog. From an ecological point of view, one might add, we clever dogs are in many ways more dangerous than our stupid counterparts.[3]

In so far as we limit our reasoning in this way, we are given over to tasks dictated by the immediate 'logic' of the situation. The social world becomes structured by actors moving in contexts with clear and immediate short-term objectives: the chief executive officer, the lobbyist, the politician and, of course, the policy analyst. Many actors will come to resemble novelist Gustave Flaubert's Charles Bovary, who 'performed his little daily task like a horse in a mill, turning forever in a circle, eyes blindfolded, with no understanding of its chore' (rpt. 1961, 23).[4]

The idea of people being captured by immediate tasks is nothing new, and is in fact depressingly familiar in the policy world. As policy theorists Charles Lindblom and David Cohen comment, the 'cognitive tactics' of policy makers include 'crisis decision-making, bottleneck breaking, attending to the squeaky wheel' (1979, 67). These techniques all highlight immediate problems and obscure everything else. David Halberstam writes of a Far

Eastern correspondent who in 1961 tried to talk to Bobby Kennedy about the developing situation in Indochina. 'Vietnam, Vietnam,' answered Kennedy, 'We have thirty Vietnams a day here,' certain that the daily minutiae of the Department of Justice were infinitely more important than a far-away land. Involvement in Vietnam, Halberstam concluded, was, 'a fateful decision unfatefully arrived at', a 'policy which had evolved not because a group of Westerners had sat down years before and determined what the future should be, but precisely because they had not' (1969, 100, 98).

One might object that the binary view has nothing to do with such a state of affairs, which is in fact the product of a simple shortage of time. But this in turn reflects, in part, the meager resources that modern societies choose to devote to spaces in which a deeper form of reflection can take place, one that challenges ends as well as means and that takes up difficult normative questions. It reflects, too, a shortage of *independent* spaces, where a more comprehensive form of reflection can take place, free of the immediate pressures facing decision makers, free as well of the pressures of lobbyists and other interested parties. I am not claiming that the binary view alone is responsible for this lack of analytical resources and independent spaces. Clearly, though, the binary view and a society characterized by such lacks fit very nicely together: the latter has no time for serious normative reflection; the former says such reflection is pointless in any case.

Being on autopilot is fine, so long as we are headed in the right direction. Are we? Given our ecological predicament, many believe that staying the course will be catastrophic. The most obvious danger today is that we will sleepwalk across a climate change threshold. Carbon Tracker, a UK climate research group, argues that the carbon content of the world's current known fossil fuel reserves is between 3.2 and 5 times the amount of carbon the world can afford to burn between now and 2050.[5] Despite this, 'the top 200 oil and gas and mining companies have allocated up to $674bn in the last year for finding and developing more reserves and new ways of extracting them' (Carbon Tracker, 2013). The companies continue to do what they have always done, continue to pressure governments to further their interests, as they have always done. Governments continue to provide the companies with tax incentives for exploration, as they have always done. Pension funds continue to invest in these companies, as they have always done.[6]

On these grounds alone, it is not a good time for a world to be on autopilot.

PART II

Non-binary analysis

What changes for policy analysis when we:

- abandon the binary view;
- understand that our beliefs form a network, that our facts and norms depend upon each other;
- understand that this network doesn't have a final foundation; and
- abandon all forms of foundational pessimism, affirming that there is always something to talk about?

What changes when we *fully* accept this outlook?

Policy analysis does not change from night to day when one embraces the key arguments advanced in this work. Because we only half believe in the binary view to begin with, many of the practices consistent with the outlook being urged here already exist within the world of policy.[1] If the binary view is something we only partly believe, the antidote to it is, to some extent, to do something we already do, but to do it *consistently*, with full consciousness of what we're doing, and why. Philosopher Jürgen Habermas suggests that we need theory to 'correct bad theories' (1993, 76). Thus, we need to undermine the ability of a bad theory, the binary view, to limit good practice, as opposed to seeking out entirely new practices. We need, we might say, to become fully aware of what we know, and act consistently on that knowledge.[2]

This entails, most obviously, that we stop reproducing the effects of the binary view; that teachers, for example, stop providing students with a simplistic binary vision, which students later have to learn to nuance as best they can.

But to say that we must learn to stop reproducing the binary view is a merely negative characterization. It is clearly not enough to say what we must *not* do. So Part II will sketch out elements of a non-binary analysis, a policy analysis fully informed by the core insights of this work. As the questions presented a moment ago indicate, I will proceed by drawing out some implications of the alternative to the binary view that was briefly sketched in the Introduction to this book. We will first fantasize, by ignoring the constraints on analysis, the interests that lead to feigned or sincere allegiance to the binary view, and so on. This fantasy will also imagine a policy analysis endowed with the luxury of *time*. Chapter 5 examines the forms of care of non-binary analysis. Any intellectual approach encourages those who follow it to pay attention to specific matters, to 'take care' in particular ways. What are the matters concerning which the non-binary analyst must learn to take care? Chapter 6 explores the implications for policy analysis of various qualities of our networks of belief. Why does it matter for policy, for example, that belief is a matter of degree? Chapter 7 extends the analysis, considering the implications of our networks of beliefs *and* practices. That is, what we do and what we believe are intertwined in complex ways. Why does this matter? The last two chapters of Part II reintroduce the real world constraints on analysis, reflecting on the wide range of actual contexts in which decisions can be made, the various weaknesses of those contexts and what we can do about those weaknesses.

Though the non-binary approach does not invent new practices, we will see that the implications of a consistent rejection of the binary view are significant. Among other things, it has serious consequences for our assessment of *where* in society policy analysis ought to take place, and for the analyst's *normative* understanding of her relation to decision makers.

5

Forms of care

In the exercise of any human skill, any craft, there are particular matters that require special attention, that demand we *take care*. When driving, for example, we know that merging on to a busy freeway, or passing on a two-lane highway, demands heightened focus.[1] Likewise, in interpersonal relations, there are situations that call for extra care, for special tact. One way to characterize intellectual crafts, then, is to identify their forms of care: to which matters does the craftsperson offer focused attention?

This chapter will examine some of the forms of care that characterize a non-binary policy analysis. I will first argue that a traditional concern with avoiding the deduction of values from facts and vice versa is replaced in a non-binary approach by careful exploration of the variety of fact and value claims that underlie any policy position. A non-binary approach should also lead us to pay close attention to the patterns of attention behind any piece of policy analysis, and critically examine the types of *trust* that support the analysis, and whether that trust is warranted. A non-binary approach must be attentive to the ways in which language shapes our reality: to the uniting or sundering of phenomena by our conceptual categories, for example. Section six further argues that a non-binary approach protects even certain normative goods associated with the binary view, better than does the binary view itself.

From is to ought, and back again

In their 2012 polemic, *Economists and the Powerful*, Norbert Häring and Niall Douglas discuss John R. Commons's 1893 book, *The Distribution of Wealth*:

> He argued that wealth distribution is the result of state policy, notably state regulation and legal rules, which protect and define property rights. He detailed the role that legal rules play in shaping the distribution of negotiation power and the distribution of income. Commons' argument was that state-created entitlements like monopolies, patent, copyright and franchises enable their owners to restrict supply and raise the price of the goods they sell. Since the state *is* one of the most important determinants of the relative values of goods, Commons argued, the state *is* implicated in income distribution and *should* intervene to improve the bargaining power of the weaker groups. (2012, 9, emphases added)

The emphasized words would seem to manifest a great error of reasoning, a careless jump across the gulf from 'is' to 'ought'. As is well known, philosopher David Hume urged readers to be on the lookout for just this sort of mistake. *That* is a form of care recommended by the binary view. Upon divorcing his wife, chess champion Boris Spassky made the painful observation that 'We were like bishops of opposite color' (Brodman, 1996). For the binary view, facts and values are bishops moving on opposite colors: they may pass close to one another, but they never touch. And to jump from one color to the other is forbidden. As C.S. Lewis put it, 'On this view, the world of facts, without one trace of value, and the world of feelings, without one trace of truth or falsehood, justice or injustice, confront one another, and no rapprochement is possible' (rpt. 2007, 702).

A non-binary approach, on the other hand, does not consider Commons's 'leap' to be a fatal logical error. We examine it, instead, in relation to existing networks of belief. Commons is arguing that governments *should* intervene in distribution. Rather than focus on his argument in isolation, let us ask how exactly is the view that government should *not* intervene in market outcomes sustained? While one can find libertarian arguments that government intervention is generally immoral and tyrannical, it is also frequently argued that such intervention is *futile*: there is an irreversibility, an inevitability, about market outcomes. Intervention is countered with a *factual* claim: your interference in the market will not accomplish its objectives, and so it is a waste of time to argue whether those objectives are even worth pursuing.[2]

A normative claim is also implicit in this well-worn argument: one *should not* even attempt the impossible. This could be challenged. Countering political 'realism', Max Weber argued that 'In a sense, successful political action is always the "art of the possible." Nonetheless, the possible is often reached only by striving to attain the impossible that lies beyond it' (1949, 23–24).

But Commons takes aim at the impossibility claim itself: there is nothing natural or inevitable about the distribution of wealth. It is, in part, the outcome of government choices. Other choices can be made. Given the influence of beliefs concerning the naturalness of the market, then, Commons's argument is in fact quite legitimate. It is, of course, incomplete: one still has to make the case that pursuing a more equal distribution of income and wealth is a normative good. That is assumed by Commons, at least as his argument is summarized by Häring and Douglas. To leave out a step, however, is not a fatal error, but a typical feature of real-life argument. The implicit step must simply be filled in. As this is generally the case in real-world discussions, the inadequacy of an argument is only demonstrated once it proves impossible to fill it in with strong supports.

Thus, rather than taking care not to deduce facts from values or vice versa, not to jump the rails between these two supposedly heterogeneous provinces, the non-binary approach must seek to explore how a policy position is supported by various explicit and implicit fact and value claims. This is not a solitary enterprise: typically, it will require searching debate to uncover even *some* of the supporting beliefs of a policy position.[3]

Paying attention to attention

Part I noted that the binary view is problematic both in what it excludes from rigorous consideration, and in the uncritical stance it encourages towards what it includes: 'facts are facts'. The non-binary approach emphasizes that we need to be *reflexive*, to reflect, among other things, on the values and interests that have led us to look at some things rather than others. We need, that is, to pay attention to our patterns of attention.

The values and interests that shape our attention need not be ours. The news media, for example, can direct our attention. The following example is old, but useful, as it displays the interplay between factual and normative beliefs in shaping attention. Herbert Gans's *Deciding What's News*, based on personal observation of various newspaper and television newsrooms, argued that 'there is, underlying the news, a picture of nation and society as it ought to be' (1980, 39). Gans identified 'clusters' of enduring values that shaped news coverage, one of which was 'social order'. For several years, marches against the Vietnam War were conventionally treated in the media as 'potential threats to the social order' (53). In 1968, however,

> most national news media had been persuaded by the Tet offensive that the Vietnam War could or should not be continued. From then on, the news started to see the demonstrators more as protesters, and to pay closer attention to the middle-class, middle-aged, and conventionally dressed young marchers. Eventually, some demonstrations even began to be seen as responses to the moral disorder on the part of the president and his hawkish policy makers. (Gans, 1980, 54)

Note the interplay of beliefs: factual and normative beliefs concerning the war (it *could* or *should* not continue) change media *perceptions*. The 'middle-class, middle aged, and conventionally dressed' get *noticed*. And, implicitly, they are somehow *worth more*, more worthy of being taken seriously.

Patterns of attention that highlight some aspects of reality and leave others in obscurity are as much a feature of scholarly disciplines as they are of popular media. In his essay on the historian's craft, E.H. Carr comments that

The facts are really not at all like fish on the fishmonger's slab. They are like fish swimming about in a vast and sometimes inaccessible ocean; and what the historian catches will depend, partly on chance, but mainly on what part of the ocean he chooses to fish in and what tackle he chooses to use – these two factors being, of course, determined by the kind of fish he wants to catch. By and large, the historian will get the kind of facts he wants. (1964, 23)

It is difficult not to feel uneasy when faced with this argument. Are historical facts, then, nothing but the product of the historian's personal preferences? It is useful here to note an observation from Karl Popper: 'Facts are something like a common product of language and reality; they are reality pinned down by descriptive statements' (1974, 1095). Historical accounts are interpretations, and interpretations may vary. But historical realities impose limits on the range of *legitimate* variation. Hannah Arendt cites Clemenceau's reply to a question about what historians would come to say about responsibility for World War I: 'This I don't know. But I know for certain that they will not say Belgium invaded Germany' (1968, 239).

But this does not entirely dispel the unease. Awareness of the role of focused attention might seem to license all sorts of historical bias, short of outright fabrication. It is a constant of irredentist movements, for example, to justify their attempt to expand their nation's territory by appealing to some historical moment when that territory was at a maximum. In regions where borders have shifted back and forth over the centuries, this naturally creates conditions for bitter conflict, as movements in neighboring states lay claim to the same turf.[4] Historians in the service of such movements need not tell falsehoods: they can simply emphasize those historical facts that are convenient for the movement, and ignore everything else.

Historians may also serve a nationalist agenda by focusing attention on their country's proudest moments and ignoring the shameful ones; again, without necessarily engaging in outright falsehood. So we can see the dangers associated with E.H. Carr's insight. But the response cannot be to pretend that history, or any other discipline, is immune to the problems of partial focus, but, to say it once again, to *take care*: to inquire into the circumstances and motives that might have contributed to a particular piece of analysis. Further, in our own work, presuming we do not simply wish to produce propaganda or one-sided pseudo-analysis, it is vital to think about the 'fish' we have set ourselves up to catch with our questions and our conceptual nets, to ask what other sorts of fish might be out there, how we might be attentive to them and so on. Ideally, a society should have a plurality of fishers, applying different nets to the same issue, to gain a richer understanding. Where this is not possible, we must try to supply whatever pluralism we can with our own resources.

Trust

Many of our beliefs depend upon trust that we have extended to someone or other. Indeed, it is hard to identify just what we would know were such trust entirely absent. An anecdote concerning Mark Twain illustrates the problem:

> As a cub reporter, Mark Twain was told never to state as fact anything that he could not personally verify. Following this instruction to the letter, he wrote the following account of a gala social event: 'A woman giving the name of Mrs. James Jones, who is reported to be one of the society leaders of the city, is said to have given what purported to be a party yesterday to a number of alleged ladies. The hostess claims to be the wife of a reputed attorney.' (Fadiman and Bernard, 2000, 543)

We must trust. But trust, obviously, is something about which we must *take care*. We need to examine critically our own patterns of trust and distrust. Whom do we trust? What sources of information? What *types* of information? Which rhetorical styles? And, of course, *why?* Are these patterns of trust defensible? In what ways are they problematic? In the face of certain contemporary policy challenges, reflection on our patterns of trust and distrust is all the more urgent.

Climate change is perhaps the most challenging issue in this respect. There is probably no single human being competent enough in all the relevant disciplines to be able to assess for herself the precise magnitude of the threat. Two decades ago, environmentalist Jo Thornton sketched an ideal future:

> In the sustainable and just society we envision ... corporate and government scientists will have to share their information in a way that makes explicit the limits of their expertise, authority, and objectivity. Their goal should be to make their 'expert' status obsolete, to make every citizen conversant at all levels of the environmental debate. (Thornton, 1991)

The complexity of the climate challenge suggests the need to revise downwards our expectations about just how scientifically literate we and our fellow citizens can ever hope to become concerning certain issues.[5]

There is a grim irony to this. Enlightenment thinkers proclaimed that modernity was a movement from reliance upon authority to the independent exercise of reason (eg Kant, rpt. 1991, 54). But modernity itself has generated problems of such complexity that trust in some authority or other is unavoidable. Unless, that is, one attempts the agnostic route, and withholds trust from all parties to a debate. In the case of climate change, however, the problem is that many vested interests are seeking precisely this outcome: not to be trusted, but simply to spread uncertainty.[6]

Resentment of this predicament can spark some curious reactions. Policy theorists Anne Schneider and Helen Ingram, whom we met in Part I, complain that scientific experts like to 'construct' problems as 'exceptionally complex phenomena' (1997, 7). So the problems are not *in fact* complex; they have simply been constructed to appear that way. Why? To further the narrow interests of scientists themselves. These self-interested scientists have 'raised issues and defined them in terms that serve the interests of science including gaining more data, funding research, and training and employing professionals' (172). As an example of this nefarious practice, they offer climate change, which 'reached the political agenda not because anyone experienced it' (173). This seems an odd criticism, but in their view, 'the responsiveness of democratic institutions' requires that policy focus be placed upon 'what the public actually cares about' (83). They apparently cannot entertain the possibility that the public *should* care about a problem that is not currently on its radar, or that we may have to trust experts who try to warn us about it.[7]

Language and reality

Our language shapes our lived reality. Here we will consider just one way in which a non-binary analysis should be attentive to the influence of language: by reflecting on the way that concepts carve up our lived world.

We perceive the world through a set of labels, labels that structure and categorize our lived reality. Further, our categories are shaped by our interests, broadly understood. This is as true in scholarly disciplines as elsewhere. As sociologist Thorstein Veblen put it, 'The ground on which a discrimination between facts is habitually made changes as the interest from which the facts are habitually viewed changes' (rpt. 1994, 5). Veblen himself illustrated the point by articulating a set of economic categories quite distinct from those wielded within economics. This further step is important, because, as philosopher Nelson Goodman writes:

> while readiness to recognize alternative worlds may be liberating, and suggestive of new avenues of exploration, a willingness to welcome all worlds builds none. Mere acknowledgement of the many available frames of reference provides us with no map of the motions of heavenly bodies; acceptance of the eligibility of alternative bases produces no scientific theory or philosophical system; awareness of varied ways of seeing paints no pictures. (Goodman, 1978, 21)

That is, awareness of how our categories shape our lived reality can serve to loosen up our thinking and thus create an openness to other ways of thinking. It does not, of itself, produce those other ways of thinking, nor does it prove that those other ways of thinking are superior to the conventional ones. After exposing the 'constructed' quality of this or that 'mainstream' or 'conventional' set of categories, we are still left with the task of providing more *suitable* ones. Suitable, that is, relative to the specific interests that shape our investigation.

The most influential innovation through which Veblen sought to change our thinking about economics was the concept of conspicuous consumption. We consume for two broad reasons, Veblen argued: for a direct benefit from the good consumed – such as nutrition, pure physical pleasure, protection from the elements – and to maintain 'reputability' (rpt. 1994, 53): to signal our respectable social status, to keep up with our neighbors. Adam Smith had already mentioned this latter aspect of consumption, as had Marx, but not until Veblen was it made central to thinking about economic life.[8]

Mainstream economics has always emphasized the relation of direct utility between consumer and product. The narrow focus is vital to arguments in favor of an unregulated market. The basic case for an unregulated transaction is that if it did not benefit both parties it would not occur. Economists accept that externalities in any activity or transaction can affect its net social benefit, for better or worse, and hence undermine the basic case, but tacitly assume that most economic transactions do not generate significant externalities. Veblen's argument, however, suggested that conspicuous consumption by its very nature produced externalities: if my consumption provides me with a superior social status, it is likely providing someone else with an inferior one.[9]

Competition for social 'place' is a zero-sum game: what some win, others lose. It is thus, Veblen insisted, wasteful. That is, all economic activity that 'does not serve human life or human well-being on the whole' represents waste (rpt. 1994, 60). The crucial dividing line that Veblen erects within economic activity is that of net or general benefit: activities within the home that contribute directly to physical comfort are productive, those that are merely 'ceremonial', oriented towards status, are not (37).[10]

So Veblen has made a simple normative judgment – not an unreasonable judgment, but one that conventional economics tacitly rejects. Having made that judgment, what one 'sees' when one looks at economic activity changes. Without the normative judgment, the economic world is full of free transactions that, in general, yield net benefit. With the judgment, much economic activity is seen to yield, in net terms, nothing positive.

Veblen insisted that *all* of society was caught up in the competition for status: 'No class of society, not even the most abjectly poor, forgoes all customary conspicuous consumption ... Very much of squalor and discomfort will be endured before the last trinket or the last pretense of pecuniary decency is put away' (1994, 53). Long before Abraham Maslow wrote, Veblen thus rejected the idea of a hierarchy of human needs that would lead people to satisfy purely physical needs before worrying about social esteem. If Veblen is correct, then it is also possible that parents who make consumption decisions for an entire family may well allow their children to undergo 'squalor and discomfort' in the name of keeping up appearances. This would naturally challenge some policy arguments in favor of transfer payments in income, rather than in the form of specific goods and services.

More generally, an obvious implication of Veblen's simple distinction between productive and wasteful consumption is that all sorts of things may provide utility to individuals, but not to society as a whole. Any policy approach that relies on the mere aggregation of individual preferences, as discerned from market choices, will thus incorporate important biases. The aggregation of market choices will be biased, relative to net social benefit, *in favor* of consumption that generates status externalities, and, by extension, *against* consumption that does not. Aggregation of individual choices generates, for example, an important bias in the income–leisure trade off: higher income presents externalities, while greater leisure apparently does not (Layard, 2005, 47). Similarly, assessing the value of education on the basis of individual choices will overvalue forms of education thought to provide a competitive advantage, and undervalue other forms.

At the most general level, Veblen's analysis calls into question the rationality of our civilization's focus on economic growth. The current standard of wealth, Veblen argued, constitutes

> the point of departure for a fresh increase of wealth; and this in turn gives rise to a new standard of sufficiency and a new pecuniary classification of one's self as compared with one's neighbors ... So long as the comparison is distinctly unfavorable to himself, the normal, average individual will live in chronic dissatisfaction with his present lot; and when he has reached what may be called the normal pecuniary standard of the community, or of his class in the community, this chronic dissatisfaction will give place to a restless straining to place a wider and ever-widening pecuniary interval between himself and this average standard. (1994, 20)

As neither 'chronic dissatisfaction' nor 'restless striving' would appear to be states conducive to happiness, the system Veblen describes appears irrational.[11] That too is a normative judgment. It can be challenged. It can be defended. *All* the categories through which we organize our lived reality, including the categories that underpin our 'value-free' disciplines, are permeated by such normative judgments.

Veblen was drawing distinctions within the category of 'the economy'. This is, unquestionably, one of our most important policy categories. Policy will be guided in different directions, depending on just how we understand the concept. Our conventional notions of economic progress don't account for the loss of nonrenewable resources, nor for the rapid depletion of our global 'carbon dioxide account'. One critique of standard economic measurements was popularized by E.F. Schumacher. Imagine that I survived by living off my current work and a stock of capital. The more I eat into my stock in any given year, the more worried I should be. Devouring my stock is a negative. But in GNP calculations, devouring our nonrenewable natural resources counts as a plus, not a minus, because the activity devoted to pulling those resources out of the ground is included, but no account is taken of the loss of the 'irreplaceable capital which man has not made, but simply found, and without which he can do nothing' (1974, 11).

The conventional form of accounting can thus set 'the environment' and 'the economy' in opposition to one another. In this grand policy clash, 'the economy' is understood in terms of economic activity as measured by GNP. Often, more stringent environmental controls simply slow down the speed with which certain resources are ripped out of the ground. This is seen as a blow to 'the economy', only because of the way that concept is conceived.

GNP will probably always be an important measure. It is a valuable denominator for calculating certain ratios, such as the relative importance of the public debt or the relative weight of taxation upon the monetary economy. Its use as a measure of overall economic performance or well-being is entirely another matter. Were we, for example, to aim above all at reducing the carbon footprint, and the overall environmental impact, of our economic activity, while minimizing the impact of changes on subjective well-being, we would need an entirely different set of conceptual resources.

We have considered just one of the ways in which language shapes our lived reality: our categories both unite some phenomena and divide them from others. Other dimensions of language, such as metaphors and narratives, have analogous effects. In all these cases, our lived reality is subtly shaped; we take on values and assumptions, often without being aware we are doing so. We need to 'take care' in these matters, but this is easier said than done. Taking care of the ways in which language shapes our lived reality is probably easiest when we find ourselves in dialogue with those who do not share our categories and narratives or who resist our metaphors.

Straddling terms

Various words necessarily combine positive and normative dimensions (eg freedom, racism). In Chapter 1, I called such words 'straddling' terms, because they straddle the line between facts and values. Other straddling terms mentioned there include: 'order', as in social order, 'national interest', 'the common good'. A non-binary analysis must remain aware of the vital importance of straddling terms within the policy world, and reflect upon the specific value and fact claims embedded within particular usages of such terms.

For some of the concepts, such as freedom or racism, the value component seems obvious. But let us now consider an apparently rock-hard concept: 'cause'. One of the most important of our concepts, cause is deeply shaped by our values. Consider Weber's strategy of using counterfactual claims to assess historical causality. We assess the historical significance of a particular fact, Weber argued, by asking whether the absence of that fact would have changed history in some important way (1949, 166). A particular event may have many roots, and Weber's approach can help us identify the truly significant ones. Imagine a tottering tower of children's blocks. A faint puff of air blows it over. The puff is the immediate cause of the event, but hardly an important cause: because the tower was unstable, sooner or later it would have collapsed, even had the puff of air not come along at that moment. Analogously, one might argue that the assassination of the Archduke Ferdinand, while an immediate trigger to World War I, was not a significant cause, because sooner or later the conflicting ambitions of the Great Powers would have led to war.[12]

But to say that the absence of this or that factor would not have changed the outcome in 'important' ways provokes questions: Important to whom? Important in light of which values, which interests? Had World War I started six months later than it did, many who died in the early months of that war might have been spared, and others, who survived the war, might have died. Clearly, for them, and for their families, the fact that the war began when it did is hardly a trivial matter, and the archduke's assassination looms rather larger as a cause of the war.

The example may seem fanciful, but in a world in which events can have an infinity of causes, how do we set about separating wheat from chaff, distinguishing the important from the trivial? Historian E.H. Carr provides a fictional anecdote to illustrate the problem:

> Jones, returning from a party at which he has consumed more than his usual ration of alcohol, in a car whose brakes turn out to have been defective, at a blind corner where visibility is notoriously poor, knocks down and kills Robinson, who was crossing the road to buy cigarettes at the shop on the corner. After the mess has been cleared up, we meet − say at local police headquarters − to inquire into the causes of the occurrence. Was it due to the driver's semi-intoxicated condition − in which case there might be criminal prosecution? Or was it due to the defective brakes − in which case something might be said to the garage which overhauled the car only the week before? Or was it due to the blind corner − in which case the road authorities might be invited to give the matter their attention? While we are discussing

these practical questions, two distinguished gentlemen ... burst into the room and begin to tell us, with great fluency and cogency, that, if Robinson had not happened to run out of cigarettes that evening, he would not have been crossing the road and would not have been killed; that Robinson's desire for cigarettes was therefore the cause of his death; and that any inquiry which neglects this cause will be waste of time, and any conclusions drawn from it meaningless and futile. Well, what do we do ? As soon as we can break into the flow of eloquence, we edge our two visitors gently but firmly towards the door, we instruct the janitor on no account to admit them again, and we get on with our inquiry. (Carr, 1964, 104–105)

Carr's question is this: on just what basis do we dismiss the explanation of the two gentlemen? Why do we reject Robinson's tobacco habit as a relevant cause?

We reject their explanation because we can *do nothing with it*. Nothing can be learned from it; no lessons that might reduce the rate of future traffic fatalities. To attribute the event to Robinson's smoking is an example of what I have elsewhere termed a 'Cubbins-explanation': 'it just happened to happen, and was not very likely to happen again' (Ryan, 2000, citing Geisel, 1991). Thus, argues Carr, 'rational and historically significant explanations' are those that 'could also be applied to other historical situations' (1964, 106). The causes upon which we focus are those that 'serve the end of broadening and deepening our understanding ... It is precisely this notion of an end in view which provides the key to our treatment of causation in history; and this necessarily involves value judgements' (107).[13]

So cause, a concept that policy analysis can't avoid, is a straddling term. So too is policy itself. Influential Canadian policy theorist Leslie Pal defines policy as 'the organizing framework for a complex web of actions' (1992, 179). By this definition, the very existence of policy requires some consistency of purpose in a certain field, such that individual decisions can be seen to obey a certain logic. It is in this sense that British cabinet minister Richard Crossman could lament, after some months in office, that 'what we still lack is that coherent, strong control which is real policy' (1991, 52). 'Policy' is thus the opposite of 'drift': 'one had only to do absolutely nothing whatsoever', Crossman quickly discovered, 'in order to be floated forward on the stream' (25).

All this might seem quite factual and clear cut. Just where is the straddling in the term? Because when we speak of policy in the way that Crossman and Pal do, we tacitly denote consistency and continuity in some *legitimate* respect. We would not honor with the label *policy* the actions of a politician who declared: 'My decisions are consistent, they all reflect my reading of the latest polls,' or 'All my actions aim at getting re-elected,' or 'With every decision, I consistently try to reward my party's backers and line my own pockets.' Thus, buried within the term 'policy' is a normative notion of legitimacy of purpose. Within a non-binary framework, we might add that 'legitimacy' is not a hopelessly subjective term: legitimate motives are those that can be openly acknowledged by the decision maker, survive critical scrutiny reasonably well and so on.

As Crossman's lament suggests, 'policy' also denotes control: riding the horse rather than being swept away by it. In practice, what gets labeled 'policy' is often an ex post consistency. At the end of Part I, I cited David Halberstam's argument that early American decisions on Vietnam were taken in a climate of inattention. The demand for consistency can turn such ill-considered decisions into a binding precedent. Near the beginning of Homer's *Iliad*, the Greeks are discussing whether to withdraw from the siege of Troy. Agamemnon declares: 'Shameful indeed that future men should hear, we fought so long here, with such weight of arms, all uselessly! We made long war for nothing' (¶2.119–122). This is a clear challenge to the model of rational calculation. It is generally held that strict rationality ignores sunk costs, that rational decisions look to the future. This is captured in the maxim that one should not throw good money after bad. The concern for consistency argues otherwise. As with Homer's Greeks, in the case of Vietnam it was argued that for the US to pull out would be to dishonor the dead.[14]

This reverses the textbook relation between policies and decisions, in which policies are riverbanks that channel the flow of decisions. The opposite can take place in real life: decisions, even ill-considered ones, create precedents, and the value of consistency demands that leaders live with those precedents. Against the textbook model in which general policies should determine specific decisions, Anthony Lake argues that 'Policy is made on the fly; it emerges from the pattern of specific decisions' (1989, 114). The word 'policy', then, can denote both a normative aspiration to coherence, and a ramshackle reality. In its aspirational mode, policy, as much as 'freedom' or 'order', has a value component. When we set out to *describe* a policy, we are tacitly approaching the matter on the basis of various values.

Protecting the normative goods

We have seen that the non-binary approach should lead us to *take care* with various matters: to pay attention to our patterns of attention, to reflect upon our criteria for extending trust, to think about the way our language shapes our lived reality and so on. But the argument is not that we will take care of these things *instead* of the normative goods traditionally associated with the binary view. On the contrary, the non-binary approach strengthens the protection of these goods, in two ways. First, commitment to normative goods such as objectivity is reduced within the binary view to the status of arbitrary preference. With a non-binary approach, on the other hand, we know that one can give reasons for the importance of any legitimate normative good. The non-binary approach also *extends* the protection, by showing how the challenges to the normative goods extend across the fact–value divide.

Autonomy of facts from values

Many people who embrace the binary view believe that it protects the autonomy of facts from values. The non-binary approach stresses that *our* facts are necessarily influenced by our values: we deem certain phenomena worthy of notice, and ignore others, and this judgment is guided by our interests. Still, what should survive the transition to a non-binary approach is the strong commitment not to let the way we want things to be to influence our perceptions of the way they are.

With the non-binary approach, our awareness of the possibility of confusion between interests, values and the facts upon which we focus should be widened. Thus, we must inquire into the interests and values that underlie *all* our analytical work and thinking, rather than assuming that the only danger is when we allow value judgments to intrude on our scientific work. To recognize the value dependence of our facts does not mean we can jump outside that state. But it can remind us that the facts of which we are aware are *our* facts, that other people may have been led to perceive and to emphasize quite different ones. This is not relativism: the claim is not that all ways of seeing are of equal value. The point is simply to be aware of just how limited is the range of things that each of us is led to perceive, to emphasize, to take into account.

A relative autonomy of facts from values is also vital to avoid the epistemological effects of premature judgment, which can block understanding: of another culture, of someone different from oneself, of an unfamiliar point of view. Historian Barbara Tuchman writes that one of the reasons the British 'lost America' was that they simply couldn't be bothered to understand it: 'The attitude was a sense of superiority so dense as to be impenetrable. A feeling of this kind leads to ignorance of the world and others because it suppresses curiosity' (1984, 229). Tuchman's observation is particularly relevant to the world of policy, since, in some fields at least, policy is often formulated and implemented from a standpoint of assumed superiority.

Once again, the non-binary approach leads us to broaden the issue. The problem with British attitudes at the time concerned not merely their value judgments, but a mesh of positive and normative beliefs. David McCullough notes that 'In the House of Lords in March of 1775, when challenged on the chances of Britain ever winning a war in America, Lord Sandwich, First Lord of the Admiralty, had looked incredulous.' House of Commons member General James Grant, McCullough adds, 'had boasted that with 5,000 British regulars he could march from one end of the American continent to the other' (2005, 6).[15] In the same way, today, the prejudiced person almost always holds incorrect factual beliefs about the target of his prejudice. We need, then, to be on the alert for fact assumptions, as well as evaluative ones, that lead us to deem certain people, cultures or situations unworthy of respect, even unworthy of understanding.

Autonomy of values from facts

Max Weber argued that the strict separation of facts and values was also needed to protect the autonomy of values from facts; to combat the fallacy, for example, that if a view is unpopular, or no longer fashionable and 'current', it must also be *wrong*. But there are problematic ways of understanding this autonomy. The whole idea of a network of beliefs holds that our normative beliefs are supported by factual ones. If a factual support for one of my norms proves false, that *should* lead me to reexamine my normative position. So the autonomy of values from facts that is worth protecting is the autonomy from *irrelevant* facts. So long as I do not embrace a normative belief because I think it is fashionable, for example, the fact that it is *not* fashionable is irrelevant, and should not affect my commitment to the belief.[16]

A proper understanding of the autonomy of values from facts is also relevant to the problem of technical expertise. Consider the following argument:

'Technical questions' are those for which a determinable answer exists, at least in principle. The answer may not be known at the moment, but further research could discover the true answer. These stand in marked contrast to 'questions of policy' which involve value-judgements and choices about the allocation of benefits and burdens among different persons or classes of persons ...

The 'democratic paradigm' can be stated in the following form: 'Questions of policy can always be separated from technical questions. Experts should make this distinction explicit and should have no greater voice in the resolution of questions of policy than the ordinary citizen or layman.' ... This treatment of expert advice asserts that all individuals are equal with respect to their opinions on questions of policy. (Clark, 1974)[17]

The argument seems reasonable at first glance. Yet its sharp distinction between technical and policy questions is clearly drawing on the binary view. That alone should lead us to scrutinize it more carefully. The issue is just what it might mean to say that all individuals are equal with respect to their opinions on questions of policy. We would certainly not expect that any person's understanding of the *facts* is as good as any other person's. Should we expect such equality in the case of individuals' normative views on a particular issue? The question in both cases is how well our normative opinions or factual understanding can hold up under scrutiny, can be 'filled in', supported. It is quite possible that, as part of their consideration of an issue, experts on a certain issue have thought through the implications of various normative positions more carefully than have other citizens. This, of course, depends on the training and orientation of experts. In a world marked by the binary view, many technical experts will be incompetent in normative matters, as was noted in Chapter 4. To the extent that their training is shaped by a non-binary approach, on the other hand, the very practice of focusing on a given policy issue, in all its dimensions, should give both their normative and their factual appraisals greater solidity.

Which is not to say that any of this should be taken on trust. The factual and the normative claims of experts must be put to the test. In such testing, equality of voice becomes important. Among other things, it can help identify collective biases shared by the experts. Within a non-binary approach, we might render the equality of voice that Clark recommends in this way: all people affected by a policy have a right to be heard, in a context in which different views can be put to the test. This does not entail, however, that all normative opinions are of equal value, or that only technical views differ in quality.

Protection from authoritarianism

Max Weber argued that the clear separation of facts from values helps protect students from having professors foist their values on the class. The non-binary approach does not dismiss the concern, but extends it. It should be obvious that students can also suffer from authoritarian professors who insist there's only one way of understanding reality. This can be done by emphasizing some facts and ignoring others. (Imagine a politics professor in some future classroom telling their students: 'Joe Biden won the 2020 U.S. presidential election, which was widely viewed as fraudulent.' This is not a normative claim. Indeed, it is not even an outright lie: at the time of writing, millions of Trump supporters continue to believe the election was stolen. Yet the professor's claim is deceptive and manipulative.) This form of authoritarianism may be more effective than seeking to impose one's values directly.[18]

The binary view, in fact, can undermine the protest against authoritarianism. At least according to Plato's account, the ancient Greek thinker Protagoras shared the binary view's understanding of norms as arbitrary: 'whatever view a city takes' concerning justice and injustice 'is truth and fact for that city. In such matters neither any individual nor any city can claim superior wisdom' (*Theaetetus*, ¶172a). From this, Frederick Copleston notes, Protagoras drew a logical conclusion: 'As far as the individual citizen is concerned, he should cleave to tradition, to the accepted code of the community – and that all the more because no one "way" is truer than another' (1962, 110). The non-binary approach challenges this. When we view norms as containing theories about the world, we are saying that their correctness is not to be decided by fiat, nor, for that matter, by opinion polls. It is precisely the relegation of norms to the sphere of the arbitrary, to the world of preferences, that allows for either an authoritarian imposition or for a slavish subjection to public opinion.

We have considered some key forms of care for the non-binary analyst. That analyst will habitually reflect upon the rich texture of her fabric of beliefs, noting the ways her values lead her to attend to certain facts, and the fact beliefs that underpin her values. She will recognize that many of her beliefs have been taken on trust, and question whether her particular patterns of trust are rational and prudent. The non-binary analyst will also recognize the varied ways in which language shapes his lived reality, and be sensitive to the values that enter into some key policy concepts. Finally, this analyst will be protective of certain normative goods traditionally associated with the binary view, but understand those goods in a consistently non-binary fashion.

Many of these forms of care are related, in one way or another, to the insight that our beliefs form a network in which positive and normative beliefs intermingle. We will now consider other aspects of our network of beliefs, and the consequences of their acknowledgment.

6

Networks of belief

This chapter considers the implications for the policy world of four key qualities of our networks of beliefs: those networks are not transparent; belief is a matter of degree; the categories of true and false can be applied to values and interests; and our networks of beliefs are foundationless.

Opaque networks of belief

Imagine a perfectly efficient library. The library catalog department notes each new item as it arrives, entering the relevant information into its computer system. At any given moment, one can thus identify every single book in the library. Our beliefs, obviously, are not at all like that. We don't consciously register each belief as it enters our head. We have picked up beliefs over the course of our lives, often embracing them without being fully conscious of doing so. This is particularly true of beliefs that do not take the form of explicit propositions: our store of labels and concepts, through which we organize our lived reality, the codes through which we interpret the behavior of others and so on. And so we are never fully aware of our personal network of beliefs.

Several implications flow from the opacity of our network of beliefs. It entails, first, that to aspire to a 'value-free' approach to research is naive, as the aspiration assumes that we can identify our values and lay them aside. Non-transparency also challenges one of the alternatives to the value-free approach: the 'confession' of one's values and biases, since one cannot confess to something of which one is unaware. Where does this leave the policy analyst? An observation from philosopher of science Helen Longino is helpful: objectivity, she notes, 'is a characteristic of a community's practice of science rather than an individual's' (1990, 74). That is, objectivity emerges from an ongoing collective practice of making and critiquing claims and arguments. Thus, it is precisely a searching dialogue between analysts who disagree sharply on a policy issue that can uncover many of their respective biases and assumptions. *Many*, but not all: one of the inevitable limits to all dialogue is that biases and assumptions shared by interlocutors will generally not be uncovered.

We are examining how objectivity is understood and preserved in a non-binary approach because it is a value worth preserving. To the extent that we can identify our personal biases, or have them identified for us, in a critical dialogue, we can understand a policy problem more adequately, respond to claims more fairly and so on. The key word here is *bias*: a preference, a gut reaction, that has not been subjected to critical scrutiny. The binary view's grave error is to identify such 'raw' biases with norms in general. Some reactions to the traditional ideal of objectivity also fail to recognize important distinctions: 'Social science', declares Stephen Leonard, 'is not, and by its very nature cannot be, objective, neutral, nonpartisan or value free' (1990, 124). Note the various terms strung together, as if rejection of one entails rejection of all. But 'partisan' refers to *parties*: what if none of the parties in a particular context seek to further certain fundamental values? What if they are all deeply flawed? One might then seek to be non-partisan *in the name of* important values. Similarly, strong normative commitments can lead one to strive for objectivity, for the ability to transcend one's narrow outlook.

Degrees of belief

A second important quality of the network of beliefs is that beliefs can be held to a greater or lesser degree. They can clash, and their respective levels of influence can vary from one context to another. A number of important implications flow from this.

Time-release beliefs

New beliefs and practices can operate like time-release drugs. E.F. Schumacher observed that, at the outset, a novel claim may be hedged in by traditional beliefs that contradict it. It is only believed to a limited degree. Thus, 'those that bring forth new ideas are seldom ruled by them' (1974, 73). Over time, though, the new belief may triumph over competitors, for good or ill. Hence, ways of thinking can have implications that do not unfold until long after the fading of the culture in which they emerged, a culture that constrained and nuanced them. This has probably been the case for ways of thinking associated with the binary view itself. Michael Polanyi argues that people can embrace the language of 'positivism', minimizing the importance of normative goods, yet 'continue to respect the principles of truth and morality which their vocabulary anxiously ignores' (1962, 233). Until they don't.

Who is at the table?

The fact that belief is a matter of degree increases the importance of who is at the table for decisions and discussions. Consider, for example, the need for gender sensitivity in policy analysis. Anyone can recognize this in the abstract, and, at least in principle, anyone can be trained to do a gender analysis. Yet for those who have been on the receiving end of gender discrimination, who have experienced marginalization in one form or another, the need for gender sensitivity in policy will likely be a much more *central* belief, one that they are less likely to neglect in the day-to-day rush to get tasks completed. More generally, we can say that a relatively representative legislature and government bureaucracy are vital so that diverse experiences in a society are not merely *heard*, through government consultations with 'stakeholders', but *felt*, in such a way that they are more likely to be taken into account.

I don't wish to exaggerate this point: it would entirely run against the spirit of this work to suppose, for example, that men can never really 'get' women's concerns, or that whites can never understand the African-American experience. One of the goals of human dialogue is for people to understand each other's experiences more fully. My argument here is simply that whether certain concerns and perspectives are *compellingly* articulated around a table can depend on who is present.

The problem of firmness, and policy training

A third implication of our varying degrees of belief is that we cannot be sure just how strong a particular belief will prove when it clashes with other beliefs, particularly in crisis situations. This is relevant to the training of policy analysts, and to the development of citizens in general, for that matter. Hannah Arendt commented that 'The sad truth of the matter is that most evil is done by people who never made up their minds to be or do either evil or good' (1978, 1:180). I would add that making up your mind on a question such as this is in part an exercise in imagination, in which one thinks through how one would confront particular crises. It is legitimate to put that issue before students.[1]

To encourage the student to ask what she would do in a crisis situation is part of training in ethical firmness. Some might object that this injects an unacceptable normative component into policy education. In the context of a non-binary approach to policy analysis, the complaint is not decisive. In any case, we should note that training in firmness does not entail the indoctrination of any particular normative positions.

The problem of firmness also raises questions about today's emphasis on critical thinking. First, a supposedly critical approach can easily become a classroom game that leaves beliefs untouched, in which students seek to demonstrate their cleverness by demolishing any idea put forth for discussion. This will encourage the view that critical reflection itself is not a serious business. Further, a critical attitude, divorced from a *self*-critical attitude, can simply reinforce dogmatism. Indeed, there is nothing quite as stupid as someone whose critical skills are marshaled to silence all ideas with which they are uncomfortable. Thus, rather than encouraging students' critical skills alone, it is useful to encourage them to use exposure to new ideas as an occasion to probe their *own* beliefs. Hans-Georg Gadamer suggested that, when reading, we should focus on the points where we are 'pulled up short by the text' (1989, 268). These are the passages that can give us insight into our own network of belief, so long as our knee-jerk response to such passages is not to mobilize our whole arsenal of critical skills.

Policy theorist Douglas Torgerson's 'Priest and jester in the policy sciences' (1992) exemplifies the limits of a one-sided critical approach. Torgerson uses two images to contrast styles of policy analysis: the priest 'sustains the cult', while the jester 'doubts all that appears self-evident'. He continues:

> The priest follows tradition, the jester is impertinent. The priest prizes unity, form, and closure. The jester, perhaps appearing ludicrous, is a friend of openness, paradox, and diversity ... In the domain of the policy sciences, the tension between priest and jester is typically resolved in favor of the priest, so that the jester perhaps needs encouragement. (1992, 225)

Given that Torgerson refers to the fool from Shakespeare's *King Lear* as 'the most renowned of jesters' (1992, 233), it is helpful to consider Michel Foucault's observation that the Shakespearean fool 'saw things better than the most sensible characters, *and was never heeded*'; the jester, that is, speaks 'irresponsible truth' (1994, 3:489, emphasis added).[2]

Under such conditions, the policy jester may, paradoxically, help *sustain* orthodoxy. J.C. Thomson's autopsy of a policy catastrophe, 'How could Vietnam happen?', suggests that dissent can become ritualized in decision-making circles. The official dissenter states his objections: this eases his conscience and helps everyone else feel that they are an open-minded bunch, willing to listen to the dissenter, before going on to do what they were always going to do (1968, 49).

Historically, the character who posed the greatest challenge to the priests was not the jester upon whom Torgerson focuses, but the prophet. Unlike the jester, the prophet is not a vehicle for a *purely* critical thought, a thought that 'doubts all'. The prophet *stands for something*, some positive vision, and it is in the name of that vision that personal risks are run and critical insights expressed. That is, the prophet does engage in critical thinking, but also in something more, which might be termed appreciative thinking, thought that seeks to identify values that are worth defending.

While talk of prophets may seem archaic, we have already noted a potentially prophetic role for the policy analyst: to alert society to problems that it is ignoring, or even prefers not to think about. That is, a prophetic policy analysis is not limited to problems that 'the public actually cares about'

(Schneider and Ingram, 1997, 83), nor, for that matter, to problems that political and economic elites actually care about.

No metaphor is perfect. The metaphor of the prophet can evoke someone who seeks the self-satisfaction that arises from speaking one's truth without regard to its effect, one who is careless about developing and applying the skills that might increase the chances of being heard, and so on.[3] So I must specify that the policy prophet I am thinking of is passionately concerned with results. The climate prophet, for example, would feel no smug satisfaction at having been in the right as they watch our slide towards an 'uninhabitable earth' (Wallace-Wells, 2019).

If, then, we wish to train students to challenge today's policy orthodoxy, and tomorrow's as well, and to challenge orthodoxy not just in the classroom but in life, we would do well to encourage students' appreciative thought as well as their critical skills. That is, we can encourage them to reflect upon questions such as: What do you stand for? What do *you* think is worthy of serious commitment? And why? What reasons can you give in support of your commitments?

True and false values and interests

If we accept that a quality of true statements is that they can hold up against all objections (MacIntyre, 1988, 358),[4] then it makes perfect sense to say that normative statements can be true or false. A shift in mental images helps clarify this. Our normative beliefs do not constitute a 'pyramid' built on unquestioned values or interests that simply *are*. Rather, as I have emphasized, our normative and positive beliefs as a whole form a foundation-less 'network'. Any particular belief, whether normative or factual, is sustained by other beliefs in our network, sustained *more or less solidly*. Any element in the network has its supports. On the other hand, any belief can be called into question, and may crumble in the face of serious scrutiny. In this sense, values can be true or false, and so too can our understanding of our interests, including the 'national interest'.

This is certainly not a novel claim. In his *Theaetetus*, Plato comments that 'when it is a question of laying down what is to the interest of the state and what is not ... the decision of one city may be more in conformity with the truth than that of another' (¶172a). This may strike the modern ear as odd; but observers regularly judge countries to have followed a *mistaken* path. They may not specify, however, just what they mean by that. The implicit claim may be that key policies will not yield their objectives. The critique can also run deeper, arguing that the policy objectives themselves should not be pursued.

An example of the first type of critique was offered by Keynes, who argued that the reparations from Germany stipulated by the Treaty of

Versailles simply could not be paid, given the losses to Germany's export capacity that also resulted from the treaty (rpt. 1963, 7ff). Adam Smith gave an important example of the comprehensive critique, when his 1776 *Wealth of Nations* argued that Britain's central policy objective of maintaining control of the American colonies was misguided. While letting go might be 'mortifying to the pride' of the nation, 'Great Britain derives nothing but loss from the dominion which she assumes over her colonies' (rpt. 1937, 582, 581).[5]

Still, while we are accustomed to speaking of policy choices as mistaken, the claim that the values and interests that underlie policies can be *true* may provoke unease. It was suggested earlier that a true claim can survive 'all objections'. But can *any* norms be held true, then? It may be easier to answer in the affirmative if we abandon a black and white understanding of truth and falsehood, and recognize that beliefs can enjoy varying degrees of truth. We already do this in the realm of facts. As philosopher of science Karl Popper argued, 'whether a statement is true or false, there may be more truth, or less truth, in what it says' (2002a, 316). Thus, Newtonian dynamics, 'even though we may regard it as refuted, has of course maintained its superiority over Kepler's and Galileo's theories' (319).

As a simple example, consider the principle of addition of velocities. This holds that if I walk at 5 km/h from the back to the front of a train that is moving at 120 km/h, I am moving relative to the earth at 125 km/h. But this is only true to a 'certain level of accuracy', and becomes increasingly inaccurate as the velocities in question increase (Taylor and Wheeler, 1966, 51). Still, the principle will serve us quite nicely for most purposes, so long as we stay away from the speed of light. So is the principle true or false? We are likely to say this is true, except under extreme circumstances that we won't encounter in ordinary life. It is true, *more or less*.

An example I have used elsewhere also points to the rich texture of our understanding of truth. Suppose I said 'Last night, I sat by the river and watched the sun go down' (Ryan, 2014a, 78). Were someone to exclaim 'Liar! The sun doesn't "go down," it's the earth's horizon that moves up,' most people would regard the objector as obtuse. Why? Because my statement is true when considered in light of its purpose, which is to tell you what I did last night, not to advance an astronomical theory. Thus, just as a tool may serve for some purposes and not others, a statement may work fine when used in one way but not when applied in other ways:

> Suppose that we confront 'France is hexagonal' with the facts ... is it true or false? Well, if you like, up to a point; of course I can see what you mean by saying that it is true for certain intents and purposes. It is good enough for a top-ranking general, perhaps, but not for a geographer. (Austin, rpt. 1975, 143)[6]

These considerations can obviously be extended to the normative realm. Thus, in claiming truth for a norm, we may be claiming that there is some *core* to that norm that will survive all critical scrutiny, as with Newtonian physics. Or we may be saying that it stands up to all objections we can conceive at this time, *better* than any rival normative claim, and that we expect it to continue performing better than its rivals in the future. Or our claim might be that the norm, like the principle of addition of velocities, is perfectly adequate for all situations that we can expect to confront in real life.[7]

There is no 'end of the line'

Chapter 1 noted how often the binary view can lead people to believe that this or that normative position constitutes the 'end of the line' for dialogue. According to this view, one can push people to explain their position to a certain extent, but eventually one reaches 'differences about which men can ultimately only fight' (Friedman, 1953, 5). The non-binary approach, in contrast, asserts that we need *never* be disarmed in the face of normative claims. Let us consider some of the forms of dialogue that emerge from this realization.

Understanding that normative claims are typically linked to implicit positive beliefs leads us to fruitful questions in the face of an unfamiliar normative argument: what would have to be true about the world for this argument to make sense? And are these premises true? The normative claim is supported by other claims, some positive, some normative. Which of these seem reasonable to us? Which do not? What support exists for the latter?

The non-binary approach does not encourage what pragmatist philosopher Charles Peirce termed 'make believe' doubt (rpt. 1966, 188).[8] Our dialogue will be contextual, focusing critical attention on some claims, not on all. This strategy both makes productive dialogue possible *and* constitutes an inevitable limitation of all serious dialogue. Thus, participants in dialogue must maintain the awareness that many of their shared beliefs, both positive and normative, have not been seriously tested, that there is always much that goes without saying, and which may be questioned by others in future dialogues. Thus, the fact that we have reached a meeting of minds in dialogue does not guarantee the correctness of our conclusions.[9]

Because each person's network consists of positive and normative beliefs that support each other in complex ways, our approach to disagreements can be flexible, seeking to identify on which front we are most likely to advance in any given case. Sometimes, clarification of disputed facts may be helpful. In many disputes, that leads nowhere, as each side has a comprehensive set of (true or false) fact claims at its disposal and resists questioning of those. In such cases, it may help to shift levels, to find the values, even the hopes, that underlie different positions and that condition each side's selection of facts.

Often, progress may occur by clarifying terminology. This can be useful because, as argued in Chapter 1, two people may affirm apparently identical statements yet remain miles apart. 'I support equality of opportunity,' as we saw, can entail radically different commitments, depending on how each person understands existing barriers to that equality. Conversely, people who appear sharply divided on an issue may be not worlds apart, but 'only words apart' (Davidson, 1985, 134). My research on Canadian multiculturalism debates, for example, found that supporters and opponents generally denote very different things by the word (Ryan, 2010b). Given this, it is unfortunate that, while pollsters regularly ask Canadians how they feel about multiculturalism, they almost never ask just what the word means to them.[10]

Clarification of terms was, in fact, one of Socrates's favorite strategies. Before challenging a particular claim, he would often press his interlocutor to clarify its meaning (eg *Republic* ¶331e). In the process, he demonstrated that not only can the meaning of terms differ between people, but also that we cannot even assume that the meaning of our own words is fully transparent to us.[11]

A particularly potent support to end-of-the-line thinking is the belief that those who differ on some issue are more or less *crazy*. For an example from the policy world, consider Aaron Wildavsky's discussion of environmentalists in his influential *Speaking Truth to Power* textbook. Wildavsky claimed that environmentalists opposed market solutions to pollution issues because they view money as 'a repulsive symbol' (1979, 192). This evidence-free assertion triggered others: environmentalists, he declared, were akin to primitive peoples fretting over the purity of the tribe (193). Non-smoking areas in restaurants, for example, aim in Wildavsky's view to separate 'the pure from the defiled' (194). Indeed, Wildavsky gasped, environmentalists even welcomed OPEC's increase in oil prices: 'No primitive people sacrificing youth to appease a vengeful god were more in the grip of a system' (195).

Wildavsky's rhetoric may strike us as comical, but its effect is not: it serves to paint the policy opponent as *beyond reason*. Today, this rhetorical style is often wielded by those opposed to 'Islamism'. For Benjamin Barber, 'Jihad' views war as 'an end in itself', rather than an 'instrument of policy' (1992, 58). If this were the case, if 'Jihad' had no objective except itself, there would be nothing we could do to avoid a war to the death. 'New Atheist' Sam Harris takes this to its logical and chilling conclusion. Islam itself, he asserts, is a 'thoroughgoing cult of death' (2004, 123). This means that the strategy of deterrence and 'mutually assured destruction' used in the Cold War will not avail us in dealing with a regime that 'grows dewy-eyed at the mere mention of paradise' (128–129). Thus, should an 'Islamist regime' obtain long-range nuclear weapons, the 'only course of action available to us' might be a nuclear first strike, even though this would 'kill tens of millions of innocent civilians in a single day' (129). In Harris's case, unreason is attributed directly to religious beliefs. For Wildavsky, the beliefs in question are depicted with religious language: 'vengeful god', 'pure', 'defiled'. Such language is a reliable symptom of dismissal, of a casual assumption that opponents are beyond reason. It is, unfortunately, all too common in policy debates.[12]

Faced with such blithe dismissal of differing views, it is helpful to note sociologist Alvin Gouldner's comment that the attribution of phenomena to madness 'is a confession of intellectual impotence' (1973, 403). It is a sign that the writer has simply given up trying to understand whatever perplexes them. The alternative is to assume that our sense of the 'craziness' of someone's position is probably triggered by a sharply different web of positive and normative beliefs, and that attempting to understand that web will weaken the initial reaction to it. This assumption is not relativist: the point is not that any network of beliefs has its own validity, or that all networks are created equal. Any network can be full of all sorts of falsehoods, and some of them may be truly monstrous. It is probably just such monstrous falsehoods that allowed the September 11 murderers to commit their evil.

But to say this is not to say that we are in the presence of madness. The latter is always a risky hypothesis, because it declares that there really is nothing further to talk about. The other party is permanently and essentially beyond our reach. To reject this assumption, of course, does not mean that we can *in practice* enter into dialogue with the other. As noted earlier, the non-binary approach asserts only that 'There is always something to talk about, if we're willing to talk.' It also recognizes that, in many contexts, people will have strong motives *not* to talk.

These motives will be particularly strong in what philosopher Eric Voegelin termed a gnostic political movement (1952). Such a movement trains its members to view any challenge to the group's beliefs as itself evil.[13] When fully indoctrinated, the member of such a group may well be 'beyond reason'. One should not assume this to be the case with the group's *leaders*, however: they may well be open to discussion, negotiation, tactical compromises. In general, it is foolish to assume that the motives and outlook of leaders and decision makers are identical with those of the people who carry out their decisions.[14]

In this chapter, we have examined some further implications of certain qualities of our networks of beliefs. Both the aspiration to value-free analysis and the injunction to be up front about our values represent impossible demands, because our networks of beliefs are not fully transparent even to us. This suggests that objectivity, to the extent that we can obtain it, is to be found through dialogue with others who think differently from us. The fact that we hold particular beliefs only to a certain degree has numerous implications: it can increase the power of certain beliefs over time, as countering beliefs wane in influence; it increases the importance of the question of who gets to sit at the policy table; and it highlights the importance of training in ethical firmness. Because our networks of belief do not bottom out at some limited set of axioms, there need be no end of the line in discussions with others. Because our normative beliefs, in particular, do not constitute a pyramid based on axiomatic norms, we can meaningfully speak of values and interests as being true and false.

Our beliefs, of course, are not isolated from our lives: they shape our practices, and are shaped by them. Having examined the policy implications of our networks of beliefs, we will now examine some implications of this broader network, the network of beliefs *and* practices.

Networks of beliefs *and* practices

Beliefs and practices are obviously intertwined. Much of what we do, we do because of beliefs we hold. Most obviously, we do many things because we believe that they are *worth doing*.[1] But the reverse is also true: our practices also shape our beliefs. This can happen, for example, because we embrace beliefs that justify our actions. Aristotle observed that 'those who have done a service to others feel friendship and love for those they have served' (*Ethics*, ¶1167b). Note the causal direction: *from* doing a service, *to* warm feelings.[2] Carol Tavris and Elliot Aronson use a striking metaphor to describe how conviction grows in the wake of our choices. A person facing a momentous yet uncertain decision is perched on the apex of a pyramid. Having chosen one way or the other, rationalization kicks in, and the person slides down one side of the pyramid or the other, becoming ever more distant from the person they would have been had they chosen otherwise. 'By the time the person is at the bottom of the pyramid', Tavris and Aronson comment, 'ambivalence will have morphed into certainty, and he or she will be miles away from anyone who took a different route' (2007, 33). Actions can shape beliefs in more indirect ways as well. The act of entering a particular social milieu, such as a new organization, will over time affect our network of beliefs.[3]

We can thus think of practices and beliefs as constituting a wider network than that of beliefs alone. Throughout this work, we have noted various characteristics of the network of beliefs. We can assume that the broader network, which includes practices, shares these qualities.[4] Let us now examine some other implications of this broader network of practices and beliefs.

Means and ends

The world is not neatly chopped into simple means and ends. Certain practices pursue multiple ends, and some things are both goods in themselves and means to other goods. We will explore the implications of this claim in an unusual way, by considering the position of someone who *denies* it.

'In any given person's value system', argues policy theorist Ralph Ellis, 'there are literally thousands of extrinsic values'. But 'there are only a very few things that could possibly be construed as valuable for their own sake' (1998, 12). From the outset, then, Ellis leaves aside the type of good that is both a means to other goods and valued in itself.[5] The point may seem minor, but a dangerous oversimplification of the world has already been imposed a priori. Every good must be slotted into one category or the other. One can therefore not grasp the complex relationships between human goods: the possibility that something might serve multiple ends, that many of these ends are means to other ends, that there are many things we value both in themselves and for what they yield, and so on.

This leads Ellis to make various claims of this sort: 'it is easy to see that the practice of creating or consuming any given art form – granted that each is unique and not precisely replaceable – has extrinsic value whose purpose is some experiential event' (1998, 50). This is not, in truth, 'easy to see' at all. Indeed, one may wonder whether talk of 'consuming' art in order to enjoy an 'experiential event' doesn't miss the point of art altogether.[6] More generally, to believe that we can pin down the 'intrinsic' reasons why we value something assumes complete self-transparency: we can look inside ourselves, and identify exactly what we are seeking through any given activity. Given our non-transparency, it is a very risky operation to assume one knows just which intrinsic goods are being served by one's various activities and commitments.[7]

There is an environmental analogue to Ellis's approach: the belief that one can identify exactly what purpose is served by this or that aspect of the natural world. James C. Scott's discussion of late eighteenth-century German 'scientific forestry' is illuminating. In this approach, forests served just one purpose: state revenue. Scott comments:

> From a naturalist's perspective, nearly everything was missing from the state's narrow frame of reference. Gone was the vast majority of flora: grasses, flowers, lichens, ferns, mosses, shrubs, and vines. Gone, too, were reptiles, birds, amphibians, and innumerable species of insects. Gone were most species of fauna, except those that interested the crown's gamekeepers. (1998, 12)

The 'next logical step' was to remake the forest itself: 'the underbrush was cleared, the number of species was reduced (often to monoculture), and plantings were done simultaneously and in straight rows on large tracts' (15). As inhabitants of a planet that has undergone centuries of such wild experiments, we know all too well how the German one ends: 'the negative biological and ultimately commercial consequences of the stripped-down forest became painfully obvious only after the second rotation of conifers had been planted. It took about one century' (20).[8]

As with the natural world, so too with the microcosmos of the person. We are to some extent a mystery to ourselves. Ellis, in fact, explicitly recognizes that we are not self-transparent.[9] Yet he proceeds as if we were:

> The way we know which values are intrinsic and which are extrinsic is by asking ourselves certain kinds of questions about our value feelings. The essential question we must put to ourselves is: What purpose does the value in question accomplish, and would it still have value if it failed to accomplish its purpose or even defeated the purpose? (Ellis, 1998, 49)

This is a dangerous way to live one's life. But there is a broader policy implication: Ellis doesn't just claim that *he* is seeking 'some experiential event' at the art gallery, he asserts that *everyone* is doing the same. Policy analysis, Ellis is suggesting, is authorized to take a resolutely external stance, one that can deduce just what social actors are doing and seeking, without asking them: 'we must make inferences to determine how people *would* interpret the structural interdependencies of their value beliefs (with the extrinsic ones depending on the intrinsic ones) *if* they were to become more reflective about these structures than people often are' (1998, 49, emphasis in original).[10] Ellis's own analyses of the 'consumption' of art, however, or of the true 'intrinsic' purpose of 'social traditions' (48), are highly questionable. This alone should give any responsible analyst reason to pause before claiming to know just which intrinsic goals her fellow citizens are pursuing.

Ellis goes quite far in applying his doctrine of intrinsic and extrinsic goods, claiming that 'there is only basic natural right whose protection has an intrinsic value: the right to have one's society organized in such a way as to achieve an appropriate balance between welfare maximization and distributive justice' (1998, 93). As it happens, this is precisely the sort of society that Ellis himself is advocating, so the one and only intrinsic 'natural right' is … to live in the sort of society in which Ellis thinks we should live!

Ellis's various simplifications are intertwined. The apparently innocuous assumption that the world is carved into means and ends, denying the possibility of something being both, entails that, as soon as one notices some end that a particular right serves, that right can be viewed as a mere means. Further, one can simply *stipulate* the end that any particular right or practice serves by adopting an external perspective that does not inquire into the motives actually articulated by social actors themselves.

Ellis is only a single policy theorist, but his stance is not idiosyncratic: the training of policy analysts often saddles us with external perspectives of which we are scarcely aware. In traditional microeconomics, for example, we are taught that the supply of labor is shaped by the worker's trade-off between two goods: leisure and money. Work is a 'disutility', whose purpose, quite simply, is to get paid, so that one can consume. The assumption is of long standing: for Jeremy Bentham, 'the desire for labour for the sake of labour … seems scarcely to have place in the human breast' (qtd in Lane, 1991,

375).[11] Armed with this a priori assumption, there is little sense in actually *asking* people just what satisfactions they get from their work.

The immediate alternative to an external approach is an interpretive approach that recognizes that people and their lived realities are not an open book, and devises ways to find out, *from the social actors themselves*, just 'what the devil they think they are up to', as anthropologist Clifford Geertz put it (1974, 29). But we must remember that there are *two* problems with Ellis's approach: its external perspective on actors' 'intrinsic' goods and its assumption of transparency. An interpretive approach, on its own, addresses only the first of these (Habermas, 1987b, 149). Thus, an interpretive approach needs to be complemented by a *critical* assessment of actors' understanding of themselves and their social reality.

Multiple ends in the workplace

If we apply an interpretive approach to the question of just what people get out of work, what ends it serves for them, we will certainly find that almost all of us work for money. But we also work for other things: human companionship, a sense of accomplishment or a sense of life meaning. These other payoffs from work are hardly trivial. Consider just one of them: Victor Frankl famously argued that the quest for meaning in life is our 'primary motivational force' (1984, 121). Whether or not he is correct, it is certainly clear that many people will not rest content with the sense that their life is meaningless, and many look to their work and careers for at least part of their sense of life meaning.

If a practice serves multiple ends, what are the implications of viewing it, even transforming it, from the perspective of just one of those ends? As was just noted, mainstream economics has traditionally assumed that work is a means to a single end: the income that sustains our consumption. Alasdair MacIntyre comments: 'So normal is this view among us that it seems natural too. But from another perspective it is precisely unnatural. On this rival view, what is essentially human is rational activity, and consumption exists to serve activity and not to be served by it' (1979, 44). To organize work to maximize only one end can lead to the atrophy of the other goods that it might further. To quote MacIntyre again: 'Only sentimentalists believe that work ought or can be always interesting, but in an order where work serves consumption it is bound to be always uninteresting' (44).[12]

An obvious objection to this line of analysis is that an organization that tried to respect the wide range of goods pursued by its members could never do anything properly: efficiency requires focus on a very limited number of objectives. Nevertheless, some type of 'constrained maximization' should be possible, in which various goods are treated as constraints on the pursuit of narrow efficiency. If the employees of an organization have a reasonable level of voice, for example, they can aim to protect the quality of the work experience even as management seeks efficiency gains.

Attention as a scarce resource: nudges and habits

Our consciousness is narrowly focused. The reason is simple: conscious attention is a limited resource. Because we can't pay attention to everything at once, we pay attention to some parts of the world around us, and let other parts sit in the background of our perception. As a result, 'Our capacity for overlooking is virtually unlimited' (Goodman, 1978, 14).

The power of what Thaler and Sunstein (2008) call 'nudges' arises from this scarcity of conscious attention. Consider organ donations. In Austria, which has a 'presumed consent' system under which one must explicitly opt out, 99.98 percent of citizens are registered as potential organ donors. In neighboring Germany, which follows the opt-in approach, only 12 percent are registered (Johnson and Goldstein, 2003). To opt in or opt out is as simple as ticking a box, usually when renewing one's driver's license, so how can the policy choice of an opt-in or opt-out approach have such an enormous impact? The power of default options shows that often we simply don't *want* to decide something one way or another. Every conscious decision draws upon our limited supply of attention: 'making a decision often involves effort, whereas accepting the default is effortless. Many people would rather avoid making an active decision about donation, because it can be unpleasant and stressful' (Johnson and Goldstein, 2003, 1338). While Sartre insisted that 'If I do not choose, I am still choosing' (1996, 63), most of us clearly do not believe that in practice: we act as if we can avoid choice if we just go with the flow, the default option, whatever it may be, unconsciously putting off a decision to some future moment that may never arrive. As Thaler and Sunstein put it, 'One of the causes of status quo bias is a lack of attention. Many people adopt what we will call the "yeah, whatever" heuristic' (2008, 35).

So the limits of attention hold as much for action as for perception. We cannot consciously focus on everything we are doing. Hence the importance of habit. Musicians and athletes understand the concept of muscle memory: repeated practice of a specific movement allows it to be performed without conscious focus. As philosopher Paul Ricoeur notes, 'the acquisition of habits liberates attention by entrusting action to habitual systems which start and unwind like supervised automatisms' (1965, 87).

Habits are not merely physical: they can be social as well. Our social roles, which facilitate 'recurrent patterns of interaction', are an obvious example of this (Berger and Luckmann, 1967, 33). The student entering a new classroom in September does not have to decide afresh how to 'be' a student, but can slip into a general pattern of 'studentish' behavior acquired over time. This reliance upon social habit 'permits attention to be devoted to the novel aspects of a situation', as Herbert Simon notes (1965, 88).

Now social roles bear norms within them: a set of expectation about how students *ought* to behave, for example. The ubiquity of roles shows how habit can produce norm-guided behavior, without conscious thought or calculation about whether those norms are to be followed or not. Some thinkers, in fact, have suggested that norms are only stable when embodied in habit. For Aristotle, 'It is from habit, and only from habit, that law derives the validity which secures obedience' (*Politics*, ¶1269a). The authors of *The Federalist*, holding that 'Man is very much a creature of habit', inferred that even the wisest government depends upon 'that veneration which time bestows on every thing' (Hamilton et al, rpt. 1937, 168, 328).

A policy approach that neglects the role of habit, perhaps assuming that individual actions are for the most part conscious and 'rational', may thus trigger unsought side effects. An emphasis on incentives, in particular, may counter the stabilizing effects of habits, perhaps by undermining people's semi-conscious sense that 'this is the way we do things here'. The whole point of a new incentive, of course, may be to counter established practice. This is not, however, always the case. Gneezy and Rustichini's famous day-care experiment illustrates the problem. A fine levied on parents who arrived late to pick up their children at Israeli day cares actually increased the number of late pickups. This obviously challenges the policy approach that assumes that 'When negative consequences are imposed on a behavior, they will produce a reduction of that particular response' (2000a, 2). An outcome that parents had previously avoided, either because they felt it violated a social norm or because they were uncertain of the consequences of late arrival, had been transformed into a simple service that carried an explicit price.

A second study by Gneezy and Rustichini also demonstrated the potential for incentives to yield unexpected results. The research subjects were high school students doing volunteer work raising money for various charities. Offering some of the students a financial incentive substantially lowered their performance. The researchers conclude that motivations are not simply additive: an extrinsic incentive can weaken the intrinsic one, 'and the net effect may be a reduction in the activity' (2000b, 802).

Both of Gneezy and Rustichini's studies suggest something that must be taken into account by a non-binary policy analysis: the potential fragility of norms and values. Strikingly, when fines were removed in the final phase of the day-care study, late arrivals did not return to their pre-fine levels. For Gneezy and Rustichini, this suggests a maxim: 'Once a commodity, always a commodity' (2000a, 14). That is, once a social interaction has come to be seen as a paid service, people do not easily revert to a pre-commodity perspective. The norm that one should do one's best to pick up one's child on time did not survive the experiment unscathed.

The point can be generalized: organizational innovations that appear efficient when considered in isolation may undermine norms that contributed to workplace productivity. Analogously, a policy that restricts the benefits from a program to those who are most needy may undermine the sense of social solidarity that sustains public support for the program. Such effects can occur even though people, when surveyed, continue to give verbal assent to the values in question.

A non-binary analysis must thus consider how a particular policy change may influence the power and salience of social norms. Influences on norms need not be negative. Problematic norms can also be fragile, which suggests that they need not always be attacked through a root causes approach. A common difficulty with the latter is that the hypothesized root causes of a problem may not be accessible to policy, or addressing them may be a task that is simply too vast to contemplate.[13] A book on environmental policy, for example, argues that 'our consumer mentality is the source of our problems'. Hence 'no Band-Aid solution will work. The domination of people by other people and the domination of the environment by certain people are both products of worldviews in need of change' (Davion, 1994, 5). This may be entirely true. Yet the argument could be a recipe for paralysis and despair, unless one recognizes that even policies that cannot fully solve a problem may still alleviate it, to a greater or lesser degree. The dismissal of 'Band-Aid solutions' may obscure this point.

That dismissal, and the root causes approach that encourages it, also suffer from an overly simple conception of the relation between beliefs and practices. Consider the matter of racist or sexist speech. It has been argued that this is deeply rooted in attitudes, and cannot be changed without changing the latter. No doubt it sometimes is. Yet such speech may often be relatively thoughtless, picked up in one's social milieu: yet another 'nasty habit', as it were. Even when it is more deeply rooted, the conception of a network of beliefs and practices recognizes that attitudes flow out of practices as much as the reverse. A direct attack on certain practices, then, may encourage a change in attitudes.

Thus, a challenge for policy is to identify strategic points of intervention in reality. There's no all-purpose a priori way of identifying these. One certainly cannot rely on root causes thinking, because often the most effective available intervention will be at a more superficial level.

In this chapter, we saw that we do not neatly divide our activities into means and ends. Since we often pursue multiple goods simultaneously, policy analysis should refrain from stipulating the goals people are pursuing in any particular activity. In work life, for example, people are pursuing multiple objectives. Forgetting this may lead to policies that damage the work experience, and even frustrate the goal of narrow efficiency. We also saw that the narrow focus of our attention leads to the importance of 'social habits', norm-laden roles into which we slip without much conscious thought. This suggests that any policy that undermines habitual norms can have unexpected side effects, which may make the policy self-defeating. The narrow focus of our attention also helps explain the power of nudges, and implies that effective policies need not always aim at root causes.

To this point, Part Two has considered various aspects of a consistently non-binary analysis. We have ignored real world constraints, such as a lack of time or clients little interested in serious and searching analysis of policy options. Let us now consider these constraints.

8

Decision contexts

A decision context is a space in which one or more people must arrive at a decision on some matter. To bring to life the non-binary approach, we need healthy decision contexts. We also need a healthy background culture: spaces of reflection that do not necessarily lead to actual policy decisions, but help inform (and form) citizens and decision makers.

Weak decision contexts

But what might 'healthy' mean here? We can approach this question by considering its opposite, an unhealthy context. In Plato's *Gorgias*, Socrates offers an arresting image: 'if a pastry baker and a doctor had to compete in front of children, or in front of men just as foolish as children, to determine which of the two, the doctor or the pastry baker, had expert knowledge of good food and bad, the doctor would die of starvation' (¶464d). Just what is wrong with that decision context?

Maybe the problem concerns *who* is doing the deciding: perhaps such important things shouldn't be decided by children. Or maybe it's the *character* of the deciders that is problematic: perhaps they are, as Plato put it, adults 'just as foolish as children'. It certainly seems unrealistic to assume that children are entirely lacking in any capacity to decide issues competently, and yet, upon reaching the age of majority, are immediately transformed into rational decision makers.[1] In truth, the transition from the child, supposedly attuned only to flashy and seductive appeals, to the adult who weighs and scrutinizes arguments carefully, is a developmental process that is never fully completed.

In developing his minimalist theory of democracy, Joseph Schumpeter suggested that, for most citizens, that transition is hardly even begun, at least on matters of public concern. In effect, Schumpeter drew certain inferences from a point that is central to this book: our attention is focused upon matters we deem relevant to us. So we are pretty good at buying shoes, Schumpeter allows. But when we move into national issues, he argues, the 'sense of reality' that marks our purchase of shoes is 'completely lost'. The average citizen, he alleges, 'expends less disciplined effort on mastering a political problem than he expends on a game of bridge', and thus 'argues and analyzes in a way which he would readily recognize as infantile within the sphere of his real interests' (rpt. 1976, 258–262).

Were we to emphasize this alone, policy analysis would clearly be moved in an elitist direction.[2] Perhaps we can avoid this outcome by turning from issues of character to the *form* in which arguments are presented and assessed: in Plato's image, the weight is put on catchy arguments, there is no contesting of the claims, no demand for evidence. Keynes once complained about decisions 'taken in a spirit of hysteria and without a calm consideration of the alternative before us', and public policy being shaped by beliefs that 'could not survive ten minutes' rational discussion' (rpt. 1963, 283). As we have all witnessed, policies sometimes don't *need* to survive ten minutes of serious scrutiny: they are debated in a haze of over-heated rhetoric, ad hominem arguments and various other distractions. Public policy debates are not supervised by a referee who could force participants to take responsibility for their words, retract false claims and so on.

This weakness in the form of the decision context is linked to the problem of time. In the *Apology*, Plato has Socrates comment that 'If it were the law with us, as it is elsewhere, that a trial for life should not last one but many days, you would be convinced, but now it is not easy to dispel great slanders in a short time' (¶37b). Clearly, the various techniques by which policy advocates avoid serious debate gain additional power when there is not enough time to counter them effectively. Even when participants in a discussion sincerely wish to argue honestly and respectfully, time pressures can preclude going into matters in sufficient depth.

A final problem of decision contexts, not manifest in Plato's image of the doctor and the pastry chef, is the issue of power disparities. Throughout this work, the central claim that there is always something to talk about has been accompanied by the condition, if we're willing to talk. There are situations in which one party believes it can safely neglect the arguments of the other.[3] In Shakespeare's *Richard II*, York warns Richard not to seize the property of Hereford (the future Henry IV). Do so, he argues, and

> You pluck a thousand dangers on your head,
> You lose a thousand well-disposed hearts

Richard brushes him aside:

> Think what you will, we seize into our hands
> His plate, his goods, his money and his lands. (2.1)

'Think what you will': Richard says, in effect, 'I do not have arguments to counter yours, but I have power, and so I do not *need* to consider your arguments.' This is not a respectful answer, but Richard might say that respect doesn't enter into it: he and York are not equals.[4] Even worse than this response is a decision context prone to 'speaking power to truth', one that wants analysts to provide support for pre-determined conclusions. At this extreme, not only is policy advice ignored, it is also doctored, to erase evidence of the original advice.[5]

The need for healthy contexts

As a society, we need healthy decision contexts: where there is enough time to explore issues in depth; where discussions are not shut down by a 'think what you will', by a simple fiat of power; where people have the integrity to honor the search for truth, to recognize that the simple and attractive arguments may be false, to accept that they must be willing to change their position if dialogue proves it to be weak. Society also needs spaces for serious analysis that can support those contexts with well-founded and 'usable' knowledge. A society that fails to give great importance to sustaining such decision contexts, and the analytical spaces that support them, is deeply unwell.

This certainly does not mean that all decision contexts will meet this standard. Many who read this chapter have suffered through meetings with overloaded agendas, where some decision must be made, and made *now*, where attempts to go deeper on an issue are met with impatient sighs, where superficial comments carry the day because the meeting must move on to the next issue. No realistic approach to policy can imagine that such contexts will disappear. Nor will we ever be free of contexts where discussion is cut short, or rendered meaningless, by a curt 'think what you will'. Nor can we expect the disappearance of 'hot button' issues concerning which political demagogy renders serious discussion unlikely.

Thus, a non-binary policy analysis cannot wait for the disappearance of problematic decision contexts, nor be premised on the existence of decision makers who stand at the opposite pole from Richard II, who habitually listen with an open mind to serious policy advice. A society willing to develop and sustain rich decision contexts must expect them to coexist with problematic ones.

But rich contexts can influence the others. As weaker contexts are problematic in different ways, the precise nature of influence will vary. In some cases, there are inevitable limitations such as time pressures. An analogy may be helpful here. A ship's captain sometimes has to make immediate decisions. But maritime charts should make those decisions more intelligent and help forestall some of the worst mistakes. Richer contexts may play a similar role. Thus, to fail to sustain rich contexts and analysis, to assume that all decision contexts must be overloaded and time-pressured, would be analogous to forcing captains to operate without the aid of charts.

In an emergency situation, the captain is of course also guided by training. We can think of the discussions that go on in richer contexts as helping train those who participate in them, some of whom will also be called upon to participate in more problematic contexts. It can train them, for example, by giving them a stronger ability to detect specious arguments (either in general, or in relation to specific policy questions) and by giving them some familiarity with previous policy experiences.

This assumes a decision maker who, though limited by time pressures, is in principle open to policy advice. But what of contexts dominated by a closed mentality?[6] What role might rich contexts play in relation to decision contexts marked by a closed or authoritarian spirit, or warped by a demagogic political environment? Independent sources of policy reflection, first, can supply citizens with more tools to assess the decisions emerging from such problematic contexts, and thus constitute a healthy constraint on the latter. Even analysis generated within government may be helpful if it becomes more common for it to be published online. This, of course, is opposed to much current practice, but the democratic legitimacy of current practice must itself be questioned. A more democratic state system might operate on the default principle that government-funded policy analysis should be at the disposal of citizens in general.[7] This need not rule out the existence of policy advisors who provide private advice to the decision maker, but it would not treat such advisors as the norm. Under the default principle, furthermore, an attempt by the government of the day to destroy institutional memory, including past policy analyses and records of decisions, would be as normatively repugnant as the Taliban's destruction of the stone Buddhas: there should be recognition that these resources do not *belong* to the government of the day, that the government is simply a steward of this rich social asset.[8]

But who should promote those contexts?

To strengthen a society's 'policy health', then, requires the nurturing of rich decision contexts, and of spaces that can provide them with supportive non-binary analysis, as well as measures to increase the influence of those spaces upon the others, such as moves towards increased public diffusion of government policy analysis. But just who might be the *agents* of this change? Ideally, society 'as a whole' must demand the development of rich contexts and of greater publicness.[9] It would be useful in this respect to have an analysis audit that identifies just where formally trained policy analysts are distributed throughout a society. How many work in each type of context? How many work, for example, in places where time is available and debate is welcome, in spaces not subordinated to immediate tasks, partisan or commercial pressures and so on? Within government itself, how are analysts distributed between those who generate publicly available analysis and those whose work remains private?

I would argue that individual analysts also have a crucial role to play. That is, analysts who fully abandon the binary view will not simply *try* to do analysis differently. They will seek, in whatever ways are feasible, to reform decision contexts so that they are *able and encouraged* to do analysis differently, so that decision makers are open to a policy analysis entirely freed from the binary view. They must also attempt to make the case to society at large that healthy decision contexts and supportive policy analysis are essential ingredients of a healthy society.

The subservient analyst model

One view of the appropriate relation between public servant and elected official would respond that, at least when working in government, analysts have no business worrying themselves about the fitness of decision contexts: their responsibility is to shut up and do as they're told. One takes one's basic orientation from one's superior, who in turn takes it from someone else, in a hierarchy ascending, in theory, to an elected official who answers to the public.[10] According to this approach, which I will term the 'subservient analyst view', experts should be 'On tap, not on top', as Luther Gulick famously put it (1937, 11). In Herman Finer's extreme formulation of this position, 'the servants of the public are not to decide their own course; they are to be responsible to the elected representatives of the public, and these are to determine the course of action of the public servants to the most minute degree that is technically feasible' (1941, 336).

A less extreme variant of the subservient analyst model makes use of the dichotomy of facts and values. In this variant, the policy analyst should not defer to the elected politician in matters of fact. The analyst would not accept, for example, political interference in the factual content of climate reports. But the analyst must defer on matters of value to the politician, who expresses a democratic mandate.[11] Thus, the approach holds

> that *both* politicians and civil servants participate in making policy, but that they make distinctive contributions. Civil servants bring facts and knowledge; politicians, interests and values. Civil servants bring neutral expertise – will it work? – while politicians bring political sensitivity – will it fly? Civil servants thus emphasize the technical efficacy of policy, while politicians emphasize its responsiveness to relevant constituencies. (Aberbach et al, 1981, 6, emphasis in original)[12]

As noted in Chapter 2, this view is convenient for a policy analysis shaped by the binary view, as it provides an exogenous source for normative orientation. Doubts concerning the feasibility of having analysts glean their normative orientation from elected officials were examined in that chapter. But there are other important difficulties with the subservient analyst view. (Note that I will not examine the descriptive accuracy of this model, focusing instead on its validity as an ideal. It would probably be extremely difficult to find an experienced cabinet minister who viewed the subservient analyst model as descriptively accurate.)

The Iraq case

An investigation of policy discussions prior to the British government's participation in the Iraq war uncovered 'a damaging vacuum in the department's advice':

> While some senior officials in Britain's intelligence agencies expressed their doubts that Saddam was genuinely stockpiling weapons of mass destruction, no serious qualms were raised by the government's foreign policy experts about the equally important problem of whether occupying Iraq could work. Analysing the likely consequences of invading one of the major Arab states should have been a crucial element in judging whether it was in Britain's interest, let alone that of ordinary Iraqis, to go to war. Yet such analysis was simply absent. Ministers never asked for it; officials never offered it. (Steele, 2008)

The practice of not answering questions that have not been asked, of not raising issues that the decision maker does not want to face, conforms perfectly to the subservient analyst model. Was the public interest well served by the strategy in this instance? What good was done by the reticence of the policy advisors? One might say that it is unfair to critique the subservient analyst model on the basis of isolated policy examples. On the other hand, it would take a great number of fabulous policy successes to outweigh a catastrophic policy decision such as the invasion of Iraq or the American involvement in Vietnam.

It is most likely that the strategy of reticence was not chosen with an eye to the public interest, but for narrow individual reasons. The self-limitation of the policy adviser fits nicely with calculations of personal prudence. To cross a certain line runs the risk of never being asked again for one's opinion, of losing one's access to the top decision makers. As J.C. Thomson said of the Vietnam policy case, 'The inclination to remain silent or to acquiesce in the presence of the great men – to live to fight another day, to give on this issue so that you can be "effective" on later issues – is overwhelming' (1968, 49).[13] Leaving aside such narrow considerations, we can see that, from the viewpoint of the public interest, there are serious difficulties with the subservient analyst view.

Imperfect democracy

In his essay entitled 'Imperfect democracy and the moral responsibilities of policy advisers', Michael McPherson comments that democracy can provide a pretext for 'passing the buck', allowing the policy advisor to argue that 'The responsibility of an adviser to an official in a democratic society … is strictly a professional one – to provide clear and accurate technical analysis and information' (1983, 74). In this approach, McPherson notes, the 'concept of democracy obviously bears quite a lot of normative freight' (69). That is, it serves to justify the actions and omissions of the subservient analyst. Can democracy bear the weight? It cannot, says McPherson, because 'our democratic process is marred by severe inequalities of political voice and power and by important defects in the channels through which public opinion is formed and communicated' (75).

Most obviously, in a political system deeply shaped by what philosopher John Rawls called the 'curse of money' (1997, 772), it is naive to assume that elected officials somehow incarnate the 'will of the people'. Even were effective barriers in place to eliminate the translation of economic power into political influence, elections might serve to choose political leaders who reflected majority preferences on some policy issues, but only some: by their very nature, elections cannot focus the public's attention on more than a few issues. Once in office, of course, the politician may face issues never discussed during the election campaign: choosing a response to the outrage of September 11, 2001 is a pertinent example.

So in viewing the elected official as representative of the 'will of the people', the subservient analyst model misrepresents how democracy in fact operates. But it also misses a vital element of how democracy *should* function. We can approach this by way of E.F. Schumacher's discussion of 'divergent' and 'convergent' problems (1974, 79–81).[14] In the latter type, work on the problem can converge upon a satisfactory and complete solution. A math problem, or a crossword puzzle, are simple examples. For divergent problems, a complete solution is not attainable, because the problem involves an ongoing balancing of values in tension. In raising children, for example, parents may seek to inculcate both a critical spirit and a respect for legitimate authority.

Schumacher suggests that 'The true problems of living – in politics, economics, education, marriage, etc. – are always problems of overcoming or reconciling opposites' (1974, 81). This is certainly true of the relation between elected officials and civil servants. As I have argued elsewhere, because a healthy democracy must not give the governing party excessive 'advantages of incumbency',

the civil servant cannot be placed in a *pure* relation of subordination to the elected official. Were that the case, the civil service would be reduced to being an instrument in the governing party's arsenal. Their relation must rather be a dialectical one, in which the bureaucrat is subordinate in some ways, and autonomous in others. Sustaining this relation will always be a challenge, as it requires an ongoing balancing and rebalancing, more like riding a bicycle than advancing on auto-pilot. (Ryan, 2014b, 461, emphasis in original)

From this perspective, the subservient analyst position represents an attempt to treat a divergent problem as a convergent one by ignoring the full range of values in tension.[15]

The foregoing critique of the subservient analyst approach applies as much to the 'values variant' as it does to more extreme versions such as that of Herman Finer. That is, the analyst is no more obliged passively to carry out a mandate of unsupported values than one of unsupported facts. All this could be read as a plea for bureaucratic dominance. It is not. Analysts are not free to act on their personal opinions concerning the facts relevant to a policy issue: their views must be put to the test. The same goes with values. To assume that a rejection of the subservient analyst position entails bureaucratic dominance keeps us yoked to the view that someone or other's subjective preferences must carry the day: if it is not the preferences of elected politicians, it is going to be those of 'faceless bureaucrats'. As I argued in Chapter 1, the correct question is not 'whose values will prevail?' but 'will serious deliberation prevail?'. The first question is relevant only when the second question meets with a 'No.'

Nevertheless, it is important to acknowledge the dangers inherent here, not in the arguments presented, but in the ways they might be used in practice. Just as those seeking to block action on climate change regularly call for more research, the public servant who wishes to avoid an unwelcome policy choice can call for a deeper and more thorough analysis.[16] This merely shows that a shift to a more consistent non-binary analysis does not magically do away with various challenges facing any democracy, such as the long-standing tension inherent in democracy's reliance upon permanent officials endowed with a certain level of expertise and institutional memory. We will return to this issue later.

Is the non-binary approach 'practical'?

I have argued that it is normatively legitimate for the analyst to seek to push analysis deeper, to raise questions that others have not, even questions that decision makers might prefer not be raised. It is legitimate to probe the normative and factual assumptions behind the policy preferences of the decision maker. Some may object that, whether or not this is legitimate, it is hardly practical: there is always too much work to be done, too many decisions to be made in too little time – and real world policy analysis and decision making can't afford the luxury of going deeper.

Much can be said in response, but for now let us consider the ambiguity of that influential adjective, 'practical'. When applied to thought and analysis, 'practical', today, almost always denotes a form that does not question reigning premises, that focuses narrowly on the task at hand. It is tacitly assumed that this narrow focus furthers the other qualities denoted by the word: useful, efficient, suitable, feasible and so on.

But imagine living in a society that passionately believes in the predictive power of Tarot cards. All policy advice is based on interpretations of the cards, and would-be policy analysts are trained in their skillful reading. Since everyone agrees that the cards – when used properly – are reliable, theoretical debates in policy journals are confined to such questions as whether Tarot reading is art or science, whether all interpretation is contextual or whether the discipline might aspire to generalized interpretations.

Such a society would benefit greatly from a theory that demonstrated the falsity of its belief in Tarot cards, *if* the society could be brought to believe that theory. But it's not clear how the society might come to accept that critical outlook. In the meantime, any given individual might well find that specializing in the interpretation of Tarot cards was a better route to advancement – more practical – than holding and advocating the critical theory. When we ask, then, whether an approach is practical, are we referring to its usefulness for Tarot-land as a whole or for the individual? In the latter case, we also need to ask whether our individual is, at least to some degree, a truth-seeker, for whom the theory will be quite useful, or a pure 'careerist', for whom it will be pernicious.[17]

A non-binary approach to policy analysis is eminently practical, in the sense of useful, when we consider the long-term interest of society as a whole. But is it a *possible* approach, from the point of view of the individual analyst? Possible, that is, without throwing one's career away or even strangling one's career in its infancy? Could the non-binary approach be of use to the individual analyst, and, in particular, to the young analyst beginning a career?

Let me address that young analyst for a moment: I recognize that you need to eat, that you probably do not wish to be so idealistic or innovative as to find yourself on the streets. I also assume, however, that you want to take pride in your work, to feel that it is important and useful to others, and that you certainly do not wish to be complicit in evil. A good society is, in part, one in which those two broad desires, to be gainfully employed and to do useful and morally decent work, are easily reconciled, one in which the pursuit of your own interest generally furthers that of society. Real-life societies, unfortunately, are only more or less good, in that sense. So there will inevitably be times when you feel torn between doing the safe and prudent thing and doing what you believe the interest of the public, perhaps even of humanity, requires. You need to give some thought now to how you will deal with such future situations.

At the same time, one must not exaggerate this dilemma by imagining that real-world policy analysis is inevitably hostile to deeper questioning. It is not. There are important variations in contexts, which we will consider in the next chapter.

This chapter has contrasted some qualities of weak and healthy decision contexts, and argued that analysts have a responsibility to do what they can to promote the latter. The objection to this view arising from the subservient analyst model was considered, and the case was made that the analyst need not accept as unquestioned axioms the beliefs, whether normative or positive, of elected officials. Finally, we examined the dilemmas with which the analyst, in particular the young analyst, might be confronted as a result of this approach.

The analyst in context

While the consistent pursuit of a non-binary approach will lead to tensions, the belief that the approach is thoroughly utopian and imprudent may arise from an exaggerated view of the conflicts that it will generate. The forms of care exercised by the non-binary analyst can be said to characterize any thoughtful analyst. In many contexts, this will be very highly appreciated. Often, the analyst is associated with a decision maker who is not absolutely wedded to a particular way of doing things, a particular understanding of their goals. In other cases, the analyst is not so fortunate.

Variations in context

Policy analysts, of course, work in a wide variety of situations. We have analysts at all levels of government, 'hired guns' working for highly partisan think tanks and lobby groups, analysts employed by more pluralistic research centers. Many people in academia, both professors and students, are engaged in ongoing policy analysis. Many citizens who may or may not be trained in policy analysis regularly engage in that activity as part of their work lives: many journalists, for example.

These contexts have a greater or lesser degree of 'givenness', of goals that must be treated as axioms, and a greater or lesser openness to normative questioning. They vary as well in the intensity of time pressures, and in the extent to which power relations limit rich dialogue. They also vary in their level of homogeneity: a partisan group that only hires people with a specific political orientation can certainly have internal dialogue, but it is inherently limited.

These qualities of contexts are not fully determined by their institutional location. Martin Rein writes that 'value-critical policy analysis' is 'by and large ... done in the university by scholars who, from this position of privilege, can remove themselves from the political fray' (1983, 106). Yet hired guns operate in today's academia, and are often more highly prized than experts whose sources of remuneration are more transparent. More subtly, ideological constraints within disciplines can also constrain the potential for academic policy analysis to go deeper.

Mirroring Rein's view, some thinkers suggest that critical thought is unlikely to occur in bureaucratic contexts. 'Hierarchy appears indefensible', argue Michael Harmon and Richard Mayer, 'since it must necessarily assume the correctness of knowledge as unilaterally decided upon by those in positions of authority' (1986, 314). In this view, each cog in the system is narrowly constrained by an array of givens, both normative and positive, that flow down from on high. Philosopher Jürgen Habermas sets up an intriguing parallel between bureaucracies (both private and public) and markets. In both 'systems', there is no need 'for achieving consensus by communicative means'. Market decisions can be 'steered' by anonymous price signals, while bureaucratic decisions are steered by power. Within bureaucracy, says Habermas, there is communication, but it occurs 'with reservation': participants need not rely on communicative action for 'coming to an understanding', because any specific matter can be decided by an exercise of power (1987b, 310).

But this is far too simple a view of organizations. Among other complications, the fact that energy must be expended to exercise power, as organization theorist Henry Mintzberg pointed out, renders power more diffused through an organization than one might deduce by looking at a formal 'org chart' (1983, 25).[1] Further, on many issues, decision makers are not set on this or that specific outcome, but on arriving at some defensible decision, one with solid supports that will hold up under scrutiny. So, even within government, there will be space for going deeper, for questioning many of the normative and factual givens of the situation.

Transforming contexts

An important consideration concerns just is what is likely to constitute effective and skillful questioning, one that creates more space for a non-binary analysis. To explore this, the analyst will need to draw on the skills of the anthropologist and the sociologist, seeking to grasp the folkways of the strange culture in which she has landed, seeking to understand the structure of power and influence in which she finds herself. She will need to ask many questions, the answers to which can only be uncovered over time by careful observation and gentle probing. What sorts of taboos are in place? How strong are they? With what sort of people is one immediately dealing? To what types of questions are they open? In what sort of context do these people in turn find themselves? To what sort of people are *they* answering? How constrained do they feel themselves to be? These last questions are vital: there is an important difference between trying to open up the people in one's immediate surroundings and giving them support and tools for doing their own opening up of others, their own push against certain constraints.[2] Over time, the analyst will find openings: moments when the givens flowing from above are ambiguous enough to permit some probing; moments when one can challenge the givens in a way that shows that an alternative way of understanding the task is more in keeping with the goals of the organization, and the goals of one's immediate superiors.[3]

In discussing the image of the doctor and the pastry chef from Plato's *Gorgias*, we considered the possibility that character was a problem in the decision context. Should the non-binary analyst attempt to deal with that? Yes, in a limited way. Strong decision contexts cannot be created from scratch: they can emerge over time through the development of citizens and decision makers who demand strong contexts. So character and context need to develop together. That is, if the decision context is problematic, if it encourages dangerous simplifications, unreflective endorsement of problematic objectives and so on, one of the analyst's tasks is to try to create a 'consumer' who is open to the analysis that needs to be offered. Clearly, some analysts are in a better position to do this than others. But all analysts need a lively sense of the imperfections of the decision context, and character will almost certainly be one of them.

Any talk of working on character, of changing people, can spark unease. But when the change in question is towards greater critical awareness, towards a greater capacity to scrutinize arguments, is the unease valid? Many today see this as a key goal of education. The supposition here is simply that this educational task should not end when a person leaves school.[4]

Putting the matter in this way is helpful because it underlines that the goal is to transform decision contexts, not merely to win on this or that particular issue. There is thus an important difference between the non-binary analyst, who has a reflex to go deeper on policy issues, a habit of not treating the preferences supporting a policy as immutable givens, and the analyst who, feeling unease with the direction of a particular policy discussion, sees going deeper merely as a useful tactic in that immediate case. The latter may view particular policy outcomes as the end and everything else as the means. The perspective advocated here, in contrast, views both policy outcomes and an improved decision context as ends.

Michael McPherson, whose arguments on imperfect democracy were cited earlier, puts the matter well: the policy adviser cannot escape making 'an independent moral judgment about the consequences of his or her involvement and about the best way to proceed'. Yet this judgment must 'show a proper concern for the integrity of the process he or she is involved in'. One is thus faced with 'a three-sided obligation: (1) to serve his or her superiors honestly, (2) to promote better policies, and (3) to respect and improve the democratic process by which decisions are made' (1983, 76).

Paralysis of analysis?

Though the non-binary analyst is seeking to improve decision contexts, is there not a danger that she will often create a 'paralysis of analysis'? Herbert Simon argues that habitual questioning of the normative premises of decisions would destroy rationality itself:

It is impossible for the behavior of a single, isolated individual to reach any high degree of rationality. The number of alternatives he must explore is so great, the information he would need to evaluate them so vast that even an approximation to objective rationality is hard to conceive. Individual choice takes place in an environment of 'givens' – premises that are accepted by the subject as bases for his choice; and behavior is adaptive only within the limits set by these 'givens.' (Simon, 1965, 79)

Two points may be made in response. First, we should not assume that a non-binary approach will in general require an extraordinary amount of extra time or lead to analytical chaos. We need to keep in mind an important point about fruitful dialogue: questions are raised and beliefs challenged on an 'as needed' basis. The process is not frivolous, random or endless. The vital difference between a rich context and many conventional decision situations is simply that hierarchy does not carry the same privileges, that normative choices are not simply decreed, that, when there *is* a need to challenge normative premises, there is freedom to do so.

Still, there are decisions for which going deeper *will* lead to paralysis. This leads to a second response: paralysis is not always a bad thing. Recall the first injunction of the Hippocratic oath: 'do no harm'. When decision makers seek to avoid paralysis at all costs, they may do so by simply ignoring the risks of their preferred path, and the grave harms their decision may inflict upon others. They will opt for confident simplifications and untruths rather than honest acknowledgment of the wretched dilemma with which they are faced. To return to the case of policy deliberations prior to the invasion of Iraq: some paralysis, in which decision makers and analysts acknowledged the limits of their knowledge, would have been most beneficial.[5]

Other spaces

The discussion to this point has tacitly assumed that the analyst is in a context in which various factors entail that much skill must be exercised to create openings for deeper analysis. As noted earlier, such spaces will never disappear. Indeed, they *should not* disappear. There will be situations that require quick decisions and that do not permit extensive dialogue, or even any dialogue at all. There will also be situations in which certain values *should* be taken as exogenous by the individual analyst. This case is analogous to that of a doctor consulted about an immediate medical problem: she may recognize that this is not an appropriate time to prod the patient to change his lifestyle in a more healthy direction, and so she will accept as a given the patient's limited understanding of health, at least for the time being.

But as noted earlier, apart from improving the quality of more limited and 'official' contexts, society must develop and sustain alternative contexts, free from both legitimate constraints such as time pressures and of illegitimate constraints such as authoritarianism ('Think what you will ... '). Let us note some of the distinguishing qualities and tasks of such alternative spaces.

Citizens as the 'addressee' of analysis

In his *Laws*, Plato comments that a doctor treating a slave 'never gives any account of the particular illness of the individual slave, or is prepared to listen to one; he simply prescribes what he thinks best in the light of experience, as if he had precise knowledge, and with the self-confidence of a dictator'. When treating a free person, on the other hand, 'he gives no prescription until he has somehow gained the invalid's consent' (¶720c).

In the first case, the doctor's client is not the patient but the patient's owner. Analogously, for most professional policy analysts, there is a distinction between their client or employer, and those who ultimately will be affected by the policy. This can encourage what policy theorist Peter DeLeon terms a 'technocratic, undemocratic orientation', with analysts 'sequestered' from the general population (1994, 82). To mitigate this, we need contexts within which policy analysts view their work as being addressed to, and *serving*, the citizenry as a whole, and shape their work accordingly. These contexts cannot come into existence, of course, unless *someone* is willing to pay for them, while granting them the autonomy to orient themselves to citizens as a whole.

To say that the analysis done in such contexts is both addressed to and serves the general citizenry means that it is not enough for government decision contexts to be supplemented by partisan think tanks and lobby groups that promote particular private interests. Some would disagree, appealing to the metaphor of the courtroom: while adversarial trials may not be perfect, no better means has been identified to test the guilt of the accused than to have two hired guns fight, each pushing for one of two possible verdicts. But in policy matters, the belief that truth will emerge from a clash of hired guns is naive. It assumes that there are only a small number of angles from which an issue can be viewed, that each of those angles is adequately represented by a skillful hired gun and that each point of view has sufficient resources to ensure that it is heard. None of these assumptions is true. For many policy issues, multiple angles are possible, some of which have yet to be identified, and could only emerge from a cooperative search for truth, rather than an adversarial contest of narrow interests.[6]

Countering groupthink

Generally speaking, it is fair to assume that analysts who have worked intensively on a particular policy issue know much more about it than the average citizen. At the same time, the knowledge they claim as their special asset can contain a fair dose of groupthink. Members of a government department can persuade themselves that truth is entirely on their side, that any difference between their consensus view on a policy and that of the public reflects the latter's ignorance, and that it is their job to get on with doing what should be done, while seeking, if possible, to enlighten the uninformed public. Public opinion can come to be seen as 'friction', impeding the smooth administration of public affairs, as Jürgen Habermas noted (1989b, 243). In this view, public opinion must not be allowed to become 'meddlesome', as Woodrow Wilson so bluntly put it (1887, 215).[7]

One may lament groupthink and the elitist attitudes that flow from it, but it is a near-inevitable sociological phenomenon. Independent sources of reflection, whose research is not easily dismissed as uninformed and emotional, can provide a vital counterbalance to the consensus view of a government department. It can both remind those within the department that there are legitimate questions that can be asked of their consensus view and contribute to the development of public opinion through channels controlled neither by the state, nor by powerful private interests. Such spaces, as noted earlier, can over time constitute a healthy constraint upon state policy.

Going deeper into the swamp

Karl Popper offers a striking metaphor:

> Science does not rest upon solid bedrock. The bold structure of its theories rises, as it were, above a swamp. It is like a building erected on piles. The piles are driven down from above into the swamp, but not down to any natural or 'given' base; and if we stop driving the piles deeper, it is not because we have reached firm ground. We simply stop when we are satisfied that the piles are firm enough to carry the structure, at least for the time being. (Popper, 2002b, 94)

Much everyday policy analysis will perforce assume that the pillars on which it rests are 'good enough'. Such analysis cannot proceed otherwise. Society also needs a parallel activity that challenges particular pillars, and asks what policy would look like were those pillars replaced.

Regarding nuclear policy, Rosemarie Tong argued in the 1980s that

> The defenders of nuclear risk simply assume that the reigning economic order is good, and that any means necessary for maintaining this good (inexpensive nuclear energy) is also good. Never do they challenge the 'goodness' of the status quo, a state of affairs that requires the United States to use, misuse, and waste two to three times the per capita energy of other Western developed nations. (1986, 27)

We cannot expect policy analysts to challenge the reigning ideologies of their society on a daily basis. But a society in which there are *no* contexts in which those ideologies might be critiqued, or in which the only contexts that do so are casually dismissed by mainstream opinion, is a society on autopilot. As argued at the end of Part I, this is a dangerous state of affairs.

A final thought on the role of other spaces of analysis: it is certainly not the case that everyone working in an official space is content with the set of givens that limit reflection within that space. Many analysts seek facts and arguments that will help them shift policy thinking and loosen up the hold of the givens. Autonomous spaces can provide an important service to such analysts. They can bring to light facts that are obscured by the dominant assumptions of the official space and provide a sense of the sort of policy insights that can emerge from 'going deeper' on a particular issue. Thus, while the autonomous spaces will challenge the official ones in many ways, they can also support them. Paradoxically, the support can only emerge from the challenge.

Conclusion: 'demarcating' practices and contexts

This chapter has noted that there are wide variations in decision contexts, even in government work: it is not the case that the analyst in government will never be allowed to 'go deeper'. Moreover, the skillful analyst will find occasions to shift decision contexts in a more open direction, and to develop her own critical capacities in the process. Despite the room that may exist within government contexts, however, a healthy society also requires alternative spaces, spaces with time for reflection, spaces not subject to the imperatives of government bureaucracy or private interests.

The binary view is big on drawing lines: between facts and values, between positive and normative statements, between worthy thought that is disciplined, objective and value-free, and unworthy thought that is not. These lines are all problematic. We need different distinctions. We need a distinction, first, between *practices*. As citizens, as well as policy analysts, we need to develop our ability to detect the moments when an interlocutor refuses to continue a serious discussion of a normative or empirical claim, and to identify the stratagems by which claims are arbitrarily exempted from critical scrutiny.[8] We need to refrain from dismissing someone's claim as normative or value-laden, and recognize that the important quality is the willingness to give reasons in support of one's claim, be it normative or positive. We need, too, a distinction between those social situations and institutions in which rational argumentation is encouraged (or even possible), and those in which it is not. These distinctions are not binary. We face a spectrum, and one of the jobs of the analyst is to try to move people, and contexts, in a direction along the spectrum that allows for richer deliberation.

Conclusion to Part II:
The instincts of the non-binary analyst

While coaching my son's soccer team some years ago, I was trying to show a player how to shoot 'with the laces' of the soccer shoe. After a few minutes, his frustration erupted: 'I know how to do it,' he exclaimed, 'I just don't know how to do it.' What was he saying exactly? He had seen the action demonstrated many times. He could see, in his mind, exactly what he should be doing. Which is to say, he had the theory down pat. Practice, the ability to translate his clear visual image into a coordinated set of movements, was another matter entirely.[1] As for *skillful practice*: in our short season together, it was beyond my ability to teach that and beyond his to learn it. For a soccer player, skillful practice does not mean hitting the ball correctly from time to time, but doing so reliably, under a wide variety of conditions and, eventually, *without thinking about it*, having the skill become second nature.[2]

Thinking about how we acquire physical skills can tell us something about learning intellectual ones and about what it *means* to have acquired a skill. The skilled builder no longer needs to focus attention on getting the head of the hammer to hit the nail properly: that has become second nature. Analogously, to master an intellectual skill is to turn a merely superficial absorption of certain insights into intellectual instincts.[3]

Sit down with an economist: describe a set of rules, those governing welfare policy, for example, or an academic program. Often, the economist will observe: 'Ah, but you've created an incentive to ...' The insight that follows may be one that anyone might come up with, if they thought long enough about the matter. To the economist, however, it comes naturally. 'Natural', in this case, refers to the product of long immersion in a disciplinary culture. The theoretical tool may seem to be applied effortlessly, but the process of acquiring the tool is anything but effortless.

In the same way, a sociologist asked to explain a bus accident

> will immediately arrive at the idea that it's not the driver's fault – that would be a simple and mono-causal way of thinking – because the road was slippery, because it was the time when everyone was returning from vacation and traffic was heavy, because drivers are poorly paid and so forced to drive a lot, and are fatigued. (Bourdieu, 2012, 575)

Intellectual training is in large part the development of disciplinary reflexes. For both physical and intellectual skills, mastery involves the development of a second nature, so that certain operations become almost automatic. So how might a consistently non-binary approach shape the instincts of the policy analyst?

Chapter 5 suggested that we can fruitfully examine any intellectual craft in terms of the forms of 'taking care' that it encourages. The non-binary analyst, for example, will be attentive to the ways in which language shapes our attention and thinking. This insight has clear affinities with a social construction approach. But as we saw in Part I, some constructionists remain wedded to highly problematic residues of the binary view. One often runs across the claim that this or that is 'merely' a social construction, as if such constructions stand opposed to a set of solid, objective, unconstructed truths (truths that such constructionists rarely get around to identifying). A non-binary approach does not see things this way. It simply encourages us to be more aware of the various tricks by which language shapes our perspectives: it does not hold out the hope of reaching a perspective-free perspective, a 'view from nowhere' (Nagel, 1986).

Rather than believing that it is enough to take care not to jump across the supposed is–ought gulf, the non-binary analyst will seek to identify, to the extent possible, the positive and normative beliefs that enter into any policy argument. She will be aware that differences of outlook may reflect the differing sources that participants in a policy discussion have chosen to *trust* and their differing patterns of *attention*.

Finally, the non-binary analyst will take care to preserve normative goods traditionally associated with the binary view. In many cases, as in the case of objectivity, the analyst will reinterpret and extend those values. The non-binary analyst is aware, for example, that it is not enough to strive to make one's analysis 'value-free': factual beliefs, such as the beliefs that underpin racism, are also permeated by bias.

Chapter 6 explored various implications for the policy world of the fact that our beliefs form a network. Because a network of beliefs is somewhat opaque even to the person immersed in it, we can move towards greater objectivity only with the help of others. It is in dialogue with those who disagree with us that we can begin to understand some of the less obvious elements in our own network of beliefs. This would suggest that to form a strong team of analysts requires a balancing act: there is a need for mutual respect, yet also for a wide range of viewpoints and the willingness to articulate them. Because any given team is unlikely to attain this ideal, society also needs institutional pluralism, a theme further developed in subsequent chapters.

Chapter 6 also emphasized that a network of beliefs is not entirely consistent: beliefs, particularly unfamiliar ones, may be hedged in by others. And so we believe many things only to a certain degree. This, as we saw, adds importance to the question about who is at the table. Some people's life experience, for example, gives them a much stronger certainty that policy thinking must take the realities of sexism or racism into account. We also saw that, because belief is a matter of degree, the traditional pedagogical emphasis on critical thinking should be supplemented by 'appreciative thinking', in which students, and all of us, are encouraged to identify society's most important goods and our own. Chapter 6 concluded with the reminder that, because a network of beliefs has no simple foundation, there is no inevitable end of the line in policy discussions. The policy analyst need not accept alleged 'bedrock differences' as an immovable obstacle to dialogue.

Chapter 7 was centered on the insight that the world is not neatly carved up into ends and means. We cannot assume that a particular phenomenon serves only one end, nor that it is *merely* a means. The analyst who deeply understands this will recognize the need for caution in dealing with both the natural and the human environment. A car designer may safely conclude that one component can perfectly well be replaced by another, but policy analysts and decision makers must think long and hard before making analogous changes in social design. The complexity of the web of means and ends also entails that efficiency is a more complicated ideal than sometimes thought. The chapter also stressed that the policy analyst must take into account the fact that attention is a scarce resource, which explains both the promise and the peril of nudges.

Apart from these specific effects of a non-binary approach, we saw in the last two chapters of Part II that there is a more general and far-reaching implication, concerning the role of the policy analyst in modern democracy. Chapter 8 rejected both the pure subservient analyst model and the influential variant that holds that the analyst must take her facts from reality, but her norms from the elected official. The chapter also argued that society as a whole must promote healthy decision contexts, and that the individual analyst must also do what he can in this regard. Chapter 9 suggested that, while the analyst should do what she can to move official government decision contexts in a healthier direction, society also needs other spaces, subordinated neither to the government nor to the control of 'deep pockets'.

PART III

Caveats

It is all too easy for us to become uncritical salespeople for our favored theories and approaches, marketing them as cure-alls with no problematic side effects. As Socrates commented in Plato's *Protagoras*, 'those who take their teachings from town to town and sell them wholesale or retail to anybody who wants them recommend all their products, but I wouldn't be surprised, my friend, if some of these people did not know which of their products are beneficial and which detrimental' (¶313d). This can in part reflect a phenomenon often observed in intellectual life: people become slaves to their own ideas. This may be entirely natural. Nevertheless, an egoistic attachment to our most cherished remedies, and the consequent obliviousness to their limits and defects, are irresponsible when we move into the world of action. Here, anyone who introduces a new approach to politics or policy has a responsibility to consider not only how it will play out when all goes as expected, but also how it might go wrong.

Part III will consider two dangers of the approach advocated in this work: the magnification of expert power, and an exaggerated optimism concerning the power of dialogue. But of course not all dangers can be anticipated, least of all by an individual author. Others may well be glaringly obvious to certain readers, while still others may emerge only over time. Part III, then, is but a 'down-payment' on the task of self-critical thought.

Experts and expertise

In considering this work's various suggestions of how policy analysis might change under the influence of a non-binary approach, a reader might legitimately fear that the approach would enhance the already great power of experts and unelected officials. The claim, for example, that the public servant need not accept the elected official's normative views as givens can spark nervousness. We must thus address the problem of experts and expertise.

In this discussion, I will define expertise broadly, as usable knowledge that requires time and effort to acquire. I do not assume that it need be 'objective', however that is understood, nor 'scientific'.[1] We will examine various critiques and concerns about experts, and ask to what extent a non-binary approach addresses those concerns.

Critiques

Expertise as 'fiction'

Philosopher Alasdair MacIntyre argues that expertise in policy matters is a 'fiction, because the kind of knowledge which would be required to sustain it does not exist' (1984, 75). 'The social sciences', he asserts, 'are almost or perhaps completely devoid of achievement. For the salient fact about those sciences is the absence of the discovery of any law-like generalizations whatsoever.' Upon examination, 'alleged laws' in the social sciences 'all turn out to be false', and many of them are *so* false 'that no one but a professional social scientist dominated by the conventional philosophy of science would ever have been tempted to believe them' (88).

Let us bypass the long-standing debate over whether the social sciences can generate 'law-like generalizations'. The question here is whether expertise depends upon the existence of such generalizations. It does not. A valuable form of knowledge in our world might be termed an 'expertise of attention': one becomes an expert on certain matters by paying sustained attention in a particular sphere. This sphere may be a particular geographical area or set of problems. Rather than being undermined by some of the insights of social constructionism, such expertise is to a large degree entailed by it. Since we do not pay attention to everything at once, our patterns of attention vary in accordance with our practical interests. Some people's particular webs of practice and belief lead to sustained attention upon a limited topic.[2] The policy analyst who has focused on a particular issue will have a clearer sense than the average citizen of what sorts of solutions have already been tried. She should also have a clearer sense of the sorts of factors that must be considered before applying the lessons of one case to another.[3] A geographical 'area expert' can be expected to have a more reliable sense of who's who in a certain country, rather valuable knowledge when deciding, for example, which factions in a conflict can be relied upon or whose versions of reality should be trusted.[4]

The epistemological problem

But if a general claim for the existence of expertise is not spurious, the same cannot be said for many specific claims. This brings us to one of the most vexing aspects of expertise, the epistemological problem: how do non-experts recognize the real thing? Return to Plato's image of the doctor and the pastry chef: let us now put the two before an audience of mature and attentive citizens. They are not seduced by flashy rhetoric, yet they may still be at sea. The problem now may be that the doctor knows much less than her audience thinks she does. Indeed, she may well know less than she herself believes. And in fact the doctor who is most persuasive, by virtue of seeming more confident and emphatic in her statements, may be the dumbest of all: a constant theme of the Socratic dialogues is that the most dangerous form of foolishness is not knowing that one does not know, not knowing the limits of one's knowledge.

This inability most powerfully afflicts, according to Philip Tetlock's fascinating study of expert political knowledge, the most self-assured experts. Tetlock found that 'the best forecasters and timeliest belief updaters shared a self-deprecating style of thinking that spared them some of the big mistakes to which their more ideologically exuberant colleagues were prone. There is often a curiously inverse relationship between how well forecasters thought they were doing and how well they did' (2005, xi). Thus, the persona of the expert may be inversely related to their actual competence. Worse still, Tetlock notes, there is 'an inverse relationship between how well experts do on our scientific indicators of good judgment and how attractive these experts are to the media and other consumers of expertise' (217).[5]

An important variant of the epistemological problem is the 'halo effect', in which someone claims special knowledge outside their area of expertise. Like the expertise of attention itself, the halo can be explained by the practical orientation of our attention: the average citizen has no more reason to distinguish between the various subspecies of political scientists than I have to distinguish between types of palm trees. When a serious-looking academic from the University of X appears on TV offering opinions on the Syrian crisis, the average citizen has no reason to suspect that the speaker is in fact a specialist in Florida municipal politics.

Confusion over the limits of a person's expertise is often not accidental. The 'expert for hire' gives particular interested claims, of a pharmaceutical company, for example, or a policy lobbyist, a veneer of scientific authority. It has been argued that this phenomenon has been exacerbated by the rise of 24-hour news channels, which create an insatiable demand for 'talking heads' and can't be too particular about the 'experts' to whom they give a soapbox (Jones, 2010).

This last point reminds us that experts may be called upon even by those who have little confidence in their claims to expertise. As Tetlock argues, 'the mystique of expertise is so rooted in our culture that failing to consult the right experts is as unconscionable a lapse of due diligence as failing to consult witch doctors or Delphic oracles in other times'. Thus, even decision makers who doubt the claims of expertise will 'continue soliciting advice from the usual suspects' (2005, 64).

The excessive power of experts

Apart from the epistemological problems associated with expertise, concern has long been expressed over the power of experts. Weber gave a classic statement of this concern: 'Under normal conditions, the power position of a fully developed bureaucracy is always overtowering. The "political master" finds himself in the position of the "dilettante" who stands opposite the "expert," facing the trained official who stands within the management of administration' (rpt. 1958, 232). This bureaucratic expertise is not limited to technical skills, such as knowledge of advanced statistical analysis, but embraces factors such as centrality within a network of information, knowledge of precedents, understanding of rules and procedures, and so on.[6]

While the critique of experts' excessive power may be based on a vision of a more participatory democracy, it can also reflect a desire on the part of powerful political and economic interests to weaken the counterweight that experts might present to their preferred policies. We see this particularly in the area of environmental policy. In the early twenty-first century, it has become clear that critique of the power of experts is in itself neither progressive nor reactionary, but ideologically flexible.

The distance between experts and other citizens

Hannah Arendt commented that 'Bureaucracy is always a government of experts, of an "experienced minority" which has to resist as well as it knows how the constant pressure from "the inexperienced majority"' (1958b, 214). The wording suggests a possible defense of the experts' power position: If the selective nature of consciousness leads ordinary citizens to pay little attention to policy issues, can one not conclude that they should have little say in the resolution of those issues?[7] And can one not say the same for politicians elected by those same uninformed citizens? This is, of course, a very old argument, dating back at least to Plato.[8] There is a straightforward response: *If* the full range of human goods could be identified by experts alone, and *if* experts could be trusted always to act only on the basis of an expert knowledge untainted by their private interests, and *if* political participation were not a good-in-itself for many people, *then* we might be more comfortable with the prospect of expert domination. But none of these conditions holds.

As no society has a perfectly egalitarian access to education and a perfectly fair recruitment process, experts will tend to be drawn from particular segments of society. There will certainly be a pattern of class exclusion, and probably also one of ethnic or racial exclusion.[9] Experts' identification and ranking of human goods can thus be expected to differ from that of citizens in general.

Further, whatever its social origins, a group of experts can become a *caste*, with its own particular interests. The most enduring interest will be the protection of its own privileged position. This can shape the way experts communicate: 'mystifying technical languages', comments policy theorist Frank Fischer, can 'serve – often intentionally – to intimidate those who attempt to deliberate with the experts' (1993, 36).[10] The same objective affects the way experts *refuse* to communicate. Weber argued that 'Every bureaucracy seeks to increase the superiority of the professionally informed by keeping their knowledge and intentions secret. Bureaucratic administration always tends to be an administration of "secret sessions": in so far as it can, it hides its knowledge and action from criticism' (1958, 233).

The non-binary approach and the problems of expertise

On its own, a non-binary approach will not resolve all the problems of expertise. This is because some of the problems are rooted in the nature of our society as a whole. The narrow social base of experts, as was noted, reflects in large part inequalities of access to education. Other problems would probably exist even in a very egalitarian society. Any institution, for example, can be expected to generate one influential form of expertise: insider knowledge. And over time, any social group will tend to promote its narrow interests, and even confuse these with the public interest. Finally, the epistemological problem of recognizing both authentic experts and the limits of expertise will exist so long as there are experts and non-experts.

Indeed, a non-binary approach could generate an additional problem of expertise. Familiarity with this approach to policy analysis should lead to some facility with the skills of argumentation. There is an obvious danger that these skills will become concentrated in a new caste of experts. Sociologist Alvin Gouldner analyzed what he termed the 'new class', among whose assets are familiarity with a 'culture of critical discourse' (1979). Within the state, this asset can easily become concentrated among those who already enjoy substantial insider knowledge. Unless we wish to believe that those skilled in a non-binary approach will be possessed of an angelic detachment, we must recognize that their skills will at times be used to bamboozle the public, rather than to serve it.[11]

The solution cannot be to retreat to a binary approach, but to address various structural issues. As argued earlier, the social location of experts is of prime importance. So too is the set of incentives they face. In the state sector, the counterposing of permanent experts with those loyal to the elected official can alleviate some, but not all, of the problems. In society as a whole, the existence of alternative spaces that can challenge expert advice is vital, as is the default principle of making policy advice public. Concerns about a new caste of argumentative experts would also be greatly reduced to the extent that the grip of a neoliberal conception of education as training for the job market is weakened, and supplemented by a vision of education for citizenship.[12] I will return to this in the next chapter.

The non-binary approach could certainly alleviate some problems of expertise, if supporting structures are in place. Apart from alternative spaces for expert deliberation, there is a need for spaces in which experts engage in serious deliberation with ordinary citizens. Various practices, such as the deliberative opinion poll (Fishkin, 1991; Luskin, Fishkin and Jowell, 2002; Ratner, 2005), use experts as resources supporting the deliberation of ordinary citizens. The further step is to draw the expert into the deliberation: the non-expert may legitimately challenge the expert to fill in factual claims, to uncover the normative assumptions behind those claims and so on.[13] (Note too that a non-binary approach makes it explicit that deliberation must embrace non-technical dimensions of policy choices. Consider minimum wage policy: discussion should never be limited to economists' guesses concerning its employment effects, but should address questions such as the normative case for or against a living wage, other social changes that governments might pursue to lessen any employment impact from such a wage and so on. Such discussion is less reliant on specialized technical training.)

Further, were the 'ordinary citizens' who work as journalists or media hosts regularly to challenge experts to fill in their claims, this might help rein in the halo effect. Addressing the halo problem of expertise, in turn, can increase, rather than diminish, the influence of legitimate experts. Thus, addressing problems of expertise does not always reduce the role of experts; it simply seeks to reap the benefits of expertise while limiting its unwanted side effects.

All that said, it is important to recognize that there is no perfect protection against the problems of expertise. To a large degree, they are rooted in the nature of life in the modern world. That world needs specialized experts, more than any previous age, and one can no more have experts without the problems of expertise than one can build a monument that casts no shadow.

11

The limits of dialogue

As we have seen, the non-binary approach insists that 'There is always something to talk about, if we're willing to talk.' Yet we must avoid a 'dialogic utopianism' that assumes that, with enough time and good will, opponents can always come to an understanding. This chapter will address some of the limits of dialogue, as well as its internal tensions.

We will first note how 'burdens of judgment' can prevent people from reaching agreement, even when they are willing to dialogue in good faith. The second section will stress that, even when agreement is reached, it should not be confused with certain truth. We will then consider some of the tensions associated with the conception of the policy analyst as facilitator. Finally, the chapter will take up certain perennial challenges of social dialogue, which cannot be overcome once and for all.

Dialogue need not lead to agreement

Philosopher John Rawls's 'burdens of judgment' concept denotes all the factors that can prevent us from reaching agreement, even when we argue in good faith and with an open mind (1996, 55). Our differing life experiences constitute one of these burdens: because we bring our whole web of beliefs and our experiences into our judgment of claims, we cannot always expect unanimity, even with good will and openness to dialogue. Imagine that we are discussing the character of a mutual acquaintance, José. Each of us has our own individual experiences of this person. My own experience naturally looms more heavily in my assessment of José than your report on something that he said or did, which, after all, simply remains your report, not my experience. You are in the same position with respect to my account of José: you may trust me, yet not give second-hand information the same weight as your own experience. So we cannot expect full agreement, simply because we are working with different sets of facts that can never be rendered entirely uniform. Openness to dialogue does not entail a willingness to take other people's experiences as one's own, nor to erase one's particular network of beliefs.

The simple example can be extended to broader cases. When people discuss the merits and core beliefs of this or that religion, for example, their respective positions depend on whether they have lived that religion from the inside or not, and, if so, how they assess that experience. People often get defensive when discussing religion, but even in the absence of defensiveness, agreement may not result. By analogy, discussions of the merits of different policies can also be shaped by our different experiences. Once-prominent US Republican Paul Ryan argued that the social safety net is becoming 'a hammock that lulls able-bodied people to lives of dependency and complacency' (qtd in Krugman, 2013). Evidence on such a question may be ambiguous, and personal experience will influence which parts of that evidence one finds most persuasive. Note that all these examples – the discussions concerning José, or a religion, or a policy – involve *factual* disagreements. That is, the 'burdens of judgment' do not divide people on normative questions alone.

Still, even dialogue that does not reach agreement may yield important fruits. Parties to the dialogue may come to understand that those with whom they disagree have good reasons for their position, and identify shared elements in their respective views. As I have argued elsewhere, 'Even when a debate does not reach agreement, it is a step forward when the parties are freed from the dogmatic assumption that anyone with common sense must think as they do' (2014a, 8). A further achievement of reasoned dialogue can be to rule out certain options.[1] Two people debating the legitimacy of capital punishment, for example, may not reach full agreement, yet may agree that capital punishment, if it is *ever* legitimate, could only be applied under certain extremely stringent conditions. This is no small achievement.

Recognizing that honest dialogue can yield great benefits, even when full agreement eludes us, can help guard against a danger inherent in the concept of 'burdens of judgment': believing that one cannot communicate across gulfs of experience, that men can never understand women's point of view, that people from the rich North will never understand a Third World perspective and so on. Such pessimistic beliefs can become self-fulfilling, if they excuse people from the responsibility of seeking to understand unfamiliar experiences and perspectives, and excuse other people from the difficult task of trying to articulate their point of view and their experiences in such a way that others can understand them.

In particular, recognition of the burdens of judgment should not be taken as support for the claim that dialogue will reach a bedrock of irreconcilable differences. The existence of those burdens does not negate the idea that there's always something to talk about. In the case of José, for example, we may decide that we could probe further and discuss each other's claims based on our respective experiences. Of course, we may instead decide that this is simply not worth the effort, that our differing views concerning José don't matter all that much after all.[2]

Elusive truth

We have just seen that when we dialogue in good faith, we may find that we cannot reach agreement, and that others have good reasons for their differing views. Now it would be a rash person who would assert that they were in full possession of the truth when they knew that others could reasonably disagree with them. So one of the byproducts of dialogue will often be the realization that truth can be hard to pin down.

It may be harder to accept, however, that even when there *is* agreement, the participants in a dialogue cannot assume that they have arrived at the truth on a particular matter. Even the best dialogue by its very nature has a limited reach. It deals with the issues that the participants bring to it, draws on their knowledge, focuses only on those matters on which they differ and so on. So we cannot expect dialogue to settle a contentious question 'for ever', but only 'for now', though we may hope that 'now' turns out to be a substantial period of time.

But if this is the case, why need we fret about the question whether we can apply the categories of 'true' and 'false' to normative claims? Indeed, what need have we of the very concept of 'truth'? Why not rest content with the goal of consensus, since that's the best we are going to achieve in any case? One answer is simple: we need 'true' because we desperately need 'false'.[3] When we read, for example, Marie Danziger's endorsement of the sophists' view that 'the highest truth for any man is what he believes it to be' (1995, 436), we can see that the possibility of error has vanished along with the idea of objective truth. To apply the categories of true and false to normative statements in particular is to recognize that even a norm supported today by an entire society could well prove to be false. Thus, to Patsy Healey's claim that '"Right" and "good" actions are those we can come to agree on, in particular times and places' (1993, 238), we can respond that, throughout human history, some of the greatest evils have appeared 'right' and 'good' to many of those who 'came to agree on' the need to carry out those acts.[4]

Policy dialogue and the analyst as facilitator

These last observations are relevant to our understanding of policy dialogue and the analyst's role in it. Given the importance attributed throughout this work to the task of filling in our normative and positive claims, it would be reasonable to conclude that, for many analysts, the facilitation of dialogue will be an important part of their job description. This inference is reasonable, but it can be understood in different ways. To view the analyst merely as a facilitator who seeks to help others clarify the factual and normative elements of their networks of belief would be to lose sight of the implications of a non-binary approach for our understanding of policy dialogue, of facilitation and of its challenges.

Unavoidable truth-judgments

In the current map of broad approaches to policy analysis, it is fair to say that those who are skeptical of the quest for truth tend to believe that policy analysts should see themselves more as facilitators of dialogue than as technical experts. Marie Danziger argues that

> Students of policy analysis should be taught that their professional goal is not necessarily the attainment of consensus about the nature of the truth in any given policy issue. Rather, they should be concerned that all relevant parties have access to sufficient data and a level of understanding that will enable them to be true players in the policy process. (1995, 445)

In the same vein, after urging us to abandon the quest for objective truth, Kelly and Maynard-Moody declare that the role of the analyst is to 'bring together various stakeholders' and to 'facilitate rational deliberation' (1993, 138). Clemons and McBeth summarize this general outlook:

> Postpositivism suggests that the role of the analyst is not to find the truth, but rather to be suspicious and distrustful of all policy claims and ultimately to provide access and explanation of data to all parties, to empower the public to understand analyses, and to promote political issues into serious public discussions ... In short, this view of analysis seeks to turn the expert policy analyst into the democratic facilitator. (2001, 178)

But the analyst-as-facilitator cannot avoid truth-judgments. First: With *whom* does the analyst facilitate? With 'all relevant parties', says Danziger (1995, 445). With 'various stakeholders', say Kelly and Maynard-Moody (1993, 138). Presumably, they are thinking of people who are affected by a particular issue. The analyst-as-facilitator will thus face truth-questions of this sort: 'Is it *true* or *false* that this person or group may be significantly affected by this issue?'

Now consider an issue such as climate change or AIDS. On these matters we are all stakeholders in one way or another. The analyst can't bring us all together, so she will seek a sample of stakeholders, representing 'a variety of perspectives' (White, 1994, 509). *All* perspectives? If the topic were policy responses to AIDS, would she give a seat at the table to a group that denies the link between HIV and AIDS? If the topic were global climate change, would she invite someone who holds that the problem is non-existent? Recall that the authors just cited hope that facilitation will promote not an aimless gabfest, nor a harvest of phrases that will help the government sell an already-chosen policy course, but 'rational deliberation' and 'serious public discussions'. This goal will at some point require the exclusion of viewpoints that can no longer reasonably claim even the possibility of truth, because it is neither 'rational' nor 'serious' to continue discussing matters considered settled by all fair-minded observers.[5] In selecting stakeholders, then, and in choosing to exclude certain viewpoints from further participation, the analyst-as-facilitator must make truth-judgments.[6]

And what of the dialogue itself? All the references to 'serious' and 'rational' discussions remind us that the participants are not seeking any old consensus. They are likely to see themselves as searching for the 'right' conclusion, or the 'best' policy choice. From a non-binary perspective, one can claim that the participants are searching for truth, whether or not they would put matters that way. That is, truth-judgments are not just required to get stakeholders around a table, but can be the goal of the dialogue itself.

But how does this objective square with the previously noted limitation on dialogue, that its outcome depends on the specific participants, and that it can hence only resolve an issue 'for now'? Serious dialogue, as Jürgen Habermas puts it, is 'Janus-faced': validity claims must be raised 'here and now', yet 'outstrip every given context' (1993, 146, 1996, 21), in the sense that participants claim not merely that a position is acceptable to other participants, but that it *should* be acceptable, because it is correct.[7] As I have argued elsewhere, the situation is roughly the same with scientific investigation (2014a, 146–147).

Possible tensions between dialogue objectives

To the question 'Just *why* are we engaging in broader consultation?,' one legitimate answer is because truth cannot be found otherwise. The quality of a policy that affects a range of citizens cannot be assessed without their views. A 'pre-fabricated' evaluation may not be sufficient, as it may ignore important dimensions of experience. Public servants setting up an evaluation of corrections policy, for example, may not think to examine what prisons do to the *spirit* not just of prisoners, but of those who work there.

As has been stressed throughout this work, a practice can pursue multiple objectives. Because of this, processes of deliberation and decision can have significance 'independent of the final products they generate' (Tribe, 1972, 79).[8] Whether or not it is seeking truth, a broad deliberation process can be used to strengthen a group, foster active citizenship, and create 'buy-in', increasing the legitimacy of the eventual policy decision.[9] The latter goal is particularly important in cases where carrying out a decision will require the cooperation of citizens.[10]

Leaving aside the possibility of a sham consultation, we can assume that the pursuit of various objectives of public deliberation cannot be entirely divorced from a concern for truth, in particular the truths concerning which policies will work, and are sustainable. This can introduce certain tensions into the process. Of particular importance is the possible tension between a quest for truth and the effort to have people recognize an eventual decision as theirs.

Most obviously, on many issues there will be a tension concerning the identification of participants in a policy dialogue. Participation structured to help us find truth on an issue may differ greatly from participation that seeks to arrive at a decision that citizens, or some particular group of citizens, can embrace as their own. How best to manage this tension will vary from issue to issue. A guiding thread will be to recognize that responsible policy analysis, in grappling with both matters of fact and normative matters, must be seen as a serious search for truth, whatever else it is alongside that. So the non-binary analyst will always be asking how one organizes that search for truth on particular policy questions. There will be no uniform answer to this. Important dimensions of many issues require expertise. There will also be dimensions that require the identification of the interests at stake, which calls for a wider deliberative process. Wider participation will often also be necessary to establish some of the key facts at issue. At some point in the policy-making process, broad participation in some form will be vital to challenge the claims of expertise. All of these factors are relevant to the search for truth, and must still be coordinated with the goal of having citizens recognize a decision as their own.

Note that, in this approach, policy issues are not divided between technical and non-technical, since the dimensions of an issue will straddle that divide. In the case of climate change, for example, we need expertise to understand its basic mechanics and likely trajectory. But we also need broad participation to understand its current impacts in different areas of life, to gain ideas about mitigation and adaptation strategies, and so on.

Perennial challenges

If we want social dialogue to be a reasonably democratic enterprise, and to contribute to the clarification and resolution of policy issues, there are challenges that cannot be overcome once and for all, but that we must address as best we can. I will touch on two of these here.

Skewed dialogue

Social dialogue will never be completely fair. As was noted earlier, not everyone has the same time available to dedicate to dialogue. Further, there is a wide range in the skills associated with dialogue – the ability to articulate one's thoughts readily, to counter criticisms, follow and critique complex arguments, and so on. To the extent that this range of ability reflects differing levels of education, differing levels of skill are yet another symptom of an inegalitarian society.

In his *Rhetoric*, Aristotle suggested that it is more important for people to learn to defend themselves 'with speech and reason' than to learn physical self-defense, since 'the use of rational speech is more distinctive of a human being than the use of his limbs' (¶1355b). Adapting the observation to our needs, we might urge schools to offer more training in a wide range of argumentative skills. This would be a vital component of education for citizenship. But it is important to avoid illusions here: in all areas on which schools currently focus, there is in practice a wide range of learning outcomes. For a variety of reasons, schools can level the distribution of skills only to a certain point.

We might seek to mitigate the problem in another way. Return to Aristotle's observation: it seems archaic today, to the extent that our sense of security rests primarily not on individual self-defense, but on various social institutions. What might be the equivalent forms of protection in matters of dialogue, so that the wide variation in argumentative skills does not skew the outcome of social deliberation? On important issues, society must find ways to structure dialogues and build in protections for those less confident in such contexts, so that all participants can feel they can contribute, without running the risk of being belittled or humiliated. Such protective structures will also help deal with our second perennial challenge.

Dialogue and mixed motives

No consideration of the potential of public consultation, 'dialogic democracy', the analyst as facilitator and so on should neglect the simple question: just *why* do people dialogue? The most realistic assumption is that people generally enter into dialogue with mixed motives, at best. As individuals, we may be seeking truth, or the best policy choice. Apart from this, however, we are almost certainly seeking to affirm ourselves, to gain recognition from others, to defend points of view to which we are viscerally attached and so on.[11] In specific cases, we may stand to profit personally from a decision, which weakens our concern for the group as a whole.

Such mixed motives can be very productive. In his *Homo Ludens*, Johan Huizinga argues that competitive play has been a central factor in the rise of human culture: history manifests 'a development *of* culture *in* play-like contest' (1955, 75, emphasis in original). Against the 'hierarchy of needs' view that human beings first look after serious matters before turning to frills such as play, Huizinga insists that culture is 'played from the very beginning. Even those activities which aim at the immediate satisfaction of vital needs – hunting, for instance – tend, in archaic society, to take on the play-form' (46).

Throughout human history, one form of competitive play has been verbal duels. 'The sophist's art is an ancient one,' says Protagoras in Plato's dialogue of the same name (¶316d). The claim, observes Huizinga, 'goes to the heart of the matter. It is indeed the ancient game of wits which, starting in the remotest cultures, vacillates between solemn ritual and mere amusement' (1955, 147). His reference to the 'remotest cultures' suggests that we might do well to view this competitive spirit as a relatively durable component of human nature, or at the very least not build our approach to policy making on the assumption that it will wither away any time soon.[12]

And this is problematic: while competitive 'play' contributed to the development of human culture, there is a dangerous side to the competitive spirit as well. Discussing the civilization in which the culture of competitive debate reached its apogee, Hannah Arendt points out that classical Athens was 'a polis whose life consisted of an intense and uninterrupted contest of all against all' (1990, 82). This spirit, she goes on, 'eventually was to bring the Greek city states to ruin because it made alliances between them well nigh impossible and poisoned the domestic life of the citizens with envy and mutual hatred' (82).[13]

Both the power and the dangers of competitive dialogue are vividly portrayed in the *Peloponnesian War*. Thucydides had Pericles declare that 'what cripples action is not talk, but rather the failure to talk through the policy before proceeding to the required action' (¶2.40). But Thucydides also depicted the vulnerability of deliberative assemblies to demagogy. He recorded, in particular, how the Athenians talked themselves into the disastrous Sicilian expedition, under the sway of 'a number of attractive falsehoods' (¶6.8).[14]

Note that neither Arendt nor Thucydides argued that the destructive impact of public dialogue imbued with a competitive spirit arose from an excessive concentration of rhetorical skills. Returning to contemporary policy analysis, the implication is that the problematic aspects of policy dialogue will not be neutralized simply by generalizing argumentative skills. In his fascinating case for the centrality of argument and persuasion in the policy world, Giandomenico Majone recommends that the analyst 'understand the rules of the game well enough to know the standard moves and have a repertoire of effective countermoves' (1989, 13). Even were these debating skills a standard part of the training of policy analysts, and indeed of citizens in general, we must still admit the possibility that policy dialogue can lead a society down a dangerously mistaken path.

As noted earlier, this is a perennial challenge. We address it first by being aware of it, by resisting utopian illusions about the power of democratic dialogue, even while promoting that dialogue wherever we can. A realistic awareness of risks can lead us to experiment with forms of dialogue that are not so conditioned by competitiveness, and recognize that the social supply of mediation skills must grow along with the development of argumentative skills.

Conclusion

In the Introduction, I acknowledged that the binary view is a 'half-belief': no one can fully endorse it, because no one can truly live by it. But I also argued that it is an extremely influential half-belief. Throughout this work, I have avoided claims concerning just how prevalent is the binary view in today's policy world. Some readers may be frustrated by this caution, suspecting that I am trying to avoid committing myself (refusing to put forward a testable claim, a follower of Popper might say). But the policy world is simply too vast for a summary judgment. I hope, however, that individual readers will try to judge for themselves just how powerful is the binary view within the particular fragment of the policy world of which they have direct experience.

Still, if we review the effects of the binary view discussed in Part I, we can identify various elements that are influential throughout our culture as a whole, and within the policy world in particular. Starting specifically with the policy world: there is little question that it is deeply shaped by a dilemma rooted in the binary view. Policy analysis is about 'what *should* be done', and since that question always involves human values, any approach framed by the binary view will be seriously constrained in addressing it. As we saw in Chapter 2, this dilemma has led policy analysts on a quest for exogenous values. These might be found through summation strategies such as cost-benefit analysis. Alternatively, in some mysterious fashion, values will be found in the political process: 'the political process has the responsibility of choosing values in a democracy' (Robert and Zeckhauser, 2011, 638).

There have, of course, been strong reactions within policy theory against the whole premise that policy analysis must depend on exogenous values. But as we saw in Chapter 3, it is not so easy to escape the binary view: aspects of that view show up in approaches that appear hostile to it. Social constructionism, originally rooted in insights that help shape a non-binary approach, has often taken a strongly binary form among policy theorists, who argue that this or that value or idea with which they disagree is 'socially constructed', and leave the unfortunate impression that everything else is not. We also saw that one may reject the binary view's belief that thought can be value-free, yet hold on to the prejudice that values, being merely subjective, are not matters for critical analysis. This combination favors an explicitly biased approach to the writing and teaching of history, with the claim that each nation has the right to a history shaped by its own (unexamined) values.

Policy analysis, of course, is embedded within particular cultures. Important effects of the binary view upon analysis, then, are not peculiar to the policy world itself. There is a widespread cultural view, for example, that all values are *someone's* values. When values clash the question is '*Whose* values will prevail?' When scientists are having an open discussion, on the other hand, to say that they are fighting over '*Whose* science will prevail?' would reflect a misunderstanding of science itself. This contrast recalls a suggestion offered in Part I: a good procedure to detect the presence of the binary view in everyday thinking is to transpose a statement about normative matters into one about factual matters. If the original statement seems sensible, while the transposed one does not, the binary view is probably at work. People often say, for example, 'We just disagree about whether X is right or wrong, and that's all there is to it.' But it would strike us as odd for someone to say: 'We just disagree on whether climate change is happening, and that's all there is to it.'

The foregoing brings us back to the problem of learning, 'deep' learning. We can nod our heads at critiques of the binary view and say 'Yes it is terribly simplistic, it ignores the ways in which values enter into the constitution of facts, the way factual arguments support normative ones,' and so on. We can give ready assent to all of this. But if we stop there, we will fail to see that the binary view is also embedded in beliefs that we may be less ready to abandon, that might seem quite commonsensical to us. Perhaps the durability of the view in the face of ongoing critiques arises from the failure to take this extra step, thus limiting the critique to the low-hanging fruit of the crude binary view.

A vitally important example of a commonsensical belief is what I have termed 'end-of-the-line' thinking: the assumption that if we probe the beliefs of a person who profoundly disagrees with us, we eventually reach a bedrock of irreconcilable difference. This belief seems confirmed 1,000 times over by our lived experience. Indeed, the view asserted here, that discussion need never reach a bedrock of difference, would seem to be more an article of faith than anything else.

Perhaps it is.

But it is a faith born of careful analysis of the nature of arguments and beliefs. And it asserts that when we reach an impasse in an argument, it is not because we've reached some logically impassible chasm of differences. It is not *beliefs* that argue against one another, but flesh-and-blood people, with all their passions, their commitments, their personal histories. It is concrete human beings who reach impasses, not the beliefs themselves. And when flesh-and-blood people reach impasses, it is very psychologically convenient to excuse ourselves by saying that something we *failed* to do simply *cannot* be done, that it is logically impossible. The view that arguments must reach a bedrock of difference is thus psychologically appealing, as it provides an alibi for the failure of dialogue and a pretext for avoiding dialogue altogether.

So while the binary view can at most be a half-belief, it is powerful, shaping our culture in general and the policy world in particular. Not surprisingly, then, a consistently non-binary analysis differs in many ways from one influenced by the binary view. As we saw in Part II, the non-binary analyst pays attention to a quite different range of issues. More generally, a non-binary approach leads us to a different understanding of the role of the policy analyst in a democracy. Let us conclude with some thoughts on that matter.

I noted in Chapter 8 that an important variant of the subservient analyst model uses the binary view as a basis for circumscribing the analyst's role. Robert and Zeckhauser were cited as an example of this: 'there is always a deep interaction between politics and analysis. Each facilitates the other, with politics helping to *supply the values* underpinning analysis and analysis helping to supply the information and clarity necessary to a well-functioning political process' (2011, 616, emphasis added). As with any policy approach rooted in the binary view, the assumption is that analysis requires a 'supply' of exogenous values to get underway.

But is the political process really up to the task of supplying the values for analysis? This is related to another question: do elected officials incarnate the will of the people? That is, can analysis plausibly view the elected leader as a transmission mechanism for the values of the sovereign people, and hence depend on that leader for its value bases?

As Schumpeter argued, we need an understanding of electoral democracy that is 'truer to life' than the view that '"the people" hold a definite and rational opinion about every individual question and that they give effect to this opinion – in a democracy – by choosing "representatives" who will see to it that that opinion is carried out' (1976, 269). Electoral democracy produces neither government 'of the people', nor government embodying the will of the people, but, at best, 'government approved by the people' (246).[1] This is not to be sneered at: electoral democracy provides ordinary citizens with a course-correction mechanism, a means of discipline that no elected government can entirely ignore.[2]

But let us consider a more difficult case. Imagine that a precise policy question has been put to the public in a referendum, one in which the power of money did not tilt the scales, and that a specific position has been approved by a strong majority. Should we consider the analyst to be ethically bound to take the values represented by that policy choice as an unquestioned axiom for analysis? Not necessarily. Consider, by way of counter-example, policy catastrophes of the past. Out of many possible examples, we can note two cases of ethnic cleansing that occurred centuries apart: Spain's 1492 expulsion of its Jews and Muslims, and the 1972 expulsion of citizens of Asian origin from Idi Amin's Uganda. Both these policies tyrannized minorities within the respective countries, and both inflicted lasting harm on the countries themselves. If such decisions had been made by a democratically elected parliament or through a referendum, if they represented the tyranny of the majority rather than the tyranny of an autocratic ruler, it is hard to argue that the policy analyst would have been ethically bound to accept the normative premises of these actions. Thus, we can imagine a *democratic* context in which an analyst would legitimately resist the norms supplied by politics.

One may well object that these are extreme examples, irrelevant to the situation of a policy analyst in a contemporary developed country. The argument seems to be that the analyst can let the political process supply the normative premises, let her own critical faculties lie dormant, unless she finds herself in a situation of clear-cut evil, such as Nazi Germany, in which case she must resist as best she can. One implausible assumption behind this view is that the analyst accustomed to a normative slumber will *recognize* when the time has come to awaken. Unfortunately, as Hannah Arendt noted, with 'nonthinking', people 'get used to never making up their minds' (2003, 178). This is all the more so in that awakening from normative slumber may be very unpleasant, creating tensions with colleagues and superiors, afflicting one with an uneasy conscience and so on. The analyst whose understanding of duty involves never questioning directives from above shields herself from possibly grave ethical dilemmas.

A further assumption is that grave normative problems only arise in extreme situations, and that catastrophic policy decisions can easily be recognized, being quite distinct from the vast majority of policy decisions, the latter resting on solid normative premises that can be accepted without further ado by the analyst. It is more realistic to assume that polities lie on a spectrum. Let us place Nazi Germany at one extreme of the spectrum.[3] What lies at the other end? An ideal, not a reality: a polity in which the widely shared values of citizens are normatively solid. Thus, people are so respectful of human rights, including those of minorities, that no politician can gain traction through divisive tactics. The values of the citizenry are also sensitive to the rights of other peoples and of future generations. Looking towards the future, they in effect adopt the Golden Rule, treating future generations as they would like to have been treated themselves (Rawls, 2001, 160). Finally, in this ideal polity, the solid normative framework of the citizenry is, somehow or other, translated by the democratic political process into guidance for concrete policy decisions.

We can see that, at one extreme of this spectrum, the analyst would be morally bound to oppose by any means possible the preferences of political leaders. At the other extreme, analysts would be bound to carry out those preferences. Note that the toxic end of the spectrum can be occupied both by tyrannies and by democracies in which the majority of citizens are vicious: hateful of minorities, belligerent and contemptuous towards other peoples and entirely unconcerned for the welfare of future generations.

Now: along this spectrum, is there a clear line between a democracy in which the analyst should be limited to faithful execution of normative preferences and a regime, whether tyrannical or democratic, in which there is a duty of resistance to those preferences? There is not: there is a vast middle ground where the proper stance is neither absolute resistance nor automatic implementation, but questioning, pushing back, calling the political master to normative reflexivity.

Further: imagine a society drifting over time to a more toxic point on the spectrum. That drift may not be obvious for all to see. No politician, for example, will explicitly declare: 'I couldn't care less about future generations' or 'Who cares if our country has to commit war crimes to get what we want?' Rather, the shift will first be manifest through more subtle changes in the concrete application of specific norms: concern about the future, for example, will be increasingly neutralized by more immediate factors.[4] Humanity has millennia of practice at paying lip service to important norms, gradually hollowing out those norms so that their influence on practice is increasingly feeble. We can take it as a general rule that important norms are almost never overturned from one moment to the next: they wear out.[5] To detect such shifts, the analyst must be attentive to the normative underpinnings of specific decisions and policy orientations, to the rhetoric being applied to justify those, to the excuses being deployed to bypass normative constraints and so on.

And so the analyst must be continually alert to her normative environment, within her organization and in society as a whole. Which values seem to be truly weighty? To which is mere lip service paid? This sort of sensitivity will help the analyst identify and avoid the possible paths of least resistance, of 'thoughtlessness' (Arendt, 1964, 287), the paths down which he will be led unless he 'takes care', to use that phrase again.

Thinking about a spectrum of societies, running from solidly benign to absolutely toxic, may seem terribly abstract, though the implication we have drawn from that idea is not: a critical normative awareness is not an outlook that the responsible analyst can pack away, to be dusted off only when needed. It is always needed. It is certainly needed today: we cannot simply assume that today's developed democratic societies are benign. On the contrary, even leaving aside the extreme toxicity of the Trump regime, one could argue that today's democracies are tyrannical, tyrannical in their disregard of the rights and needs of future generations. G.K. Chesterton once referred to 'the small and arrogant oligarchy of those who merely happen to be walking about' (1990, 48). He was making a case for respect for the past, for tradition. But we can apply his words looking forward as well: in relation to all who will come after us, a democracy that fails to protect the environment is an 'arrogant oligarchy'. Clearly, the normative challenges facing an analyst in an oligarchy are more serious than those that arise within a truly benign democracy.

I wish to conclude with two important points. First: no matter how many arguments I advance on this matter, many a reader may be left with the suspicion that there is something undemocratic in my position. There is not. I have not argued that we must shift ultimate decision-making authority from elected officials to bureaucratic experts. A democracy endows elected officials with the responsibility to decide policy questions, subject to the constitution and existing laws. I know of no democratic constitution that proclaims that the values of elected officials are to reign supreme, that elected officials are to decide matters without reflection, that they may not be questioned. The subservient analyst model does not emerge from democratic theory: it is a perversion of it, because it undermines one of the key premises for a healthy democracy, the widespread practice of deliberative judgment.[6]

Second: in sketching the nature of a non-binary analysis, and in arguing for the conception of the role that a responsible analyst should adopt, I am not naively imagining that the world will embrace with open arms the sort of policy analysis being advocated here. There are many powerful forces at work today that are hostile to the very idea of independent policy advice and critical reflection. As a consequence, as discussed in Chapter 8, the responsible analyst will often confront tensions between the goal of self-preservation and the normative demands of her situation. Still: however tyrannical modern societies may be in relation to the future, however flawed modern democracies are in the present, we still have the good fortune to live in democratic societies, ones in which the space for critical (and appreciative) thought, and for dissent, will never entirely disappear. Unless we allow that to happen.

Notes

Introduction

[1] *Seems* justified – but in truth many arguments that generate 'more heat than light' concern fact claims. The core claims of religious doctrine, over which much blood has been spilled throughout history, often concern matters of fact.

[2] Textbooks that try to present a simple positive-normative dichotomy get around this problem with example-rigging. Recent editions of Lipsey's *Economics* offer nice tables showing students the unproblematic difference between types of statements. Thus, 'Higher interest rates cause people to save more' is paired with 'People should save more', while 'High income taxes rates discourage effort' is contrasted with 'Governments should tax the rich to help the poor' (Lipsey and Chrystal, 2007, 17). So long as one chooses one's examples carefully, classification of statements into positive or normative will present no difficulty, and the dichotomy itself will seem natural, a matter of common sense.

[3] The point may seem obvious, but is worth stating, to forestall the sort of confusion engendered by certain problematic claims of social constructionists, such as 'all "reality" is socially constructed' (Kelly and Maynard-Moody, 1993, 136). Such statements become compatible with sanity if we take their use of 'reality' to denote *our* lived reality. That is, one can be a constructionist, in the sense of recognizing that *our* facts about the world are constructed, without denying 'ontological objectivity', to use John Searle's term (1995, 8).

[4] I present an example of such a dismissal, from the work of Aaron Wildavsky, in Chapter 6.

[5] 'Theories, during their tenure of office, are highly immune to falsification; that tenure of office is ended by the appearance on the scene of a better theory' (Putnam, 1974, 234); 'There is no falsification before the emergence of a better theory' (Lakatos, 1970, 119); 'once it has achieved the status of paradigm, a scientific theory is declared invalid only if an alternate candidate is available to take its place' (Kuhn, 1970b, 77).

[6] In Chapter 5, we will examine two advocates of a constructionist approach to policy analysis who exemplify this confusion on climate change.

[7] As Diotima said to Socrates: 'There's no need to ask further, "What's the point of wanting happiness?"' (Plato, *Symposium*, ¶205a).

[8] Anyone who thinks that it is a simple matter to make happiness the foundation of one's network of beliefs and practices should reflect on Kant's warning that 'what brings true, lasting advantage, if this advantage is to be extended to one's entire existence, is shrouded in impenetrable obscurity' (rpt. 2002, 36).

[9] This is an epistemological rather than a metaphysical claim. That is, no claim is being made concerning the ultimate nature of reality.

[10] To someone who insists on the opposite claim, that there is no difference at all between facts and values, we can offer a similar answer: what concretely depends on that claim? How would one's analysis or practice change were it true?

[11] This is the sort of usage assumed when philosophers speak of knowledge as 'justified true belief'. I take no position on that particular formulation, but make use of its implied sense of belief.

[12] To guard against certain simplifications, I should add that we are not conscious of all our beliefs (see Chapter 6). And, as noted earlier in the discussion of half-beliefs, we are not always fully committed to a particular belief.

Part I

[1] The policy analyst in particular can ask how often, in meetings, in reading policy briefs, practice-oriented articles in policy journals and so on, you encounter those symptoms.

Chapter 1

[1] Levitt, who depicts himself as a 'Rogue Economist', thus demonstrates that even rogues have difficulty escaping orthodoxy.

[2] Simon was extraordinarily influential in a wide range of disciplines, earning among many distinctions the Nobel Memorial Prize in Economics in 1978. Of his impact in just one field, Daniel Kahneman comments that Simon is 'perhaps the only scholar who is recognized and admired as a hero and founding figure by all the competing clans and tribes in the study of decision making' (2011, 237). His commitment to the binary view, then, may be assumed to have influenced countless scholars.

[3] 'Straddling terms' bear some resemblance to the 'thick' ethical concepts discussed by philosopher Hilary Putnam. With thick concepts, facts and values are necessarily entangled. Putnam offers the example of 'cruel', which 'simply ignores the supposed fact/value dichotomy and cheerfully allows itself to be used sometimes for a normative purpose and sometimes as a descriptive term' (2002, 35; see also Sayer, 2011, 7). One cannot fully disentangle the descriptive and evaluative components of such thick concepts. The *Concise Oxford Dictionary*, for example, defines cruel as 'Having or showing indifference to or pleasure in another's suffering' (Sykes, 1976) But what is 'indifference'? It may not necessarily involve a total non-response to the other's suffering, but a response we consider inappropriate, insufficient in relation to the depth of the suffering. Some normative evaluation is necessarily involved in applying the term in this or that case. Many straddling terms will be thick in Putnam's sense. But not all. To say that 'free press' is a straddling term is not to say that it is impossible to provide a strictly observational definition of this or that understanding of the term (eg 'press not owned or censored by the government'). But the choice of just which definition to settle upon must invariably contain a normative component. That is, norms enter into the definition of the concept, but not necessarily into its application.

[4] Julien Benda commented in 1946 that it was 'amusing' to see so many intellectuals 'condemn communism in the name of order. As if the victory just won by the Soviet state in the war did not require order! But that's not the order they want' (rpt. 1975, 59).

[5] We can imagine this, that is, if we assume for a moment that a social science can develop in entire isolation from its political and economic context.

[6] Of James Buchanan and the Virginia school of political economy, whose approach has an affinity with that of Riker, political philosopher Brian Barry comments: 'they seem to me to display a kind of willful, arrogant ignorance about the entire history of historical and social thought' (1992, 336).

On the history of Buchanan's work and his relation to the Koch brothers, see Nancy MacLean, *Democracy in Chains* (2017).

[7] Dismayed, but perhaps not surprised, in this age of 'post-truth democracy' (Habermas, 2006, 18). Monica Prasad et al studied people's reactions to 'information that contradicted their beliefs' concerning the alleged role of Saddam Hussein in the 9/11 attacks. This led to one exchange:

> INTERVIEWER: ... the September 11 Commission found no link between Saddam and 9/11, and this is what President Bush said. [pause] This is what the commission said. Do you have any comments on either of those?

RESPONDENT: Well, I bet they say that the Commission didn't have any proof of it but I guess *we still can have our opinions and feel that way* even though they say that. (Prasad et al, 2009, 154, emphasis added)

In 1950, Hannah Arendt visited Germany for the first time since she fled the Nazis. She commented that

perhaps the most striking and frightening aspect of the German flight from reality is the habit of treating facts as though they were mere opinions ... [I]n all fields there is a kind of gentlemen's agreement by which everyone has a right to his ignorance under the pretext that *everyone has a right to his opinion* ... [T]he average German honestly believes this free-for-all, this nihilistic relativity about facts, to be the essence of democracy. In fact, of course, it is a legacy of the Nazi regime. (rpt. 1994, 251–252, emphasis added)

We cannot blame the Nazis for today's widespread confusion of fact and opinion: so what are its causes?

8 Anyone who doubts this interpretation of the force of these claims may wish to examine how often the 'reasonable people can disagree' formulation is followed by further analysis, examining *why* they disagree, what *reasons* each 'reasonable person' can offer for their position, and so on.

9 Decades before Friedman, Lionel Robbins argued that

If we disagree about ends it is a case of thy blood or mine – or live and let live, according to the importance of the difference, or the relative strength of our opponents. But, if we disagree about means, then scientific analysis can often help us to resolve our differences. If we disagree about the morality of the taking of interest (and we understand what we are talking about), then there is no room for argument. (1932, 134).

10 In Part II, we will see just how far this foundational pessimism may take someone, when we briefly examine the musings of 'New Atheist' Sam Harris on how to deal with 'Islamist' regimes.

11 Foundational pessimism relies on another important assumption, which will simply be noted here: that we can *know* when it is impossible to argue further. Amartya Sen distinguishes basic and non-basic value judgments: 'A value judgment can be called "basic" to a person if no conceivable revision of factual assumptions can make him revise the judgment' (1967, 50). While one can demonstrate that people revise particular judgments in the face of new facts, showing those judgments to have been non-basic, one *cannot* demonstrate that a value judgment would survive any 'conceivable revision' of facts. Hence, Sen argues, 'some value judgments are demonstrably non-basic, but no value judgment is demonstrably basic' (53). See also Hilary Putnam's discussion of this early work of Sen (2002, 67ff).

12 For Friedman, 'fundamentally, there are only two ways' of organizing an economy: the technique of the 'modern totalitarian state' and that of the 'market place' (1962, 13).

13 A 1975 letter from Friedman to Pinochet contained not a hint of concern over the widespread torture, assassination and 'disappearance' of regime opponents. Instead, Friedman commented on the 'trends toward socialism that started forty years ago, and reached their logical – and terrible – climax in the Allende regime. You have been extremely wise in adopting the many measures you have already taken to reverse this

trend' (rpt. 1998). Pinochet could certainly be forgiven if he understood this as a blanket endorsement of his crackdown on human rights.

14 Articles of religious faith are not in fact 'beyond debate': believers of all stripes have debated them for millennia. Despite this, the phrase 'article of religious faith' is used as a shorthand to signify a belief supposedly placed beyond debate by its adherents.

15 Note the definitional gambit here: Friedman simply *equates* equality of opportunity with the 'free market', thus begging the question. But one can leave such ploys aside when examining the structure of his argument.

16 Friedman's full point is: 'Life is not fair. It is tempting to believe that government can rectify what nature has spawned. But it is also important to recognize how much we benefit from the very unfairness we deplore. There's nothing fair about Marlene Dietrich's having been born with beautiful legs that we all want to look at' (1979, 127). It is unlikely that a Rawlsian would think to drag Marlene Dietrich's legs into a discussion of inequality. Is that because Rawlsians are less vulgar than Friedmanites or because they are less likely to believe that 'nature' has much to do with economic inequality?

17 Further examples could have been explored. Joseph Schumpeter claimed that

> Americans who say, 'We want this country to arm to its teeth and then to fight for what we conceive to be right all over the globe' and Americans who say, 'We want this country to work out its own problems which is the only way it can serve humanity' are facing irreducible differences of ultimate values. (rpt. 1976, 251)

At this point, the reader can probably think of various questions that could be put to either camp, to flesh out just what they mean, and how seriously their broad declarations are to be taken. Prior to discussion of those questions, it is unlikely that even those who offer such statements are fully sure of what they believe.

18 Friedman himself spent much time arguing in favor of his personal understanding of values such as freedom and equality. In practice, it is clear that *he* didn't believe these are matters about which we can 'only fight'.

19 Madison's use of 'liquidate' here points to a profound change of meaning over time. The *Oxford English Dictionary* dates to 1575 the word's usage to mean 'To make clear or plain (something obscure or confused); to render unambiguous; to settle (differences, disputes).' Even words whose meaning we think quite obvious have undergone mutation over time. The student of *policy* would do well to consult a historical dictionary such as *Oxford*, to gain a sense of the word's evolution. When Mr. Darcy declares, in Jane Austen's *Pride and Prejudice*, 'These bitter accusations might have been suppressed, had I, with greater policy, concealed my struggles' (rpt. 1996, 140), he is drawing upon a meaning that dates back at least to the time of Shakespeare.

20 Amitai Etzioni observed that incrementalism is 'both a descriptive and a normative model' (1967, 387). That is, one might agree that incrementalists have described certain typical aspects of human decision making quite well, without accepting the theory as a guide to how policy *should* be developed. (This goes to show that, notwithstanding the complexities of the is–ought distinction, it can sometimes play a useful role.)

21 Note also Laurence Tribe's suggestion that 'the whole point of personal or social choice in many situations is not to implement a given system of values in the light of the perceived facts, but rather to define, and sometimes deliberately to reshape, the values – and hence the identity – of the individual or community that is engaged in the process of choosing' (1972, 99).

22 Consider this exchange:

Antigone: We have a duty to the dead.
Creon: Not to give equal honour to good and bad.
Antigone: *Who knows?* In the country of the dead that may be the law. (140, emphasis added).

23 Creon brings to this issue, we might add, a fair bit of gender anxiety:

Better be beaten, if need be, by a man,
Than let a woman get the better of us. (144)

24 The personalization of values will often be applied quite selectively. For Hayek and his acolytes, interference with the 'free play of economic forces' inevitably limits our freedoms in the name of 'somebody's ideal of justice' (2007, 132). Needless to say, the state of affairs that results from the unhindered play of market forces, the particular understanding of property rights that has evolved in the modern world and the doctrine that corporations enjoy the rights of persons, to take a few examples, are not acknowledged to reflect someone or other's subjective conception of justice.

25 The Texas state panel charged with approving biology textbooks for school use is said to include six members, out of 28, 'known to reject evolution' (Rich, 2013).

26 While all science may contain a political aspect, science is not politics. An observation from anthropologist Clifford Geertz is relevant here:

> I have never been impressed by the argument that, as complete objectivity is impossible in these matters (as, of course, it is), one might as well let one's sentiments run loose. As Robert Solow has remarked, that is like saying that as a perfectly aseptic environment is impossible, one might as well conduct surgery in a sewer. (1973, 30)

27 Defending the participation of anthropologists in the CIA's and USAF's counter-insurgency efforts in Iraq and Afghanistan, anthropologist Montgomery McFate comments that 'Despite the fact that military applications of cultural knowledge might be distasteful to *ethically inclined anthropologists*, their assistance is necessary' (2005, 37, emphasis added). Here, the subjectivization has gone one step further: even the will to be ethical at all is reduced to a mere 'inclination'. For a critique of the military application of anthropology see Price (2011).

28 Some constructionist or 'postmodern' theorists apply the same personalization to facts. Policy theorist Marie Danziger, for example, quotes with approval the sophists' view that 'the highest truth for any man is what he believes it to be' (1995, 436). This is an example of the strategy of overcoming the fact–value gulf by dragging down our factual beliefs to the same level of subjectivity that the binary view attributes to our normative beliefs. As I have argued elsewhere, truth is not the only casualty of this approach: error vanishes along with it (Ryan, 2015).

Chapter 2

1 Along with 'What is worth doing?', we have, for example, the obvious question: 'What means are permissible to do it?'

2 Tony Benn, who served in the UK's Labour government from 1974 to 1979, later wrote that civil servants offer the minister a trade-off: 'If you follow the policies we recommend, we will help you, in every way we can, to pretend that you are implementing the policy on which you were elected' (1989, 136).

3   There is much more to say concerning the relation between analysts and elected officials, and we will return to the question in Part II.

4   Quantitative evaluation of programs can bypass an issue such as the monetary value of life, by engaging in strictly comparative cost-effectiveness analysis: 'According to one study, better allocations of health expenditures could save, each year, 60,000 additional lives at no additional cost -- and such allocations could maintain the current level of lives saved with $31 billion in annual savings' (Sunstein, 2001, 11). Such claims can be made without putting any monetary value on life.

5   It is striking that Posner and Weisbach (2010, 149) label Nordhaus a 'positivist', contrasting him with the 'ethicists' who 'reason from first principles' to shape a climate change policy. Nordhaus and Boyer, as we will see, also rely on first principles, principles that are not free of (dubious) ethical content.

6   United Nations development program figures for 2017 show that Swiss gross domestic product per capita is 62 times that of Niger. In addition, Swiss life expectancy is 38 percent higher, so the Swiss child can be expected to have more productive years (http://hdr.undp.org/en/data#).

7   But have they correctly identified 'existing values'? Consider the public reaction to explicit suggestions that some lives are worth less than others. Early in the pandemic, a Canadian Conservative MP had to beat a hasty retreat after tweeting that restrictions should be eased because 'Most deaths are in care homes where average life expectancy is 2 years' (Zimonjic, 2020).

8   I am drawing here on John Rawls's concept of 'reflective equilibrium', which calls for deductions from general principles to be tested against our 'considered judgments' (1971, 47). In this particular case, the fact that one's method has led to a normatively repugnant conclusion should send one back to the drawing board, as they say, to arrive, if possible, at a general method that can avoid such pitfalls. (And if this is not possible? That would call into question the whole search for a general method to 'infer' society's values.)

9   Many economists simply assume that a response to climate change requires the specification of a 'social cost of carbon', which can then be used for policies such as a carbon tax or a cap-and-trade system. But even leaving aside matters such as the value of human life, that social cost may simply be incalculable. Consider just one possible long-term effect of climate change. The US Geological Survey states that 'If all of the glacier ice on Earth were to melt, sea level would rise 70 m (≈230 ft), flooding every coastal city on the planet.' To account for this one possible effect of climate change, we would have to: (a) put a monetary value on the total cost of this occurrence; discounted by (b) the probability of the occurrence. But we can do neither.

> Does this leave economists with no contribution to make to climate policy? No. We have had, for over forty years now, a clear sense of global emissions targets that need to be met in order to avert a climate cataclysm (Rich, 2018), and that clarity has sharpened over time. The policy question is thus: what suite of measures, including a price on carbon as one arrow in the quiver, can bring us to the level of emissions the planet can tolerate? Note that this procedure requires no pricing of intangibles (human lives, polar bears, etc.). Economists can certainly contribute through statistical analysis of policies taken to date and of their observable effects.

10   Thomas Piketty's monumental *Le capital au XXIᵉ siècle* argues that the substantial reduction in income inequality in the developed world throughout much of the twentieth century was largely the product of the great political shocks of the two world wars and various

political repercussions of those events (2013, 47). The outcome certainly did not reflect a process in which societies 'chose' to reduce income inequality.

[11] This procedure recalls Milton Friedman's likening of consumer spending to voting, with the difference that market 'voting' is more satisfying: 'When you vote daily in the supermarket, you get precisely what you voted for, and so does everyone else' (1979, 57). Such market 'voting is', of course, rather oligarchical. In the case of globalized financial markets, many of those with the greatest influence over the interest-rate decisions of 'society' are not even members of the society itself.

[12] Sunstein is assuming positive real interest rates and the absolute security of the investment.

[13] The history of the theory of pure time preference is reviewed by Herbener (2011).

[14] The target here is 'pure' time preference. In some cases, there are reasons to weight current goods and ills more heavily, reasons that depend neither on myopia nor on egotism. Legitimate uncertainty concerning the future may play a role: a dollar today is, after all, a bird in the hand, while a dollar in a year from now is not. There are also circumstances in which we judge, non-myopically, that our need for resources is greater than it will be at some future point: this is the basis of demand for many loans (eg mortgages, student loans).

But such cases cannot constitute a *general* justification for time discounting.

[15] The problem of myopia and egotism, it should be noted, is simply one instance of a broader problem with CBA and the utilitarian philosophy that has inspired it. If one regards preferences as purely subjective, then consistency dictates that one should also believe that 'No matter how trivial, how stupid, or how evil, a preference is a preference is a preference' (Tong, 1986, 20). All preferences thus become raw material for one's CBA calculations. Rawls critiques pure utilitarianism on similar grounds: 'if men take a certain pleasure in discriminating against one another, in subjecting others to a lesser liberty as a means of enhancing their self-respect, then the satisfaction of these desires must be weighed in our deliberations according to their intensity, or whatever, along with other desires' (1971, 30).In practice, however, analysts are unlikely to argue that policy should take into account the 'utility' that racists derive from discrimination. This shows that policy analysis, even when influenced by utilitarianism, in practice departs from it at many points. The departures, though, tend to be tacit and unexplained.

[16] Two of the difficulties with CBA discussed here are intimately linked. As Stephen Gardiner shows, it is the refusal to take distributional questions into account that supplies a key justification for time discounting in discussions of climate change. Bjorn Lomborg defends discounting by arguing: 'If the welfare of future generations means just as much (or almost as much) to us as our own, then we ought to spend an extremely large share of our income on investment in the future, because the dividend payable on investments will be much greater in the future' (qtd. in Gardiner, 2011, 335). To which Gardiner replies: 'Clearly, commonsense morality tells us that distribution matters, and some sacrifices ought to be prohibited. So, what is happening here is that bad theory is being invoked to attack better ethics, and the blame is put on the ethics' (335).

[17] Imagine that we were able to devise a democratic decision procedure, so that social savings were set by public decision, rather than through individual market choices. Even here, as Rawls argues, 'There is nothing sacrosanct about the public decision concerning the level of savings; and its bias with respect to time preference deserves no special respect. In fact the absence of the injured parties, the future generations, makes it all the more open to question' (1971, 296). Thus, 'the collective will concerning the provision for the future is subject, as all other social decisions are, to the principles of justice' (297).

[18] A corollary is that the 'rational voter' cares little if the party that promises maximum individual benefits happens to cheat: 'That these voters would punish their own leaders for successful ruthlessness is improbable at best' (Riker, 1986, 72). One can expect this

'rational voter' to lead to the emergence of politicians of a particular type. This was eloquently expressed in a 1972 *New Yorker* cartoon: 'Look, Nixon's no dope. If the people really *wanted* moral leadership, he'd give them moral leadership' (rpt. Mankoff, 2004 [1972], 715, emphasis in original).

[19] McCloskey comments that 'a watered down version of Friedman's essay is part of the intellectual equipment of most economists, and its arguments come readily to their lips' (1983, 485). We might add that important parts of Friedman's essay itself were already a 'watered down', badly muddled and unacknowledged rendering of Karl Popper's philosophy of science.

[20] Erich Maria Remarque's World War I novel *All Quiet on the Western Front* emphasized that Germany's defeat was economic as much as military: 'Our lines are falling back. There are too many fresh English and American regiments over there. There's too much corned beef and white wheaten bread. Too many new guns. Too many aeroplanes' (rpt. 1982, 280).

[21] 'The introduction of new methods of production and new commodities is hardly conceivable with perfect – and perfectly prompt – competition from the start. And this means that the bulk of what we call economic progress is incompatible with it' (Schumpeter, rpt. 1976, 104). In less than perfect competition, firms can get away with a fair bit of 'X-inefficiency', as Harvey Leibenstein termed it (1966). That can allow firms some latitude to pursue goals other than pure profit maximization alone.

[22] On this, see Plato's *Republic*, ¶357b.

[23] Do not many managers believe that 'a happy workforce is a productive workforce'? Does this then make happiness a merely instrumental value? While it may be instrumental for such managers, it is not so in general.

Chapter 3

[1] As Andrew Sayer notes, such a confessional approach assumes that values are not only subjective but synonymous with 'bias' and distortion. It's further assumed that they are personal biases that one ideally should confess to, so that others will at least be able to 'take them into account', that is, discount them. This is self-deprecating insofar as it invites the reader to discount what may be reasonable evaluative judgements. Tactically, it's disastrous since it invites readers with different values to ignore them (2011, 10).

[2] Analogously, as Andrew Collier puts it, 'Those who demand that theory, for instance in politics, be judged by practical criteria rather than by its adequacy to reality are generally saying that the criteria of some *existing* practice should judge the theory' (1994, 15, emphasis in original).

[3] Historian Tanika Sarkar, warning of the falsification of recent history by the Hindu Right, called for 'absolute opposition to their proclamation that they will make and unmake facts and histories according to the dictates of conviction … We need, as a bulwark against this, not simply our story pitted against theirs, but the story of what had indubitably happened' (qtd in Nussbaum, 2013, 254).

[4] I will use 'lived reality' to denote a person's set of beliefs about the world.

[5] As Charles Taylor explicates Spinoza's *omnis determinatio est negatio*, 'concepts can only have determinate sense against a background of others with which they are contrasted' (1975, 110).

[6] There can also be difficulties with more specific comparisons. Michel Foucault raised the provocative question of whether today's world is freer than, for example, seventeenth-century France. There was little political freedom in the earlier period. On the other hand, the machinery of state was 'heavy, unsupple', and hence unable to observe and control the population at the level of fine detail. The modern state, on the other hand,

accepts certain political freedoms, but also seeks to act upon citizens' 'health, work, way of life' and so on. Thus, suggests Foucault, 'to judge the quantity of freedom between one system and the other doesn't, I believe, make much sense' (2004, 64).

[7] This leads to revealing contradictions. Frank Fischer, to take one example, declares that 'what is identified as objective "truth" by rational techniques is as often as not the product of deeper, less visible, political presuppositions' (2003, 14). His ideal policy analyst will thus engage in 'scepticism and critique rather than truth-seeking per se' (46). Yet the same Fischer informs us of 'discoveries' and 'new historical and sociological *observations* about the nature of scientific practices', and assures us that 'historical and sociological analysis *makes clear*', helps us '*recognize*' the true nature of scientific communities (1998, 132–134, emphases added). It seems that 'scepticism and critique' are abandoned when it comes to 'historical and sociological' claims.

[8] The following few paragraphs draw upon my work 'Positivism: Paradigm or culture?' (Ryan, 2015).

[9] Lekachman's account emphasizes just how fitful was the application of Keynesian ideas in both the UK and the US. Of the UK, he comments that 'there was something depressingly familiar in the "stop-go" tactics of Conservative Chancellors of the Exchequer between 1951 and 1964' (1967, 226). In the US, Lekachman locates the 'triumph' of Keynesian ideas in the Kennedy and Johnson years. Writing in 1967, he could not know that the end was nigh.

Chapter 4

[1] Amy's observation is seconded by Mary Hawkesworth's comment that 'the legitimacy accorded policy scientists is parasitic on beliefs sustained by the discredited fact/value dichotomy' (1988, 187).

[2] I emphasize the young analyst, as the constraints can loosen for more senior officials, assuming their willingness to raise serious normative questions has survived their ascent through the ranks. There is an old French phrase: 'The vicar can smile at an anti-religious comment, the bishop laugh outright, and the cardinal join in with a comment of his own' (Chamfort, 1796).

[3] Alasdair MacIntyre offers the provocative suggestion that methodological rigor in the social sciences is 'essentially a histrionic subject: *how to act the part of a natural scientist on the stage of the social sciences* with the more technical parts of the discipline functioning as do greasepaint, false beards and costumes in the theater' (1979, 50, emphasis in original).

[4] The fan of the Harry Potter series can think of the rationalizations for any problematic practice as so many horcruxes, which must be found and vanquished before the practice itself will be decisively buried.

Conclusion to Part I: A world on autopilot

[1] The claim here is not that *because* policy analysis is limited, so too is society's reflection. One might just as well say that, *because* society has little interest in disciplined normative reflection, it ends up with a certain type of policy analysis. To do justice to the complexity of the relation between the policy world and its civilization, we might draw on Weber's concept of 'elective affinity': two social phenomena may fit well together, reciprocally furthering each other (1978, 341). This stable fit can emerge without one phenomenon causing the other.

[2] Some policy theorists advance rather curious statements about instrumental rationality. Schneider and Ingram declare that 'instrumental rationality undermines democracy because it disempowers ordinary people' (1997, 55). John Dryzek, for his part, believes

that 'instrumental rationality destroys the more congenial, spontaneous, egalitarian, and intrinsically meaningful aspects of human association' (1990, 4).

But instrumental rationality is simply the form of thought that aims at getting something done. Even the most critical policy theorist engages in it when planning how she will get something to eat today. The problem is not with instrumental rationality, but with a world in which it becomes synonymous with rationality itself, and thus marginalizes other forms of rationality (Habermas, 1987b, 304).

3   The collapse of the Grand Banks cod fishery off the coast of Newfoundland, to take one example, occurred because the technical capacity to catch fish developed rapidly, while the policy capacity to keep the catch within bounds did not.

The Grand Banks collapse, in turn, has had knock-on effects around the globe (Mora, 2012).

4   In a world in which we are absorbed by the 'logic of the situation', the sorts of accounts produced by rational choice thinkers take on a degree of truth. That is: reality is shaped and reshaped by the immediate decisions of atomized actors, *and nothing more*.

5   The carbon we can 'afford' to burn, that is, if we are to enjoy 'an 80% chance of limiting global warming to 2°C' (Carbon Tracker, 2013).

6   Carbon Tracker points out that, based largely on their reserves, these companies have a combined stock market valuation of $4 trillion and have been able to contract a corporate debt of $1.27 trillion (2013).

Part II

1   Dan Durning made a similar point concerning the 'postpositivist' critique of policy analysis: 'I maintain that traditional policy analysts are likely not so distant in their actual work from the practice envisioned by many postpositivist theorists, but remain distant in their beliefs about how policy analysis should be conducted' (1999, 390).

2   Michael Polanyi notes that when we do something like swimming, riding a bike or playing an instrument, we do not entirely know how we're doing what we're doing. It takes analysis of the performance to understand that. Polanyi cites W.L. Balls on the scientific study of cotton spinning: 'most of the initial decade's work on the part of the scientist will have to be spent merely in defining what the spinner knows' (1962, 52).

Chapter 5

1   A number of jurisdictions have banned the use of hand-held cell phones while driving. Many researchers, however, have found that hands-free phones are every bit as dangerous. A National Safety Council review of the relevant research suggests that both types interfere with the need to take special care in particular driving situations: 'Talking on cell phones has a different social expectation because not responding on a cell phone can be considered rude. In addition, callers cannot see when a driving environment is challenging and cannot suppress conversation in response. Passengers can see the roadway and may moderate the conversation' (2012, 8).

2   Albert Hirschman's wonderful book *The Rhetoric of Reaction* (1991) argues that the 'futility thesis' has for hundreds of years been one of the standard elements in the rhetorical arsenal of opponents to social change.

3   I say 'some' because productive dialogue typically focuses on contentious points and ignores matters on which the discussants agree.

4   Those of us who live in the Americas, with its relatively fixed borders, can underestimate the magnitude of this phenomenon. Visiting a town in Western Ukraine, journalists Laurent Geslin and Sébastien Gobert find a resident who observes that 'My grandfather

lived in five countries without ever leaving his village.' Beginning the twentieth century within the Austro-Hungarian empire, the village belonged successively to Czechoslovakia, the Nazi Reich, the USSR and Ukraine. After all that, the town's residents are emotionally attached to Hungary: 'They watch Hungarian TV, and set their clocks to Budapest time, one hour ahead of Kiev' (2013).

5 A challenge such as climate change has thus brought to the awareness of citizens something that observers of science have known for some time: 'nobody knows more than a tiny fragment of science well enough to judge its validity and value at first hand. For the rest he has to rely on views accepted at second hand on the authority of a community of people accredited as scientists' (Polanyi, 1962, 163).

6 Mark Hertsgaard notes that this strategy was first developed to weaken 'public understanding of the health effects of smoking', and cites an internal memo from the tobacco lobby, which declared that 'Doubt is our product' (2011, 259).

7 I leave aside the difficult question of identifying criteria by which we might distinguish between wise and foolish trust, or – just as importantly – between wise and foolish mistrust.

8 Smith wrote that 'With the greater part of rich people, the chief enjoyment of riches consists in the parade of riches; which, in their eye, is never so complete as when they appear to possess those decisive marks of opulence which nobody can possess but themselves' (rpt. 1937, 172). Marx, for his part, observed that a house may be perfectly adequate. But if a palace should be built next door, 'the little house shrinks to a hut'. The house is a *signal* to others, as well as a consumption good. With the large house beside it, 'The little house now makes it clear that its inmate has no social position at all to maintain, or but a very insignificant one' (Marx and Engels, rpt. 1969, 1:163).

9 On orthodox economics' hostility to such psychic externalities, see also Amartya Sen's classic essay 'Rational fools' (1977, 328).

10 While some forms of consumption may be *purely* wasteful, Veblen recognized that 'An article may be useful and wasteful both' (1994, 62).

11 Richard Layard describes this state of affairs as a 'hedonic treadmill' (2005, 48).

12 The claim is controversial: any detailed history of the months preceding the war (eg Hastings, 2013) will suggest countless points at which things might have taken a different turn. On the other hand, the fact that the main theaters and stakes of the eventual war were far removed from the Balkans suggests that the assassination was a triggering event rather than a fundamental cause.

13 Weber himself drew the same lesson from his approach to causality. Even the simplest causal relation, he argued, 'can be infinitely subdivided and analyzed. The point at which we halt in this process is determined only by our causal *interests* at the time' (1949, 179, emphasis in original).

14 Fear of dishonoring the dead was of course not the only factor encouraging the concern for consistency. In one of her last public appearances, Hannah Arendt reflected with some sadness on the path taken by her beloved adopted country:

> Madison Avenue tactics under the name of public relations have been permitted to invade our political life. The Pentagon Papers … proved beyond doubt and in tedious repetition that this not very honorable and not very rational enterprise was exclusively guided by the needs of a superpower to create for itself an *image* which would *convince* the world that it was indeed 'the mightiest power on earth'. (rpt. 2003, 263, emphasis in original)

15 Such *factual* underestimation of American capacity was not universal. 'Any notion of conquering America was "wild and extravagant," said the Earl of Coventry' (qtd in

McCullough, 2005, 13). And John Wilkes, then Lord Mayor of London, warned that 'We are fighting for the subjection, the unconditional submission of a country infinitely more extended than our own, of which every day increases the wealth, the natural strength, the population' (qtd in Ibid., 15). Wilkes, incidentally, is relevant to another argument in this book: the problem of state secrecy, discussed in Chapter 8. As Jürgen Habermas notes, Wilkes was instrumental in overturning the British law that parliamentary debates could not be made public (1989c, 61).

16 This points to a problem with the indiscriminate use of concepts such as 'policy learning' or 'social learning'. Diane Stone, for example, declares that 'think tanks aspire to effect social learning. They want to promote knowledge and understanding of new ideas, programs and policies.' She goes on to offer as an example of such 'learning' the work of various think tanks that 'wish to instill faith in the market' (2000, 60). Thus, policies or ideologies that happened to win in a political conflict are equated with learning, with an increase in knowledge.

17 In like spirit, Philip Tetlock defends 'the principled neopositivist conviction that scientists should not mix their roles as fact gatherers and analysts, where they have a comparative advantage, and their roles as policy advocates, where their opinions merit no greater weight than those of their fellow citizens' (2005, 230).

18 Weber himself recognized this possibility: ' "To let the facts speak for themselves" is the most unfair way of putting over a political position to the student' (1958, 146).

Chapter 6

1 For one attempt to do that, see Ryan (2003). Max Weber once warned an audience that 'every one of us who is not spiritually dead must realize the possibility of finding himself at some time' in the position of having to say 'Here I stand; I can do no other' (rpt. 1958, 127). The fact that many in Weber's audience for that 1918 speech probably went on to become pliant servants of the Nazi machine adds poignancy to his warning.

2 Rousseau commented of the Abbé de Saint-Pierre: 'he was allowed to say whatever he wished, because it was easy to see that no-one was listening to him' (rpt. 1972, 2:149).

3 This apparent unconcern for effectiveness is made explicit in the Biblical book of Ezekiel: 'And whether they hear or refuse to hear (for they are a rebellious house) they will know that there has been a prophet among them' (2.5). Indeed, the book of Jonah depicts a prophet positively miffed because his prophecy *has* been effective.

4 The formulation suggests that we can view truth as a matter of degree. I will return to this in a moment. Note that the formulation does not rule out an understanding of truth as 'correspondence', but it does rule out an excessively literal understanding of that concept. I have addressed the 'post-positivist' hostility to the notion of correspondence in Ryan (2015).

5 It is worth noting that, while Smith and Keynes are among the most influential thinkers of modern history, neither was heeded on these particular matters, at least not initially. Indeed, Keynes presents his *Essays in Persuasion* as 'the croakings of a Cassandra who could never influence the course of events in time' (rpt. 1963, v). Smith, for his part, interrupted his argument for letting go of the colonies with the sober comment that 'The most visionary enthusiasts would scarce be capable of proposing such a measure, with any serious hopes at least of its ever being adopted' (rpt. 1937, 582).

Clearly, these two great thinkers on matters of policy did not confine themselves to proposals likely to find favor among decision makers.

6 This does not entail acceptance of the pragmatist claim that truth is *defined* by 'usefulness', as Austin himself goes on to stress (rpt. 1975, 145). His point is rather that 'in the case of stating truly or falsely, just as much as in the case of advising well or badly, the intents and

purposes of the utterance and its context are important; what is judged true in a school book may not be so judged in a work of historical research' (143).Austin's example is part of his broader argument that the distinction between statements that state facts and other types is less cut and dried than is often believed. He concludes that 'the familiar contrast of "normative or evaluative" as opposed to the factual is in need, like so many dichotomies, of elimination' (149).

7   Robert Goodin critiques an approach that relies upon 'crazy cases' as a basis for ethical reflection. These are, he insists, 'inappropriate for policy analysis' (1982, 8).

8   Hilary Putnam comments that 'Pragmatists believe that doubt requires justification just as much as belief, and there are many perceptions that we have no real reason to doubt' (2002, 110).

9   I will return to this in Part III.

10 Clark and Schober (1992) is a useful overview of the problem of meaning in surveys.

11 A striking passage in Plato's *Euthydemus* satirizes an attitude towards the problem of meaning quite close to that of many modern pollsters:

> Now whenever I don't understand your question, do you want me to answer just the same, without inquiring further about it?
> You surely grasp something of what I say, don't you? he said.
> Yes, I do, said I.
> Then answer in terms of what you understand.
> Well then, I said, if you ask a question with one thing in mind and I understand it with another and then answer in terms of the latter, will you be satisfied if I answer nothing to the purpose?
> I shall be satisfied, he said, although I don't suppose you will. (¶295b–c)

12 In my study of opposition to Canadian multiculturalism, I noted the prevalence of the 'tired religious metaphors of "cult" and "faith"' (Ryan, 2010b, 209). Indeed, the most influential attack on multicultural policy was subtitled 'The cult of multiculturalism' (Bissoondath, 1994).

13 Voegelin cites Richard Hooker's portrait of the Puritan: 'Let any man of contrary opinion open his mouth to persuade them, they close up their ears, his reasons they weight not, all is answered with rehearsal of the words of John: "We are of God; he that knoweth God heareth us"' (1952, 137). But we should not assume that this aspect of gnosticism is found only in exotic religious movements. To take one example: reflexive distrust of unwelcome views shapes many people's choice of news sources today, right across the political spectrum (Iyengar and Hahn, 2009).

14 G.K. Chesterton asked: 'Does anybody in the world believe that a soldier says, "My leg is nearly dropping off, but I shall go on till it drops; for after all I shall enjoy all the advantages of my government obtaining a warm-water port in the Gulf of Finland"?' (1925, 158). Those who send the soldier off to war, on the other hand, are certainly thinking of the advantages of the warm-water port, or whatever grand objective is being pursued.

Chapter 7

1   We must not exaggerate this point: we do many things habitually. I will return later to the question of habit.

2   An interesting experiment run by Jon Jecker and David Landy provides some support for Aristotle's claim (1969).

3   Ryan (2014a, 14), notes that 'Nearly all the leading voices on both sides of the New Atheist debate assume that *we do what we do because we believe what we believe.*' That is, beliefs

provide a firm foundation for actions. The traditional Marxist challenge to this 'idealism' put forth a different foundation: 'It is not the consciousness of men that determines their existence, but their social existence that determines their consciousness' (Marx and Engels, rpt. 1969, 1:503). A foundation-less alternative to these two perspectives is that

> both actions and beliefs are *shaped* (not determined) by our life in society. Moreover, this life can sometimes act directly on our beliefs, and through our beliefs indirectly on our actions, but it can also shape our actions directly, which in turn reshape our beliefs. That is, as we make our way through life, we seek some degree of harmony between what we believe and what we do. To attain this, sometimes we shape our actions according to our beliefs, sometimes we do the reverse. Action is not a moon orbiting the planet of belief. Action and belief circle each other, under the influence of our social milieux, and these milieux are over time reshaped by our actions and beliefs. (Ryan, 2014a, 13).

4   Some might object, however, that our practices *do* have a unitary foundation: the search for happiness and the avoidance of pain. But casual observation hardly supports the view that people do this with any consistency. It is not easy to reject Robert Lane's observation that 'people often choose of their own accord paths that do not lead to their well-being: they escalate their standards in proportion to their improved circumstances, choose short-run benefits that incur greater long-term costs, fear and avoid the means to their preferred ends' (2000, 9).

5   In Chapter 2, we saw that Richard Layard also ignores such goods, with important consequences.

6   A similar point can be made with respect to Ellis's claim that 'the virtues practiced within social traditions give our lives meaning. But the feeling that life has meaning is for this very reason the *intrinsic* value at stake in these traditions; the practices themselves are merely extrinsic values whose purpose is to give people a sense that life has meaning' (1998, 48, emphasis in original). As with the view of art as consumption, tradition as an extrinsic good may yield only the most superficial of pay-offs.

7   It is striking that the final judgment is frequently depicted in the Koran as a moment when people will understand what they have done. The implication is that they do *not* fully understand this, prior to that moment.

8   Scott's tale of scientific forestry gives plausibility to Karl Polanyi's dramatic claim that the treatment of vital dimensions of human reality – human beings, the natural world, money – *merely* as commodities, merely as profit-generating resources, would entail the 'annihilation of society' (1957, 3), precisely because it leads to the ignoring of the many other ends that these things serve, ends that may not yield anyone a profit, but which are vital for the maintenance of the human world.

9   'It is very difficult for anyone other than the individual involved (*and it is often difficult even for that individual*) to understand exactly which intrinsic values are served by the extrinsic values to which she is committed, or to explain why the intrinsic value in question is best served, under the circumstances, by just this particular extrinsic value and no other. For example, a visual artist will have *difficulty understanding* why she values visual art, and why the purposes served by it could not be served equally well by music or football' (Ellis, 1998, 40, emphases added).

10   Ellis's claim oddly echoes Hungarian Marxist Georg Lukács's concept of 'imputed class consciousness': 'By relating consciousness to the whole of society it becomes possible to infer the thoughts and feelings which men would have in a particular situation if they

were able to assess both it and the interests arising from it in their impact on immediate action and on the whole structure of society' (1971, 51).

[11] Earlier, Smith assumed the disutility of work in order to formulate his labor theory of value: 'Equal quantities of labour, at all times and places, may be said to be of equal value to the labourer. In his ordinary state of health, strength, and spirits; in the ordinary degree of his skill and dexterity, he must always lay down the same portion of his ease, his liberty, and his happiness' (rpt. 1937, 33).

[12] Influential psychologist Abraham Maslow proposed that 'Some kind of tax penalty should be assessed against enterprises that undo the effects of a political democracy, of good schools … and that make their people more paranoid, more hostile, more nasty, more malevolent, more destructive' (1971, 59). The proposal was perhaps made with tongue in cheek, but there is a sound insight buried within it: the 'negative externalities' generated by an organization are not always limited to physical pollution.

[13] This may be why 'root causes' are sometimes invoked in a quite cynical manner, to forestall action on a policy issue. Responding to the threat of a ban on the use of cellphones while driving, the head of the Canadian Wireless Telecommunications Association commented that 'Banning cellphones may be a false solution. If we focus on one behaviour instead of trying to get to the root cause, then we may feel we've solved the problem, but we really haven't addressed the bigger issue of driver distraction' (qtd in Abbate, 2002).

Chapter 8

[1] While the assumption is unrealistic, it is central to modern life, which relies upon a dichotomy between what Bowles and Gintis term 'learners' and 'choosers'. 'Learners', the prime example of which are children, are subject to various authoritarian institutions, under the assumption that they are not competent to make their own choices. At a certain point, they are suddenly transformed into 'choosers', whose preferences and decisions must be treated as sacrosanct, unless they should negatively affect others (1986, 124).

[2] Some observers advocate such elitism (Gilley, 2017). But as I argued in response (Ryan, 2018), this position assumes the existence of an unsullied and incorruptible caste of experts.

[3] As Kant put it, 'those who have only their old system before their eyes and for whom it is already settled beforehand what is to be approved or disapproved are not about to demand a discussion that might stand in the way of their private aim' (rpt. 2001, 9).

[4] Mind you, York fares better than the Bishop of Carlisle, who later in the same play warns Henry not to seize the crown. Northumberland answers him:

> Well have you argued, sir; and, for your pains,
> Of capital treason we arrest you here. (*Richard II*, 4.1)

For the policy advisor, there are worse fates than having one's advice disregarded.

[5] During the Bush Jr. administration, an American Petroleum Institute lobbyist hired by the White House regularly doctored 'government climate reports in ways that play down links between [greenhouse gas] emissions and global warming'. 'The dozens of changes, while sometimes as subtle as the insertion of the phrase "significant and fundamental" before the word "uncertainties," tend to produce an air of doubt about findings that most climate experts say are robust' (Revkin, 2005).

[6] This mentality itself can sometimes emerge from an environment of constant time pressures. J.C. Thomson's analysis of Vietnam policy, mentioned earlier, stresses 'the paramount role of *executive fatigue*'. The overloaded policy maker, he argues, gradually 'becomes a prisoner of his own narrowed view of the world and his own clichéd rhetoric. He becomes irritable and defensive – short on sleep, short on family ties, short on patience.

Such men make bad policy and then compound it. They have neither the time nor the temperament for new ideas or preventive diplomacy'" (1968, 50, emphasis in original).

7   Political philosopher Norberto Bobbio has emphasized the importance of publicness for democracy: 'we might define the rule of democracy as the rule of public power in public' (1987, 79). To make publicness the default principle would be to subject all current forms of government secrecy to the simple question: does this secrecy further the public interest? Or is it only in the interest of the leader or the governing party?

8   In Canada, the Conservative government of Steven Harper was much criticized for its closure of document archives and removal of information from websites. A particularly vulnerable topic was government relations with indigenous peoples. The government's online Aboriginal Portal was shut down, with the justification that 'search engines and social media have rendered the portal website obsolete'. A critic commented that 'Apparently Twitter has displaced properly vetted and archived government records' (Gogolek, 2013).In the UK, controversy was sparked by the Conservative Party's erasure not of government sites, but of its own party website. The party thus erased its public record of several years of Prime Minister David Cameron's speeches. This included, ironically, a 2006 speech to the Google Zeitgeist Europe Conference, in which then opposition leader Cameron declared: 'You've begun the process of democratising the world's information. Democratising is the right word to use because by making more information available to more people, you're giving them more power' (qtd in Ballard, 2013).

9   'Society as a whole', of course, has no voice with which to demand anything. The phrase simply denotes the 'public sphere', the space within which political opinions and norms are debated.

10 Within the model, there is no need for the analyst actually to know on whose desk the product of their work ends up, nor its fate. As odd as this may sound, this model conforms to Kafka's memorable description of state bureaucracy: 'The ranks of officials in this judiciary system mounted endlessly, so that not even the initiated could survey the hierarchy as a whole ... any particular case thus appeared in their circle of jurisdiction often without their knowing whence it came, and passed from it they knew not wither' (rpt. 1970, 119).

11 Both Finer's model and this 'values variant' apply to public servants in general, not merely to analysts. Given the context of the argument here, I focus on analysts in particular.

12 On this variant and its relation to the fact-value dichotomy, see also Hawkesworth (1988, 187–188).

13 This 'effectiveness trap', writes Thomson,

> keeps men from speaking out, as clearly or often as they might, within the government. And it is the trap that keeps men from resigning in protest and airing their dissent outside the government. The most important asset that a man brings to bureaucratic life is his 'effectiveness,' a mysterious combination of training, style, and connections. The most ominous complaint that can be whispered of a bureaucrat is: 'I'm afraid Charlie's beginning to lose his effectiveness.' To preserve your effectiveness, you must decide where and when to fight the mainstream of policy. (1968, 49)

14 Schumacher credits G.N.M. Tyrell for the concepts.

15 In 1969, Herbert Kaufman advanced the intriguing claim that reforms to public administration in the US had reflected a shifting balance regarding the importance of three values: 'representativeness, politically neutral competence, and executive leadership' (1969, 3). Just as a novice cyclist swerves first one way then the other, no administrative

reform settles the issue once and for all: 'emphasis on one remedy over a prolonged period merely accumulates the other discontents until new remedies gain enough support to be put into effect, and no totally stable solution has yet been devised. So the constant shift in emphasis goes on' (4).

16 *Yes Minister*'s Sir Humphrey was fond of this stratagem:

> He promised to do his best to put it into practice, and will set up a committee of enquiry with broad terms of reference so that at the end of the day we can take the right decisions based on long-term considerations. He argued that this was preferable to rushing prematurely into precipitate and possibly ill-conceived actions which might have unforeseen repercussions. (Lynn and Jay, 1984, 136)

17 José Nun, who taught me Latin American politics, took strong issue with the maxim that 'In the land of the blind, the one-eyed is king.' Not so, Nun insisted: 'In the land of the blind, the one-eyed would be locked up, because he would keep saying that he was "seeing things," and would be treated just like someone in our society who "hears voices."' Edwin Abbott's *Flatland* (rpt. 1992) makes an analogous argument.

Chapter 9

1 As sociologist Pierre Bourdieu put it, 'While it is true that, on the surface, the first link in the chain commands all the others, in fact, this basic, linear, transitive vision is quite simplistic, to the degree that, at each stage, delegation is accompanied by a loss of control' (2012, 478).

2 Apart from helping to identify opportunities for change, this process of questioning may prove therapeutic for the new analyst, who may find herself in an environment that often feels alien. Hannah Arendt was fond of quoting Isak Dinesen's aphorism: 'All sorrows can be borne if you put them into a story' (1958a, 175). Suffering is borne by story making, a process of meaning-creation. In observing her surroundings with the eyes of an anthropologist and sociologist, the analyst is engaged in something similar.

3 The experienced gender analyst knows that the best gender analysis is one that can show people how taking gender into account in policy making, apart from making policy more inclusive, can further at least *some* of the objectives they already hold. The non-binary analyst must seek to do something analogous.

4 Marx pointed out that the teacher must also be taught (1969, 1:13). Thus, the analyst seeking to encourage greater critical awareness among others must accept that her own critical awareness stands in need of further development, and that those around her may be helpful in this respect.

5 To a lawyer who commented that clear and precise sentencing rules reduce the 'anguish' often felt by judges, philosopher Michel Foucault answered: but they *should* be anguished, and it is worrisome that there is so little anguish in the whole system (1994, 3:297). We can adapt the observation to policy contexts in which human lives are at stake.

6 Laurence Tribe notes that if analysts are simply hired guns,

> the only values that can be served will be those strongly held by persons who seek a policy analyst's aid. The point may seem too trivial to make, but its consequences are anything but minor. For at least three categories of values and interests are likely to be excluded on this basis: those too widely diffused over space (or too incrementally affected over time) to be strongly championed by any single client of a policy analyst; those associated only

with persons not yet existing (future generations); and those not associated with persons at all (for example, the 'rights' of wild animals). (1972, 104)

7 One means to reduce such friction has been government advertising. While this is often justified as a means to 'inform' citizens, my study of the Canadian case found that government advertising is extremely short on information, structured instead around vacuous images that aim to sell a particular policy, or the reigning government as a whole. Strikingly, the government has exempted itself from its own law on misleading advertising (Ryan, 1995).

8 Putnam notes Charles Peirce's view that 'what holds good for inquiry in general holds for value inquiry in particular'. Thus, through reflection on the standards of responsible dialogue in any field, 'we can often tell that views are irresponsibly defended in ethics and the law as well as in science' (Putnam, 2002, 104–105).

Conclusion to Part II: The instincts of the non-binary analyst

1 The goal of athletic training, as Pierre Bourdieu puts it, is to progress from a merely intellectual understanding to 'being understood by the body' (2003, 208).

2 'Fast, competent action requires the actor to develop appropriate embodied dispositions, forms of sensitivity, awareness and response, so that, for example, the nurse does not have to stop and think which action comes next when assessing a patient' (Sayer, 2011, 71).

3 The discussion here draws upon Chapter 4 of Michael Polanyi's *Personal Knowledge* (1962).

Chapter 10

1 This is close to the *Concise Oxford Dictionary* definition of expert: 1) 'Trained by practice, skilful'; 2) 'Person having special skill or knowledge' (Sykes, 1976). I have added the qualifier 'usable' to rule out the sort of 'expert whose expertise is not wanted by the society at large' (Berger and Luckmann, 1967, 126). 'Usable', of course, is a context-dependent term: it refers to knowledge that is usable by specific people, in specific situations, to deal with specific challenges.

2 Tony Lawson argues that the expertise of economists arises not from their theories, but from 'the care with which they study the economic news' (qtd in Collier, 1994, 226).

3 Contrary to MacIntyre, the expert may be more wary of jumping to 'law-like generalizations' than the average citizen. Schutz notes that everyday life is strongly influenced by the tendency to generalize on the basis of past experience (1970, 138). But the competent analyst's training and experience should have made her aware of cases where such generalization has proven disastrous.

4 That such knowledge can be extremely valuable for practice does not mean that it is valued within a discipline. After 9/11, such area-experts were in high demand in the US, yet it was hard to find a 'political scientist who specializes in the Middle East or South Asia at the nation's top universities' (Kotkin, 2002). Oddly, such knowledge can also be considered suspect in the broader society. It has often been suggested, for example, that the US government's 'march of folly' into Vietnam (Tuchman, 1984) was facilitated by McCarthyism's purge of China and East Asia expertise in the State Department (Thomson, 1968, 47).

5 An expert employed by a think tank, one whose predictions Tetlock tested, defended his dismal performance by pointing out that he was not playing a 'game run by the rules of social science ... I fight to preserve my reputation in a cutthroat adversarial culture. I woo dumb-ass reporters who want glib sound bites.' Tetlock observes that 'In his world, only the overconfident survive, and only the truly arrogant thrive' (2005, 186).

[6] Though Sir Humphrey is a fictional character, the expertise he demonstrates has verisimilitude. It is striking that, throughout the entire *Yes Minister* and *Yes Prime Minister* series, one cannot identify any particular *technical* skill wielded by this bureaucratic genius: he appears entirely free of any knowledge of statistics, the natural sciences or even of economics.

[7] In Ibsen's *An Enemy of the People*, the lead character denounces the doctrine 'that the common folk, the ignorant and incomplete element in the community, have the same right to pronounce judgment and to approve, to direct and to govern, as the isolated, intellectually superior personalities in it' (rpt. 1999, 60). See also Ishiguro (1989, 196).

[8] Hannah Arendt argues that Plato's claim that knowledge constitutes the ground of legitimate power 'has remained at the root of all theories of domination which are not mere justifications of an irreducible and irresponsible will to power' (1958a, 225).

[9] One question is the extent to which historical patterns of gender-based exclusion have waned, since the days when 'the word "Miss"', as Virginia Woolf observed, had 'a curious leaden quality, liable to keep any name to which it is fastened circling in the lower spheres' (rpt. 1991, 56).

[10] In his 1911 essay 'Philosophy as rigorous science', phenomenologist Edmund Husserl critiqued 'profundity': 'Genuine science, so far as its real doctrine extends, knows no profundity. Every bit of completed science is a whole composed of "thought steps" each of which is immediately understood, and so not at all profound.' Husserl expressed his hope that 'philosophy [will] fight through from the level of profundity to that of scientific clarity' (rpt. 1965, 144). Could thought outside the natural sciences ever manage that level of clarity? And if not, why not? Are there obstacles built into the very nature of the disciplines? Or is obscurity so strongly in the interests of the guild of scholars and experts that it will never be abandoned?

[11] Plato's *Euthydemus* provides a vivid portrayal of argumentative skill being used to trap and confuse: 'Just at this moment Dionysodorus leaned a little toward me and, smiling all over his face, whispered in my ear and said, I may tell you beforehand, Socrates, that whichever way the boy answers he will be refuted' (275e). Plato's depiction of how Socrates escapes from their tactics is also worthy of close study.

[12] Habermas argues that a 'radically democratic republic' is not a matter of institutions alone, requiring as well 'a resonant political culture that meets it halfway' (1996, 371). Education can do much to foster that culture of alert and questioning citizenship.

[13] On some policy matters, this need can be met through participatory research.

Chapter 11

[1] The thought here draws from Rawls's lectures on Locke. Rawls argues that Locke did not seek to identify the *most just* political regime, but simply to rule out of consideration one type, royal absolutism (2007, 130).

[2] In the face of a particularly thorny question, we may also decide that there are *more important* things to talk about. In *After the New Atheist Debate*, for example, I announce at the outset that the book will not consider 'one of the central issues in that debate: whether it is reasonable to believe in God'. The justification is that 'we can live happily together in society, even in a single household, and disagree on that question. But there are other matters that we must discuss in order to live together' (2014a, 12). A focus on the theological question may prevent a socially necessary dialogue from getting started.

[3] Note in this respect the subtle distinction between Weber's and Peirce's definitions of truth. For Weber, 'scientific truth is precisely what is *valid* for all who *seek* the truth' (1949, 84, emphasis in original). For Peirce, however, 'The opinion which is fated to be ultimately agreed to by all who investigate, is what we mean by the truth' (rpt. 1966,

133). Peirce reminds us, as Weber does not, that all who 'seek the truth' may agree on something, and yet 'ultimately' prove to be mistaken.

4   Hannah Arendt observed that 'As Eichmann told it, the most potent factor in the soothing of his own conscience was the simple fact that he could see no one, no one at all, who actually was against the Final Solution' (1964, 116).

5   Those who stress the importance of public deliberation for policy making often glide over this point. Fishkin's work on 'deliberative opinion polls' states that a fair hearing must be given to 'the major rival viewpoints' (Fishkin, 1991, 31). So even before the randomly selected citizens enter the room to deliberate, unavoidable decisions must have been made, concerning which viewpoints will be presented to those citizens.

The legitimacy of excluding viewpoints is, of course, often a matter of timing. It was once reasonable, but no longer is, to doubt whether climate change was occurring. Note also the complexity of the judgment that the analyst-as-facilitator must make here: she must judge whether a viewpoint has a *reasonable* claim to be possibly true, taking into account the consensus of *fair-minded observers*. One cannot provide a cut-and-dried definition of 'reasonable' and 'fair-minded' that the analyst-as-facilitator can wield, though she can use rough and ready criteria of reasonableness.

6   It is thus far too simplistic to declare that 'dissent is healthy and even vital. In our view, the climate skeptics and other dissenters very likely strengthen both the policy and the scientific debates' (Robert and Zeckhauser, 2011, 626).

7   A stark contrast to this outlook is provided by Polus, in Plato's *Gorgias*. Asked if he can provide good answers, he dismissively replies: 'What does that matter, if they're good enough for you?' (¶448).

8   On the dual importance of process and outcome, see also Stone (1997, 51) and Sen (2009, 215).

9   Using public consultation as a means to policy legitimacy can be understood in different ways. The consultation may actually change outcomes or it may be a sham consultation, a process in which everyone gets to have their say, but nothing is really affected thereby.

10   One example of this is the sort of problem that 'cannot be solved until certain groups of people learn different behavior' (Lindblom and Cohen, 1979, 18).

11   These mixed motives are as powerful in 'pure' intellectual pursuits as elsewhere. 'The scientist loves both the truth he discovers and himself insofar as he discovers it,' commented Paul Tillich (1952, 46). Speaking of philosophers, Rousseau commented drily that 'Each knows very well that his system is no more solid than that of the others, but he holds it because it is his' (rpt. 1966, 348).

12   It might be objected that this analysis is androcentric, and that the centrality of competitive 'play' in human history reflects masculine dominance more than human nature. There is probably some truth in the objection, but how much truth? In the specific matter at hand: could we expect social dialogue to transcend the competitive spirit in a gender-equal society? My skepticism arises from having heard socialist thinkers make the analogous claim that egocentricity and competitiveness would vanish along with capitalism. Egoism is a mere relic of capitalism, declared Latin American revolutionary Che Guevara, a relic that will be unknown to future generations, who will be 'free of original sin', the original sin of having lived under capitalism (rpt. 1985, 2:380). It is wiser, perhaps, not to build one's imagined future upon such hopes.

13   Huizinga himself recognizes that the competitive spirit was so powerful in Greece that 'it allowed rhetoric to expand at the cost of pure philosophy' (1955, 151).

14   One of the remarkable elements in Thucydides's book is the ongoing debate about the value of debate itself. Sthenelaïdas, a Spartan, impetuously declares: 'let no one try to tell us that when we are wronged we should stop to think about it' (¶1.86), a comment

that recalls certain contemporary responses to attack. For his part, the Athenian Cleon berates his fellow citizens: 'Frankly you are in thrall to the pleasure of listening, and you sit here more like spectators at the sophists' displays than men taking decisions for their city' (¶3.38). The criticism is disingenuous, as Cleon himself was one of the leading demagogues, and as such is harshly rebuked by another speaker: 'Anyone who contends that words should not be the school of action is either a fool or an interested party' (¶3.42).

Conclusion

1   Thus, we cannot expect electoral democracy reliably to produce leaders who pursue the public interest. This should not be taken to mean that no such interest exists. It is reasonable to say that every society has an 'objective interest' in its long-term sustainability and in the flourishing of its members. This is an objective interest in the sense that it does not depend on the subjective outlooks of citizens and leaders at any particular moment. We may disagree on just what 'flourishing' involves, and on just which policies further the public interest. But disagreement concerning the nature of some good does not mean the good is nothing more than an empty shell into which competing subjective notions can be poured, any more than disagreement concerning the nature of a healthy diet means that the whole concept is mired in subjectivity.

2   The power of vested interests limits ordinary citizens' ability to 'discipline' government, and represents another source of control over officials, one that weakens even further the government's claim to be sensitive to the will of 'the people'.

3   Some might wish to locate other regimes there as well. No matter: the point is to imagine a regime so evil that it is clear that 'I was just following orders' does not exonerate the bureaucrat working within it.

4   Stephen Gardiner's *A Perfect Moral Storm: The Ethical Tragedy of Climate Change* (2011) includes a striking chapter that uses Jane Austen's *Sense and Sensibility* as an analog for various forms of moral corruption that insensibly corrode thinking around climate change and the moral obligations with which it confronts us.

5   A possible exception is when a society undergoes a severe shock, one that makes previously respected institutions appear hollow and greatly weakens shared norms. It is often said that the experience of the trenches of World War I was one such shock. As the narrator in Remarque's *All Quiet on the Western Front* exclaimed, 'It must be all lies and of no account when the culture of a thousand years could not prevent this stream of blood being poured out' (1982, 263).

6   We should also note that any particular policy decision is just one moment in an ongoing stream of decisions and government actions. Once a policy decision has been made with due diligence (including open discussions), elected leaders have a right to expect officials to make a good-faith effort at implementation. It will often happen, however, that the implementation process will reveal flaws in the policy that were not identified during the formulation phase. Here, too, the responsible analyst cannot simply be 'subservient', proceeding with blithe disregard for the policy's weaknesses or its unforeseen side effects.

Works cited

Abbate, G. (2002) 'Jury's cellphone stand buoys politician', *Globe and Mail*, September 17.

Abbott, E. (1992) *Flatland*, New York: Dover.

Aberbach, J.D., Putnam, R.D. and Rockman, B.A. (1981) *Bureaucrats and Politicians in Western Democracies*, Cambridge, MA: Harvard University Press.

Amy, D. (1984) 'Why policy analysis and ethics are incompatible', *Journal of Policy Analysis and Management*, 3(4): 573–591.

Anderson, C.W. (1979) 'The place of principles in policy analysis', *The American Political Science Review*, 73(3): 711–723.

Anderson, J.E. (2011) *Public Policymaking: An Introduction* (7th edn), Boston, MA: Wadsworth.

Arendt, H. (1958a) *The Human Condition*, Chicago: University of Chicago Press.

Arendt, H. (1958b) *The Origins of Totalitarianism* (2nd edn), New York: Meridian.

Arendt, H. (1964) *Eichmann in Jerusalem: A Report on the Banality of Evil* (Revised edn), Harmondsworth: Penguin.

Arendt, H. (1968) *Between Past and Future*, Harmondsworth: Penguin.

Arendt, H. (1978) *The Life of the Mind*, San Diego, CA: Harcourt Brace.

Arendt, H. (1990) 'Philosophy and politics', *Social Research*, 57(1): 73–103.

Arendt, H. (1994) *Essays in Understanding*, New York: Schocken.

Arendt, H. (2003) *Responsibility and Judgment*, New York: Schocken.

Aristotle (1941) *The Basic Works of Aristotle*, New York: Random House.

Austen, J. (1996) *Pride and Prejudice*, New York: Modern Library.

Austin, J.L. (1975) *How to Do Things with Words* (2nd edn), Oxford: Clarendon Press.

Ayer, A.J. (1946) *Language, Truth and Logic* (2nd edn), London: Victor Gollancz.

Babbie, E. (2013) *Social Research Counts*, Belmont, CA: Wadsworth.

Ballard, M. (2013) 'Conservatives erase internet history', *Computer Weekly*, November 12. Available from: http://www.computerweekly.com/blogs/public-sector/2013/11/conservatives-erase-internet-h.html [Last accessed June 24, 2021].

Barakso, M., Sabet, D.M. and Schaffner, B. (2014) *Understanding Political Science Research Methods*, New York: Routledge.

Barber, B. (1992) 'Jihad vs McWorld', *The Atlantic Monthly*, March: 53–65.

Barry, B. (1992) 'Welfare economics and the liberal tradition', in J.M. Gillroy and M.L. Wade (eds) *The Moral Dimensions of Public Policy Choice: Beyond the Market Paradigm*, Pittsburgh, PA: University of Pittsburgh Press, pp 325–339.

Benda, J. (1975) *La Trahison Des Clercs*, Paris: Bernard Grasset.

Benn, T. (1989) 'Obstacles to reform in Britain', *The Socialist Register 1989*, 25: 130–145.

Berger, P. and Luckmann, T. (1967) *The Social Construction of Reality*, Garden City, NY: Doubleday.

Bissoondath, N. (1994) *Selling Illusions: The Cult of Multiculturalism in Canada*, Toronto: Penguin Books.

Bobbio, N. (1987) *The Future of Democracy*, Minneapolis: University of Minnesota Press.

Bourdieu, P. (2003) *Méditations Pascaliennes*, Paris: Editions du Seuil.

Bourdieu, P. (2012) *Sur l'État: Cours au Collège de France, 1989–1992*, Paris: Seuil.

Bowles, S. and Gintis, H. (1986) *Democracy and Capitalism*, New York: Basic Books.

Bradford, N. (1998) *Commissioning Ideas: Canadian National Policy Innovation in Comparative Perspective*, Toronto: Oxford University Press.

Brodman, J. (1996) *The Grolier Library of International Biographies*, Danbury, CT: Grolier Educational Corp.

Brownstein, H.H. (2013) *Contemporary Drug Policy*, New York: Routledge.

Burrell, G. and Morgan, G. (1979) *Sociological Paradigms and Organizational Analysis*, London: Heinemann.

Caidan, N. and Wildavsky, A. (1980) *Planning and Budgeting in Poor Countries*, New Brunswick, NJ: Transaction Books.

Carbon Tracker (2013) *Unburnable Carbon 2013: Wasted Capital and Stranded Assets*. Available from: http://carbontracker.live.kiln.it/Unburnable-Carbon-2-Web-Version.pdf [Last accessed June 24, 2021].

Carley, M. (1980) *Rational Techniques in Policy Analysis*, London: Heinemann.

Carr, E.H. (1964) *What is History?*, Harmondsworth: Penguin.

Chesterton, G.K. (1925) *The Everlasting Man*, London: Hodder and Stoughton.

Chesterton, G.K. (1990) *Orthodoxy*, New York: Image.

Clark, H. and Schober, M. (1992) 'Asking questions and influencing answers', in J. Tanur (ed) *Questions about Questions: Inquiries into the Cognitive Bases of Surveys*, New York: Russell Sage Foundation, pp 15–48.

Clark, I.D. (1974) 'Expert advice in the controversy about supersonic transport in the United States', *Minerva*, 12(4): 416–432.

Clemons, R. and McBeth, M.K. (2001) *Public Policy Praxis*, Upper Saddle River, NJ: Prentice Hall.

Copleston, F. (1962) *Greece & Rome*, A History of Philosophy, vol. 1, Part 1. New York: Image Books.

Collier, A. (1994) *Critical Realism: An Introduction to Roy Bhaskar's Philosophy*, London: Verso.

Crossman, R. (1991) *The Crossman Diaries*, London: Mandarin.

Dahl, R. (1947) 'The science of public administration: Three problems', *Public Administration Review*, 7(1): 1–11.

Daigneault, P.-M. (2014) 'Reassessing the concept of policy paradigm: Aligning ontology and methodology in policy studies', *Journal of European Public Policy*, 21(3): 453–469.

Danziger, M. (1995) 'Policy analysis postmodernized: Some political and pedagogical ramifications', *Policy Studies Journal*, 23(3): 435–450.

Davidson, D. (1985) 'On the very idea of a conceptual scheme', in J. Rajchman and C. West (eds) *Post-analytic Philosophy*, New York: Columbia University Press, pp 129–144.

Davion, V. (1994) 'Introduction: Where are we headed?', in F. Ferré and P. Hartel (eds) *Ethics and Environmental Policy: Theory Meets Practice*, Athens: University of Georgia Press, pp 1–6.

Dawkins, R. (2006) *The God Delusion*, Boston, MA: Houghton Mifflin.

de Chamfort, N. (1796) *Maximes, Pensées, Caractères et Anecdotes*, Paris: T. Baylis.

DeLeon, P. (1994) 'Reinventing the policy sciences: Three steps back to the future', *Policy Sciences*, 27: 77–95.

Downs, A. (1957) *An Economic Theory of Democracy*, New York: Harper and Row.

Dryzek, J.S. (1990) *Discursive Democracy*, Cambridge: Cambridge University Press.

Durning, D. (1999) 'The transition from traditional to postpositivist policy analysis: A role for Q-methodology', *Journal of Policy Analysis and Management*, 18(3): 389–410.

Easterly, W. (2001) *The Elusive Quest for Growth: Economists' Adventures and Misadventures in the Tropics*, Cambridge, MA: MIT Press.

Ellis, R. (1998) *Just Results: Ethical Foundations for Policy Analysis*, Washington, DC: Georgetown University Press.

Etzioni, A. (1967) 'Mixed-Scanning: A "third" approach to decision-making', *Public Administration Review*, 27(5): 385–392.

Fadiman, C. and Bernard, A. (eds) (2000) *Bartlett's Book of Anecdotes* (Revised edn), Boston, MA: Little, Brown.

Feser, E. (2008) *The Last Superstition*, South Bend, IN: St. Augustine's Press.

Fetter, F.A. (1927) *Economic Principles*, New York: The Century Co.

Finer, H. (1941) 'Administrative responsibility in democratic government', *Public Administration Review*, 1(4): 335–350.

Fischer, F. (1993) 'Policy discourse and the politics of Washington think tanks', in F. Fischer and J. Forester (eds) *The Argumentative Turn in Policy Analysis and Planning*, Durham, NC: Duke University Press, pp 21–42.

Fischer, F. (1998) 'Beyond empiricism: Policy inquiry in postpositivist perspective', *Policy Studies Journal*, 26(1): 129–146.

Fischer, F. (2003) *Reframing Public Policy*, Oxford: Oxford University Press.

Fisher, M. (2013) 'John Kerry chose a strange country from which to defend Egypt's military takeover', *Washington Post*, August 1.

Fishkin, J. (1991) *Democracy and Deliberation*, New Haven, CT: Yale University Press.

Flaubert, G. (1961) *Madame Bovary*, Paris: Le Livre de Poche.

Florida House of Representatives (2006) *An Act Relating to Education*, House Bill No. 7087. Available from: https://www.myfloridahouse.gov/Sections/ Documents/loaddoc.aspx?FileName=_h7087er.docx&DocumentType= Bill&BillNumber=7087&Session=2006 [Last accessed June 24, 2021].

Foucault, M. (1994) *Dits et Écrits: 1954–1988*, Paris: Gallimard.

Foucault, M. (2004) *Naissance de la Biopolitique, Cours au Collège de France: 1978–1979*, Paris: Gallimard.

Frankl, V. (1984) *Man's Search for Meaning*, New York: Washington Square Press.

Friedman, M. (1953) *Essays in Positive Economics*, Chicago: University of Chicago Press.

Friedman, M. (1962) *Capitalism and Freedom*, Chicago: University of Chicago Press.

Friedman, M. (1998) 'Letter to Excmo Sr. Augusto Pinochet Ugarte (1975)', in Milton and Rose Friedman, *Two Lucky People*, Chicago: University of Chicago Press, pp 591–594.

Friedman, M. and Friedman, R. (1979) *Free to Choose*, New York: Avon.

Friedman, T. (1999) 'Protesters pulling in wrong direction', *National Post*, December 2.

Gadamer, H.-G. (1989) *Truth and Method* (2nd edn), New York: Continuum.

Gans, H. (1980) *Deciding What's News*, New York: Vintage Books.

Gardiner, S. (2011) *A Perfect Moral Storm: The Ethical Tragedy of Climate Change*, Oxford: Oxford University Press.

Gebremedhin, T.G. and Tweeten, L.G. (1994) *Research Methods and Communication in the Social Sciences*, Westport, CT: Praeger.

Geertz, C. (1973) *The Interpretation of Cultures*, New York: Basic Books.

Geertz, C. (1974) 'From the native's point of view: On the nature of anthropological understanding', *Bulletin of the American Academy of Arts and Sciences*, 28(1): 26–45.

Geisel, T. (1991) 'The 500 Hats of Bartholomew Cubbins', in *Six by Seuss*, New York: Random House.

Geslin, L. and Gobert, S. (2013) 'Voyage aux marges de Schengen', *Le Monde Diplomatique*, April.

Gilley, B. (2017) 'Technocracy and democracy as spheres of justice in public policy', *Policy Sciences*, 50: 9–22.

Gneezy, U. and Rustichini, A. (2000a) 'A fine is a price', *Journal of Legal Studies*, 29 (January): 1–17.

Gneezy, U. and Rustichini, A. (2000b) 'Pay enough or don't pay at all', *The Quarterly Journal of Economics*, 115(3): 791–810.

Gogolek, V. (2013) 'Harper government centralizing, slashing federal web info', *Huffington Post*, March 10.

Goldstein, R. (2014) *Plato at the Googleplex: Why Philosophy Won't Go Away*, New York: Pantheon Books.

Goodin, R. (1982) *Political Theory and Public Policy*, Chicago: University of Chicago Press.

Goodman, N. (1978) *Ways of Worldmaking*, Indianapolis, IN: Hackett.

Gouldner, A. (1973) *For Sociology: Renewal and Critique in Sociology Today*, New York: Basic Books.

Gouldner, A. (1979) *The Future of Intellectuals and the Rise of the New Class*, New York: Seabury Press.

Guevara, C. (1985) *Obras Escogidas: 1957–1967*, Havana: Editorial de Ciencias Sociales.

Gulick, L. (1937) 'Notes on the theory of organization', in L. Gulick and L. Urwick (eds) *Papers on the Science of Administration*, New York: Institute of Public Administration (Columbia University), pp 1–46.

Habermas, J. (1987a) *The Philosophical Discourse of Modernity*, Cambridge, MA: MIT Press.

Habermas, J. (1987b) *The Theory of Communicative Action II: Lifeworld and System*, Boston, MA: Beacon Press.

Habermas, J. (1989a) 'Dogmatism, reason, and decision', in S. Seidman (ed) *Jürgen Habermas on Society and Politics*, Boston, MA: Beacon Press, pp 29–46.

Habermas, J. (1989b) 'The Public Sphere', in S. Seidman (ed) *Jürgen Habermas on Society and Politics*, Boston, MA: Beacon Press, pp 231–236.

Habermas, J. (1989c) *The Structural Transformation of the Public Sphere*, Cambridge, MA: MIT Press.

Habermas, J. (1993) *Justification and Application*, Cambridge, MA: MIT Press.

Habermas, J. (1996) *Between Facts and Norms*, Cambridge, MA: MIT Press.

Habermas, J. (2006) 'Religion in the public sphere', *European Journal of Philosophy*, 14(1): 1–25.

Haines, S. (2010) 'A world full of terror to the British mind: The Blair doctrine and British defence policy', in D. Brown (ed) *The Development of British Defence Policy: Blair, Brown and Beyond*, Farnham: Ashgate, pp 63–79.

Halberstam, D. (1969) *The Best and the Brightest*, Greenwich, CT: Fawcett Crest.

Hall, P. (1990) 'Policy paradigms, experts, and the state: The case of macroeconomic policy-making in Britain', in A.G. Gagnon and S. Brooks (eds) *Social Scientists, Policy and the State*, New York: Praeger, pp 53–78.

Hall, P. (1993) 'Policy paradigms, social learning, and the state: The case of economic policymaking in Britain', *Comparative Politics*, 25(3) (April): 275–296.

Hamilton, A., Jay, J. and Madison, J. (1937) *The Federalist*, New York: Modern Library.

Hansell, W. (2007) 'The council-manager plan', in R.L. Kemp (ed) *How American Governments Work: A Handbook of City, County, Regional, State, and Federal Operations*, Jefferson, NC: McFarland, pp 111–116.

Häring, N. and Douglas, N. (2012) *Economists and the Powerful*, London: Anthem Press.

Harmon, M. and Mayer, R. (1986) *Organization Theory for Public Administration*, Boston, MA: Little, Brown, and Co.

Harris, S. (2004) *The End of Faith: Religion, Terror, and the Future of Reason*, New York: W.W. Norton & Company.

Harvard Crimson (1964) 'Friedman cautions against rights bill', *Harvard Crimson*, May 5. Available from: https://www.thecrimson.com/article/1964/5/5/friedman-cautions-against-rights-bill-pmilton/ [Last accessed June 24, 2021].

Hastings, M. (2013) *Catastrophe: Europe Goes to War 1914*, London: William Collins.

Hawkesworth, M. (1988) *Theoretical Issues in Policy Analysis*, Albany: State University of New York Press.

Hawkesworth, M. (1992) 'Epistemology and policy analysis', in W. Dunn and R.M. Kelly (eds) *Advances in Policy Studies since 1950*, New Brunswick, NJ: Transaction Press, pp 295–329.

Hayek, F. (2007) *The Road to Serfdom*, Chicago: University of Chicago Press.

Healey, P. (1993) 'Planning through debate: The communicative turn in planning theory', in F. Fischer and J. Forester (eds) *The Argumentative Turn in Policy Analysis and Planning*, Durham, NC: Duke University Press, pp 233–253.

Herbener, J.M. (2011) 'Introduction', in J.M. Herbener (ed) *The Pure Time-preference Theory of Interest*, Auburn, AL: Ludwig von Mises Institute, pp 11–58.

Hertsgaard, M. (2011) *Hot: Living Through the Next Fifty Years on Earth*, Boston, MA: Houghton Mifflin Harcourt.

Hirschman, A. (1991) *The Rhetoric of Reaction*, Cambridge, MA: The Belknap Press.

Hodgson, S.M. and Irving, Z. (2007) 'Studying policy: A way forward', in S.M. Hodgson and Z. Irving (eds) *Policy Reconsidered: Meanings, Politics and Practices*, Bristol: Policy Press, pp 191–207.

Homer (1975) *The Iliad*, Garden City, NY: Anchor Books.

Horkheimer, M. (2004) *Eclipse of Reason*, London: Continuum.

Huizinga, J. (1955) *Homo Ludens: A Study of the Play Element in Culture*, Boston, MA: Beacon Press.

Husserl, E. (1965) 'Philosophy as rigorous science', in *Phenomenology and the Crisis of Philosophy*, New York: Harper & Row, pp 71–147.

Ibsen, H. (1999) *An Enemy of the People*, Mineola, NY: Dover.

Ishiguro, K. (1989) *The Remains of the Day*, London: Faber and Faber.

Iyengar, S. and Hahn, K. (2009) 'Red media, blue media: Evidence of ideological selectivity in media use', *Journal of Communication*, 59: 19–39.

Jecker, J. and Landy, D. (1969) 'Liking a person as a function of doing him a favour', *Human Relations*, 22(4): 371–378.

Johnson, E.J. and Goldstein, D. (2003) 'Do defaults save lives?', *Science*, 302 (21 November): 1338–1339.

Jones, S. (2010) 'Qui paie les experts de la télévision américaine?', *Le Monde Diplomatique*, July.

Kafka, F. (1970) *The Trial*, New York: Schocken.

Kahneman, D. (2011) *Thinking, Fast and Slow*, New York: Farrar, Straus, and Giroux.

Kant, I. (1991) *Kant: Political Writings* (2nd edn), Cambridge: Cambridge University Press.

Kant, I. (2002) *Critique of Practical Reason*, Indianapolis, IN: Hackett.

Kaufman, H. (1969) 'Administrative decentralization and political power', *Public Administration Review*, 29(1): 3–15.

Kelly, M. and Maynard-Moody, S. (1993) 'Policy analysis in the post-positivist era: Engaging stakeholders in evaluating the economic development districts program', *Public Administration Review*, 53(2): 135–142.

Kelman, S. (1992) 'Cost-benefit analysis: An ethical critique', in J.M. Gillroy and M.L. Wade (eds) *The Moral Dimensions of Public Policy Choice: Beyond the Market Paradigm*, Pittsburgh, PA: University of Pittsburgh Press, pp 153–164.

Keynes, J.M. (1963) *Essays in Persuasion*, New York: W.W. Norton & Co.

Kotkin, S. (2002) 'A world war among professors', *New York Times*, September 7.

Krugman, P. (2013) 'A war on the poor', *New York Times*, October 31.

Kuhn, T. (1970a) 'Reflections on My Critics', in I. Lakatos and A. Musgrave (eds) *Criticism and the Growth of Knowledge*, Cambridge: Cambridge University Press, pp 231–278.

Kuhn, T. (1970b) *The Structure of Scientific Revolutions* (2nd edn), Chicago: University of Chicago Press.

Kuhn, T. (1998) 'Objectivity, value judgment, and theory choice', in M. Curd and J.A. Cover (eds) *Philosophy of Science: the Central Issues*, New York: Norton, pp 102–118.

Lakatos, I. (1970) 'Falsification and the methodology of scientific research programmes', in I. Lakatos and A. Musgrave (eds) *Criticism and the Growth of Knowledge*, Cambridge: Cambridge University Press, pp 91–195.

Lake, A. (1989) *Somoza Falling*, Boston, MA: Houghton Mifflin.

Lane, R. (1991) *The Market Experience*, Cambridge: Cambridge University Press.

Lane, R. (2000) *The Loss of Happiness in Market Democracies*, New Haven, CT: Yale University Press.

Layard, R. (2003) 'Happiness: Has social science a clue?', Lionel Robbins Memorial Lectures. Available from: http://eprints.lse.ac.uk/47429/ [Last accessed June 24, 2021].

Layard, R. (2005) *Happiness: Lessons from a New Science*, London: Penguin.

Leibenstein, H. (1966) 'Allocative efficiency vs. X-efficiency', *American Economic Review*, 56(3): 392–415.

Lekachman, R. (1967) *The Age of Keynes*, London: Allen Lane.

Leonard, S. (1990) *Critical Theory in Political Practice*, Princeton, NJ: Princeton University Press.

Levitt, S.D. and Dubner, S.J. (2005) *Freakonomics: A Rogue Economist Explores the Hidden Side of Everything*, New York: William Morrow.

Lewis, C.S. (2007) 'The abolition of man', in *The Complete C.S. Lewis Signature Classics*, New York: Harper Collins, pp 693–738.

Lindblom, C. and Cohen, D. (1979) *Usable Knowledge*, New Haven, CT: Yale University Press.

Lipsey, R., Sparks, G. and Steiner, P. (1973) *Economics*, New York: Harper & Row.

Lipsey, R. and Chrystal, K.A. (2007) *Economics*, Oxford: Oxford University Press.

Longino, H. (1990) *Science as Social Knowledge: Values and Objectivity in Scientific Inquiry*, Princeton, NJ: Princeton University Press.

Lukács, G. (1971) *History and Class Consciousness*, Cambridge, MA: MIT Press.

Lukacs, J. (1999) *Five Days in London: May 1940*, New Haven, CT: Yale University Press.

Luskin, R., Fishkin, J. and Jowell, R. (2002) 'Considered opinions: Deliberative polling in Britain', *British Journal of Political Science*, 32: 455–487.

Lynn, J. and Jay, A. (1984) *The Complete Yes Minister*, London: BBC Books.

McCloskey, D. (1983) 'The rhetoric of economics', *Journal of Economic Literature*, 21(2): 481–517.

McCullough, D. (2005) *1776*, New York: Simon and Schuster.

McFate, M. (2005) 'Anthropology and counterinsurgency: The strange story of their curious relationship', *Military Review*, March–April: 24–38.

MacIntyre, A. (1979) 'Social science methodology as the ideology of bureaucratic authority', in M.J. Falco (ed) *Through the Looking Glass: Epistemology and the Conduct of Enquiry*, Washington, DC: University Press of America, pp 42–58.

MacIntyre, A. (1984) *After Virtue* (2nd edn), Notre Dame, IN: University of Notre Dame Press.

MacIntyre, A. (1988) *Whose Justice? Which Rationality?*, Notre Dame, IN: University of Notre Dame Press, pp 42–58.

MacLean, N. (2017) *Democracy in Chains: The Deep History of the Radical Right's Stealth Plan for America*, New York: Viking.

McPherson, M. (1983) 'Imperfect democracy and the moral responsibilities of policy advisers', in D. Callahan and B. Jennings (eds) *Ethics, the Social Sciences, and Policy Analysis*, New York: Plenum Press, pp 69–81.

Majone, G. (1989) *Evidence, Argument and Persuasion in the Policy Process*, New Haven, CT: Yale University Press.

Manheim, J. and Rich, R. (2006) *Empirical Political Analysis* (6th edn), New York: Longman.

Mankoff, R. (ed) (2004) *The Complete Cartoons of the New Yorker*, New York: Black Dog & Leventhal.

Marx, K. (1959) *Capital*, vol. 3. Moscow: Progress Publishers.

Marx, K. and Engels, F. (1969) *Selected Works in Three Volumes*, Moscow: Progress Publishers.

Maslow, A. (1971) *Eupsychian Management: A Journal*, Homewood, IL: Irwin and Dorsey Press.

Menger, C. (2007) *Principles of Economics*, Auburn, AL: Ludwig von Mises Institute.

Mintzberg, H. (1983) *Power In and Around Organizations*, Englewood Cliffs, NJ: Prentice-Hall.

Mishan, E. and Page, T. (1992) 'The methodology of cost-benefit analysis, with particular reference to the ozone problem', in J.M. Gillroy and M.L. Wade (eds) *The Moral Dimensions of Public Policy Choice: Beyond the Market Paradigm*, Pittsburgh, PA: University of Pittsburgh Press, pp 59–113.

Monbiot, G. (2004) 'Bottom of the barrel', *Guardian Weekly*, January 22.

Mora, J.-S. (2012) 'Ravages de la pêche industrielle en Afrique', *Le Monde diplomatique*, November.

Nagel, T. (1986) *The View from Nowhere*, Oxford: Oxford University Press.

National Safety Council (2012) 'Understanding the distracted brain: Why driving while using hands-free cell phones is risky behavior', Available from: https://www.nsc.org/getmedia/2ea8fe8b-d7b7-4194-8ea5-306d3 0a73972/cognitive-distraction-white-paper.pdf [Last accessed June 24, 2021].

Neuman, W. L. (2011) *Social Research Methods: Qualitative and Quantitative Approaches* (7th edn), Boston, MA: Allyn & Bacon.

Nordhaus, W., and Boyer, J. (2000) *Warming the World: Economic Models of Global Warming*, Cambridge, MA: MIT Press.

Nussbaum, M. (2013) *Political Emotions: Why Love Matters for Justice*, Cambridge, MA: Belknap Press.

Pal, L. (1992) *Public Policy Analysis* (2nd ed), Scarborough: Nelson.

Pal, L. (1997) *Beyond Policy Analysis*, Scarborough: Nelson.

Panel on Alternative Policies Affecting the Prevention of Alcohol Abuse and Alcoholism (1981) *Alcohol and Public Policy: Beyond the Shadow of Prohibition*, Washington, DC: National Academies Press.

Pedroletti, B. (2001) 'School textbook rewrites Japan's role in Second World War', *The Guardian Weekly*, April 26.

Peirce, C.S. (1966) *Selected Writings*, New York: Dover.

Piketty, T. (2013) *Le Capital au XXIe Siècle*, Paris: Editions du Seuil.

Plato (1997) *Complete Works*, ed. John M. Cooper. Indianapolis, IN: Hackett Publishing Company.

Polanyi, K. (1957) *The Great Transformation*, Boston, MA: Beacon Press.

Polanyi, M. (1962) *Personal Knowledge*, Chicago: University of Chicago Press.

Popper, K. (1974) 'Replies to my critics', in P.A. Schilpp (ed) *The Philosophy of Karl Popper*, La Salle, IL: Open Court, pp 961–1197.

Popper, K. (2002a) *Conjectures and Refutations* (5th edn), London: Routledge.

Popper, K. (2002b) *The Logic of Scientific Discovery*, London: Routledge.

Posner, E.A. and Weisbach, D. (2010) *Climate Change Justice*, Princeton, NJ: Princeton University Press.

Prasad, M., Perrin, A.J., Bezila, K., Hoffman, S.G., Kindleberger, K., Manturuk, K. and Powers, A.S. (2009) ' "There must be a reason": Osama, Saddam, and inferred justification', *Sociological Inquiry*, 79(2): 142–162.

Price, D. (2011) *Weaponizing Anthropology*, Petrolia, CA: Counterpunch.

Putnam, H. (1974) 'The "corroboration" of theories', in P.A. Schilpp (ed) *The Philosophy of Karl Popper*, La Salle, IL: Open Court, pp 221–240.

Putnam, H. (1981) *Reason, Truth, and History*, Cambridge: Cambridge University Press.

Putnam, H. (2002) *The Collapse of the Fact/Value Dichotomy and Other Essays*, Cambridge, MA: Harvard University Press.

Ratner, R.S. (2005) 'The BC Citizens' Assembly: The public hearings and deliberations stage', *Canadian Parliamentary Review*, Spring: 24–33.

Ravallion, M. (2003) 'The debate on globalization, poverty and inequality: Why measurement matters', *International Affairs*, 79(4): 739–753.

Rawls, J. (1971) *A Theory of Justice*, Cambridge, MA: Harvard University Press.

Rawls, J. (1996) *Political Liberalism*, New York: Columbia University Press.

Rawls, J. (1997) 'The idea of public reason revisited', *The University of Chicago Law Review*, 64(3): 765–807.

Rawls, J. (2001) *Justice as Fairness: A Restatement*, Cambridge, MA: The Belknap Press.

Rein, M. (1983) 'Value-critical policy analysis', in D. Callahan and B. Jennings (eds) *Ethics, the Social Sciences, and Policy Analysis*, New York: Plenum Press, pp 83–111.

Remarque, E.M. (1982) *All Quiet on the Western Front*, New York: Fawcett Crest.

Remler, D.K. and Van Ryzin, G.G. (2015) *Research Methods in Practice: Strategies for Description and Causation*, n.p.: Sage.

Revkin, A. (2005) 'Bush aide softened greenhouse gas links to global warming', *New York Times*, June 8.

Rich, M. (2013) 'Creationists on Texas panel for biology textbooks', *New York Times*, September 28.

Rich, N. (2018) 'Losing earth: The decade we almost stopped climate change', *New York Times Magazine*, August 1.

Ricoeur, P. (1965) *Fallible Man*, Chicago: Henry Regnery.

Riker, W.H. (1962) *The Theory of Political Coalitions*, New Haven, CT: Yale University Press.

Riker, W.H. (1964) 'Some ambiguities in the notion of power', *American Political Science Review*, 58(2): 341–349.

Riker, W.H. (1977) 'The future of a science of politics', *American Behavioral Scientist*, 21: 11–38.

Riker, W.H. (1983) 'Political theory and the art of heresthetics', in A. Finifter (ed) *Political Science: The State of the Discipline*, Washington, DC: American Political Science Association, pp 47–67.

Riker, W.H. (1986) *The Art of Political Manipulation*, New Haven, CT: Yale University Press.

Riker, W.H. (1992) 'Applications of political theory in the study of politics – introduction', *International Political Science Review*, 13(1): 5–6.

Riker, W.H. and Ordeshook P.C. (1973) *An Introduction to Positive Political Theory*, Englewood Cliffs, NJ: Prentice-Hall.

Robbins, L. (1932) *An Essay on the Nature and Significance of Economic Science*, London: Macmillan.

Robert, C. and Zeckhauser, R. (2011) 'The methodology of normative policy analysis', *Journal of Policy Analysis and Management*, 30(3): 613–643.

Rousseau, J.-J. (1966) *Émile*, Paris: Garnier-Flammarion.

Rousseau, J.-J. (1972) *Les Confessions*, Paris: Librairie Générale Française.

Ryan, P. (1995) 'Of Miniature Mila and Flying Geese: Government advertising and Canadian democracy', in S. Phillips (ed) *How Ottawa Spends*, Ottawa: Carleton University Press, pp 263–286.

Ryan, P. (2000) 'Structure, agency, and the Nicaraguan revolution', *Theory and Society*, 29(2): 187–213.

Ryan, P. (2003) 'Ethics and resignation: A classroom exercise', *The Journal of Policy Analysis and Management*, 22(2): 313–315.

Ryan, P. (2010a) 'Beware shared memory', *Canadian Issues*, Winter: 28–31.

Ryan, P. (2010b) *Multicultiphobia*, Toronto: University of Toronto Press.

Ryan, P. (2014a) *After the New Atheist Debate*, Toronto: University of Toronto Press.

Ryan, P. (2014b) 'The multicultural state and the religiously neutral state: Comment on Cliteur', *International Journal of Constitutional Law*, 12(2): 457–463.

Ryan, P. (2015) 'Positivism: Paradigm or culture?', *Policy Studies*, 36(4): 417–433.

Ryan, P. (2018) '"Technocracy," democracy ... and corruption and trust', *Policy Sciences*, 51(1): 131–139.

Sabatier, P. and Jenkins-Smith, H. (1999) 'The advocacy coalition framework: An assessment', in P. Sabatier (ed) *Theories of the Policy Process*, Boulder, CO: Westview Press, pp 117–168.

Samuelson, P. (1976) *Economics* (10th edn), New York: McGraw-Hill.

Sartre, J.-P. (1996) *L'Existentialisme Est un Humanisme*, Paris: Gallimard.

Sayer, A. (2011) *Why Things Matter to People*, Cambridge: Cambridge University Press.

Schneider, A. and Ingram, H. (1993) 'Social constructions and target populations', *American Political Science Review*, 87: 334–347.

Schneider, A. and Ingram, H. (1997) *Policy Design for Democracy*, Lawrence: University Press of Kansas.

Schumacher, E.F. (1974) *Small Is Beautiful*, London: Abacus.

Schumpeter, J. (1976) *Capitalism, Socialism and Democracy* (3rd edn), New York: Harper Torchbooks.

Schutz, A. (1970) *On Phenomenology and Social Relations: Selected Writings*, Chicago: University of Chicago Press.

Scott, J.C. (1998) *Seeing Like a State: How Certain Schemes to Improve the Human Condition Have Failed*, New Haven, CT: Yale University Press.

Searle, J. (1995) *The Construction of Social Reality*, New York: Free Press.

Sen, A. (1967) 'The nature and classes of prescriptive judgements', *The Philosophical Quarterly*, 17(66): 46–62.

Sen, A. (1977) 'Rational fools: A critique of the behavioral foundations of economic theory', *Philosophy and Public Affairs*, 6(4): 317–344.

Sen, A. (2009) *The Idea of Justice*, Cambridge, MA: Harvard University Press.

Shakespeare, W. (1988) *The Annotated Shakespeare*, New York: Greenwich House.

Simon, H. (1965) *Administrative Behavior*, New York: Free Press.

Smith, A. (1937) *The Wealth of Nations*, New York: Modern Library.

Smith, A. (2009) *Theory of Moral Sentiments*, London: Penguin.

Sophocles (1947) *The Theban Plays*, London: Penguin.

Steele, J. (2008) 'Guys, I'm afraid we haven't got a clue', *The Guardian*, January 21.

Stokey, E. and Zeckhauser, R. (1978) *A Primer for Policy Analysis*, New York: Norton.

Stone, Deborah (1997) *Policy Paradox: the Art of Political Decision-making*, New York: W.W. Norton.

Stone, Diane (2000) 'Non-governmental policy transfer: The strategies of independent policy institutes', *Governance*, 13 (January): 45–70.

Streeck, W. (2016) *How Will Capitalism End?*, London: Verso.

Sunstein, C. (2001) 'The arithmetic of arsenic', *John M. Olin Law & Economics Working Paper*, no. 135.

Sykes, J.B. (ed) (1976) *Concise Oxford Dictionary* (6th edn), London: Oxford University Press.

Tavris, C. and Aronson, E. (2007) *Mistakes Were Made (But Not by Me)*, Orlando, FL: Harcourt.

Taylor, C. (1975) *Hegel*, Cambridge: Cambridge University Press.

Taylor, E. and Wheeler, J. (1966) *Spacetime Physics*, San Francisco, CA: W.H. Freeman.

Tetlock, P.E. (2005) *Expert Political Judgment: How Good Is It?, How Can We know?*, Princeton, NJ: Princeton University Press.

Texas Education Agency (2010) *Texas Essential Knowledge and Skills*, Available from: https://tea.texas.gov/sites/default/files/all_HS_TEKS_2ndRdg.pdf [Last accessed June 24, 2021].

Thaler, R. and Sunstein, C. (2008) *Nudge*, New Haven, CT: Yale University Press.

Thomson, J.C. (1968) 'How could Vietnam happen?', *The Atlantic Monthly*, April: 47–53.

Thornton, J. (1991) 'Risking democracy', *Greenpeace Magazine*, March/April: 14–17.

Thucydides (2009) *The Peloponnesian War*, Oxford: Oxford University Press.

Tillich, P. (1952) *The Courage to Be*, New Haven, CT: Yale University Press.

Tong, R. (1986) *Ethics in Policy Analysis*, Englewood Cliffs, NJ: Prentice-Hall.

Torgerson, D. (1992) 'Priest and jester in the policy sciences: Developing the focus of inquiry', *Policy Sciences*, 25: 225–235.

Toulmin, S. (2003) *The Uses of Argument* (Updated edn), Cambridge: Cambridge University Press.

Tribe, L.H. (1972) 'Policy science: Analysis or ideology?', *Philosophy and Public Affairs*, 2(1): 66–110.

Tuchman, B. (1984) *The March of Folly*, New York: Ballantine.

Veblen, T. (1994) *The Theory of the Leisure Class*, New York: Dover.

United States Geological Survey (n.d.) 'How would sea level change if all glaciers melted?', Available from: https://www.usgs.gov/faqs/how-would-sea-level-change-if-glaciers-melted [Last accessed June 24, 2021].

Vickers, G. (1965) *The Art of Judgment*, London: Chapman & Hall.

Voegelin, E. (1952) *The New Science of Politics*, Chicago: University of Chicago Press.

Wallace-Wells, D. (2019) *The Uninhabitable Earth: Life after Warming*, New York: Tim Duggan Books.

Walzer, M. (1990) 'The communitarian critique of liberalism', *Political Theory*, 18: 6–23.

Weber, M. (1949) *The Methodology of the Social Sciences*, New York: Glencoe.

Weber, M. (1958) *From Max Weber: Essays in Sociology*, New York: Oxford University Press.

Weber, M. (1978) *Economy and Society*, Berkeley: University of California Press.

White, L. (1994) 'Policy analysis as discourse', *Journal of Policy Analysis and Management*, 13(3): 506–525.

Wildavsky, A. (1979) *Speaking Truth to Power*, Boston, MA: Little, Brown.

Williams, L.P. (1970) 'Normal science, scientific revolutions and the history of science', in I. Lakatos and A. Musgrave (eds) *Criticism and the Growth of Knowledge*, Cambridge: Cambridge University Press, pp 49–50.

Wilson, W. (1887) 'The study of administration', *Political Science Quarterly*, 2(2): 197–222.

Woolf, V. (1991) *Three Guineas*, London: Hogarth Press.

Zimonjic, P. (2020) 'Tory MP notes "most" pandemic deaths are in care homes, asks if it's time to reopen economy', *CBC News*, April 13.

Index